4G

COMMUNICATION

Applying The Lord's Prayer For Today's Believers

DR. LONNIE E. RILEY

Author of *Yes, You Can! You Just Need Help*
and *The Power Of Praying For Your Pastor*

4G COMMUNICATION

Applying The Lord's Prayer For Today's Believers

DR. LONNIE E. RILEY

Author of *Yes, You Can! You Just Need Help*
and *The Power Of Praying For Your Pastor*

4G Communication

Published by Freedom Place Publishing

A Division of Freedom Ministries International

Myrtle Beach, SC

www.fmintl.org

Cover Design: Kimberly T. Riley

ISBN ISBN-13:
978-0988445550 (Freedom Place Press)

ISBN-10: 0988445557

Library of Congress Control Number: 2014921214

Printed in the United States of America

Table of Contents

OPENING MATERIAL

Dedication 9

Acknowledgements 11

Introduction...13

SECTION 1: FIRST G = GAIN INSIGHT

Chapter 1: Our Father 23

    Gaining Insight Into Your Relationship

Chapter 2: In Heaven 59

    Gaining Insight Into His Sovereignty

Chapter 3: Hallowed Be Your Name 77

    Gaining Insight Into His Character

Chapter 4: Your Kingdom Come 97

    Gaining Insight Into His Kingdom

Chapter 5: Your Will Be Done.................................123

    Gaining Insight Into His Will

SECTION 2: SECOND G = GROWTH

Chapter 6: Give Us This Day Our Daily Bread 149

    We Grow In Faith

Chapter 7: And Forgive Us Our Debts............................171

    We Grow In Grace

Chapter 8: As We Forgive Our Debtors 191

    We Grow In Mercy

SECTION 3: THIRD G = GUARD

Chapter 9: And Lead Us 223

    We Will Be Guarded By His Leadership

Chapter 10: Not Into Temptation 247

    We Will Be Guarded From Temptation

Chapter 11: But Deliver Us From Evil 269

    We Will Be Guarded By His Deliverance

SECTION 4: FOURTH G = GIVE PRAISE

Chapter 12: For Yours Is The Kingdom 297

    We Give Praise By Our Submission

Chapter 13: And The Power 319

    We Give Praise In Our Weakness

Chapter 14: And The Glory Forever, Amen 339

    We Give Praise By Our Recognition

CLOSING MATERIAL

Afterword (A 5th G) 369

Notes 387

Index 391

Dedication

I Lovingly Dedicate This Book
To The Life And Memory
Of My Praying Grandmother,
Ella Mae Riley.
"Mother Riley"

Jesus knew the importance of prayer.

-Dr. Lonnie E. Riley-

Acknowledgments

I am so thankful that God has placed so many people in my life that are encouragers and helpers. A work of this size requires both. First of all, I praise my Heavenly Father for placing the desire within me to communicate through writing. He aided me in my recovery from a stroke 10 years ago and has impregnated me with the desire to share my thoughts and experiences through books.

Secondly, I appreciate my companion and helpmate, Kim Riley. She has encouraged me in the difficult times of life and helped me by designing the book's cover and editing the initial manuscript.

My mother, Ann Wiggins, is a constant source of encouragement. Nearly each time we speak she wants to know about my writing and when the next book will appear.

My son, Jason Riley, is an endless inspiration to me. He encourages me to think "outside of the box" and to ponder new and exciting angles of consideration.

The inspiration of the afterword is credited to a friend and business partner of mine, Bobby Doty. In a business meeting he suggested its focus and it hit a nerve of inspiration in me.

I believe that prayer, in its basic form, is just communicating with God.

- Dr. Lonnie E. Riley-

Introduction

Communication is always changing. Over my lifetime, it has been developing rapidly. As I was growing up in southern Georgia, we had only one main means of communication, our home phone. There were no "features" available such as call waiting, 3-way calling, voicemail or call forwarding. There was just one line and maybe a couple of handsets connected to that line. Wireless, mobile, cell or smart phones did not exist. Having a phone in your car would have been considered science fiction, only Batman or a bad man had something like that.

My first mobile phone was in the early 1990's. It was a heavy bag phone. You could actually carry it from car to car, as opposed to the car phones that were actually installed in the vehicle. Between regular phone minutes and "roaming" charges, it was an expensive commodity.

In what seems like a flash we moved from that technology to actually having mobile (cell) phones. The way they work and are billed has changed dramatically over the last 10 to 15 years. We now we have unlimited minutes and even though our signal is still bouncing off towers we are no longer paying the roaming charges.

Suddenly a new "generation" of cell phones hit the market. With these, you can make phone calls, send texts and emails, Skype and surf the internet. It has all the features like voice dialing, call waiting, 3-way calling, voicemail, etc. As this new generation of phones has developed it has continued to do even more, faster and with more reliability. We are now in the 4th generation (4G) of these new intelligent (smart) phones, and no doubt we will soon change once again. At one time it was unusual for a family to have more than one mobile phone, now it seems almost everyone in a family is "sharing" minutes and has their own smart phone. I have had little children help me understand how to use my cell phone features. It can be embarrassing. Here I am with an earned doctorate, working on a second one, and I need an 8 year old to teach me how to change or access things on my cell phone. Now, I understand when I hear people say, "My phone is smarter than me."

This type of communication has enabled us to stay in contact with people across the globe. Classmates that have moved across the country or even to another country are able to stay in touch. When my oldest son, Jason, was in the United States Marine Corps, he was deployed to Iraq for two tours over the course of one full year. Needless to say, it was the longest year of my life. I can only imagine the uncertainty the loved ones of those who fought in Vietnam, Korea and WWII went through. I could regularly talk to my son. He could call at certain times and we knew he was still alive and doing well.

I have shared this information because I believe that prayer, in its basic form, is just communicating with God. It is an extremely vital part of the life and growth of each person who has named the name of Jesus Christ as their Savior. It is our life-line with the God of the universe. It is wireless, mobile and immediate. It always works and "calls" are never "dropped." God is always anxious to speak with us.

Jesus knew the importance of prayer. Even a cursory look at His life reveals the significance prayer had in His daily walk with the Father. Evidently a prayer life like His was something that His disciples had never witnessed. Though they had been reared as Israelites, were used to the prayers of priests, Pharisees or Sadducees, something about Jesus' prayer life was different. Was it different because of its length or perhaps because of its effectiveness? Maybe it was different in that it was so intimate and personal that they could see a different way of approaching God that they had never thought was possible. Whatever the difference, it was so radical that they actually are recorded asking Him to teach them how to pray (Luke 11:1).

Hidden within that request is the understanding that Jesus knew how to pray. Think about it, we only ask someone for help, or to teach us something if we know they are able. Over the years as a pastor I have met many people from different professions. If I wanted to learn to drive a bulldozer, work with electricity, fly a plane or build a house, I know where to find the people who have experience in those areas. I would find them and ask them for their assistance in teaching me. If I have spoken to my friend, John, and asked him to give me flying lessons, I would listen intently to his instruction. I would follow his advice to the letter. I know that one miscalculation could do more than just "fail" me as a pilot; it could kill me and possibly others.

One of my great childhood memories was my introduction to Dr. Charles L. Allen of First United Methodist Church of Houston, Texas, where my aunt and uncle were members. He was a kind gentleman who took the time to encourage a young future minister. I have nearly every volume he penned and he took the time to autograph them all. He wrote in his book, "*All Things Are Possible Through Prayer*" on this request of the disciples, as follows:

> "It seems strange that Jesus' disciples would have said, 'Lord, teach us to pray' (Luke 11:1). These men doubtless had grown up in strictly religious homes. They had gone to church and they had prayed all their lives. A year before if you had asked the disciples, 'Do you know how to pray?' they would have been indignant. 'Of course, we know how to pray,' they would have insisted. 'We have prayed regularly every day for years.'
>
> They could have quoted you many verses in the Bible in reference to prayer. They could have answered the arguments against prayer and given the reasons for prayer. However, when they saw Jesus pray, they realized they did not know how to pray. They saw how much time He gave to prayer and what it meant in His own life. They saw Him go into prayer in one mood and come out in another. As a result of His prayers, they saw things become different. To them prayer had been a form, but to Christ it was a force.
>
> As those disciples saw Jesus pray, they realized it was something quite different from what they had been doing when they prayed. They realized they didn't know how, after they had seen Jesus pray, and so they said, 'Lord, teach us too pray.' Their request has been on the lips of many people since that day."[1]

Jesus gave a model prayer for His followers (including us) to emulate. Most of us have known it as, "The Lord's Prayer."

> *"In this manner, therefore, pray:*
> *Our Father in heaven, Hallowed be Your name.*
> *Your kingdom come.*
> *Your will be done on earth as it is in heaven.*
> *Give us this day our daily bread.*
> *And forgive us our debts, as we forgive our debtors.*
> *And do not lead us into temptation,*
> *but deliver us from the evil one.*
> *For Yours is the kingdom and the power and the glory*
> *forever. Amen"*
> Matthew 6:9-13

Jesus began this section with the words, "In this manner," not "Say these words." Not that actually memorizing and praying this prayer is wrong; it was just not His intent. The motive that Jesus is trying to cultivate is an attitude or spirit of prayer and dependence on our heavenly Father: God. Many people use this prayer as scaffolding around which they pray. It provides structure. Noted author and Professor Dr. C. Peter Wagner has used the prayer in this fashion:

"This works well for me, for when you *pray* the Lord's Prayer, instead of simply *saying* the Lord's Prayer, you have a ready-made structure to cover everything you possibly need to pray about at one time."[2]

Though the actual prayer is not that long (only 70 words depending on the version you use) it is full of dramatic implications. Prayer does not always have to be long and drawn out. It can be specific and succinct, short and powerful. Elijah's prayer on Mt. Carmel which brought the fire of God down (1 Kings 18:36-37) was only 63 words. The 36 word prayer Jesus prayed at the tomb of Lazarus (John 11:41-42) was pretty effective, don't you think? And what is probably Jesus' most merciful and notable prayer on the cross was a simple 10 words, *"Father, forgive them for they know not what they do."*

As we delve into a fresh understanding of this noble prayer let us hear the reverberation of Adam Clarke's comments from centuries ago:

> "What satisfaction must it be to learn from God himself, with what words, and in what manner, he would have us pray to him, so as not to pray in vain! A king, who draws up the petition which he allows to be presented to himself, has doubtless the fullest determination to grant the request. We do not sufficiently consider the value of this prayer; the respect and attention which it requires; the preference to be given to it; its fullness and perfection: the frequent use we should make of it; and the spirit which we should bring with it. "Lord, teach us how to pray!" is a prayer necessary to prayer; for unless we are divinely instructed in the manner, and influenced by the spirit of true devotion, even the prayer taught us by Jesus Christ may be repeated without profit to our souls."[3]

I am sure that some might be wondering why I would want to study this prayer AGAIN. This prayer is old and millions of people say it every week, if not every day. Isn't there some new revelation we should seek as to what the Spirit of God is saying to the Church today? Can't there be some "new" nugget of truth that has gone unexplored? What about the defense of the Gospel from those who have tried to water down the message?

I can appreciate the honesty in those questions and I understand the excitement of a new revelation. As I have ministered and studied over the decades, I have found that true change and real revival often comes out of the dust of forgotten truths and the renewal of overlooked vows and commitments from years gone by. Listen to the words of H. Richard Niebuhr as he explains this thought:

> "The great Christian revolutions come not by the discovery of something that was not known before. They happen when somebody takes radically something that was always there."[4]

I am confident that the model prayer of Jesus still gives us a fresh revelation of the awesome privilege it is to communicate with God. May the new revelation you seek, come as a fresh wind when the pieces of this prayer take on a new meaning for you.

Praying for your praying,

Dr. Lonnie E. Riley

True change and real revival often comes out of the dust of forgotten truths and the renewal of overlooked vows and commitments from years gone by.

-Dr. Lonnie E. Riley-

SECTION ONE

FIRST
"G"

GAIN INSIGHT

"In this manner, therefore, pray:
Our Father in heaven, Hallowed be Your name.
Your kingdom come.
Your will be done on earth as it is in heaven.
Give us this day our daily bread.
And forgive us our debts, as we forgive our debtors.
And do not lead us into temptation,
but deliver us from the evil one.
For Yours is the kingdom and the power and the
glory forever. Amen"
Matthew 6:9-13

CHAPTER ONE

GAINING INSIGHT INTO YOUR

RELATIONSHIP:

"Our Father"

I have learned over the years that the more time you spend communicating with someone, the more you begin to understand them, learn from them, and often appreciate or perhaps even love them. (Though honestly there are some relationships that more time spent with them actually makes you appreciate that you don't want to or have to be near them.) Either way, the act of communication helps you understand and **_GAIN INSIGHT_** into that particular relationship.

As we begin this study, the first "G" of this communication we call prayer is the "G"aining of insight. The insights we will be uncovering are of vital importance to our Christian walk as well as the understanding and application of the rest of the prayer. As we pray, we should begin to see some things, some characteristics and maybe even God in a new light. We can understand them from a new (or at least different) perspective than we have ever considered them in the past.

Jesus begins this model prayer for His disciples uniquely in that He is helping them **_GAIN INSIGHT_** into the relationship they will have with God as "Father."

The church is now accustomed to this term. Perhaps you learned this prayer as a child in Sunday School or heard it recited weekly just prior to partaking of the Eucharist. Most of us are familiar with it and can quite readily make the correlation of God Almighty as our Heavenly Father.

PARADIGM SHIFT

The disciples did not have that privilege. They did not grow up with this relational concept of God. Their generation had no idea what it was like to have the manifested presence of God with them. The Jewish people of their time had not had the Ark of the Covenant for 400+ years. There is no written or verbal record of the Ark of the Covenant in the Herodian temple, therefore, there was no Shekinah glory in the temple, since it rested on the Mercy Seat between the cherubs on top of the Ark.

The actual Shekinah glory of God had not been manifested since Ezekiel saw it removed from the temple.

The faith the Apostles of Jesus had, and their contemporaries, had been placed in the adherence to a long list of rules, not based in any type of personal relationship. It was an extreme expansion of the Mosaic covenant and law. They were being led by men (Pharisees and Sadducees) who, in large part, had learned to control the people through the manipulation of the Torah, ancient Scriptures, and the scholarship and writings of previous leaders.

To the Jews of Jesus' day, the idea or concept of God was important. The faith of the average man was in God, but NOT in a God with Whom he understood it was possible to have an individual, personal relationship.

Based on their view of God, the first two words in this prayer, "Our Father" created a paradigm shift in both their mind and their faith. It was a totally different approach from entering into prayer with "The Almighty God" or "The God of the Universe" and especially "The Lord of Hosts." The few times we do find reference to God as Father in Judaism, they relate to Him as the Father of creation. He is Father of everything because He both created it and maintains it. It is not personal, devotional or relational in its application.

Jesus is now breaking new theological and relational ground in telling them to draw near to God as they would their father. What? This is a huge difference and should not be overlooked both in the reading and the consideration of the cultural and religious ramifications of such a change in perception.

As a curious student, I performed a simple word search which revealed a dramatic difference in the use of Father as a term for God from the Old Testament to the

New Testament.   In the Old Testament, the word "Father" is used of God only 15 times but is used 245 times of God in the New Testament.   That is extremely significant and shows the radical paradigm shift not only in the 12 Apostles but also for all those early first century believers' view of God in regard to both their relationship with God and their developing theology.

JESUS USES FATHER

Part of those 245 times includes the fact that Jesus used the term "Father" nearly every time He spoke of God. His first recorded words were when He was taken to the temple by Mary and Joseph to observe the Passover when He was 12 years old. After this visit, His parents left, assuming Jesus was with them among the crowd of travelers. Once they realized He was not with them, they returned to Jerusalem to discover Him speaking among the leaders and teachers of the temple. When asked of His purpose for staying behind He replied,

> *"And He said to them, 'Why did you seek Me?*
> *Did you not know that I must be about My*
> ***FATHER'S*** *business?'"*
> Luke 2:49 (emphasis mine)

From the context we understand the meaning to be a reference to God, His Heavenly Father. He was not about Joseph's (a carpenter) business.   He was not measuring for a new table for the Menorah.   He was asking and answering questions with the teachers in the Temple. It is evident that even at such a young age He was cognizant of both His relationship with Father God and the mission He was sent to accomplish. Though He may not have understood all of the implications of that mission, He showed an understanding that He *must* do the will of His Heavenly Father.

The last words spoken by Jesus on the cross as He gave His life for all who lived, had lived, and would ever live; are recorded by Luke in chapter 23 verse 46,

> *"And when Jesus had cried out with a loud voice, He said, "**FATHER**, 'into Your hands I commit My spirit.'" Having said this, He breathed His last."*
> Luke 23:46 (emphasis mine)

These are the bookends of Jesus' recorded words from childhood to death. Both display His understanding of His relationship with God to be that of a Father and Son. The only time in the Scriptures that Jesus did not refer to God as His Father was on the cross. When the weight of the sin of the world pushed down on Him and the most hideous form of reverse metamorphosis occurred as He "became sin."

For the first time ever He felt the absence of God. The Scriptures reveal that God cannot, and will not, look on sin and Jesus had just become ALL sin that had ever and would ever happen. In that moment totally covered in all the sinful acts (word, thought, and deed) of the entire world, in the midst of that overwhelming abandonment, Matthew records:

> *"And about the ninth hour Jesus cried out with a loud voice, saying 'Eli, Eli, lama sabachthani?'*

that is, 'My God, My God, why have You forsaken
Me?'"
Matthew 27:46

Interestingly, though, is the fact that even then, when He didn't use the word "Father," He still recognized His personal relationship by using the possessive pronoun "My." One may consider it is safe to presume from this compilation and the Spirit of the Word, that "My God" is also "My Father."

HE IS MY FATHER

"Okay," you may ask. "Why is that so important? What is the big deal that the perspective changed of God as Father?" I'm glad you asked (though I know I actually asked it). The answer is that of relationship. How does one relate to a king in contrast to how one relates to his/her father? Or consider the dramatic difference in communicating with a judge instead of having a heart to heart with dad. The way each one of us views this relationship is vitally important. It is even more important that God views our relationship in this fashion.

"But you, when you pray, go into your room, and
when you have shut your door, pray to your
FATHER *who is in the secret place; and your*
FATHER *who sees in secret will reward you*
openly"
Matthew 6:6 (emphasis mine)

God intends for us to call Him, "Father." He desires to show His most intimate and loving ways to us, His "Children." Though there are many attributes one expects from a father, the most notable is love.

Each time I had a child, the first feeling or emotion I had as I held him was an indescribable wave of love. Yes, there was always some trepidation and anxiety as I considered the fact that this little life was now under my care, but the "father's love" that erupted within me let me know that I would do anything for that little guy and always be there for him. It brings to mind the Scripture that says,

> *"Or what man is there among you who, if his son asks for bread, will give him a stone? Or if he asks for a fish, will he give him a serpent? If you then, being evil, know how to give good gifts to your children, how much more will your* **FATHER** *who is in heaven give good things to those who ask Him!"*
> Matthew 7:9-11 (emphasis mine)

Based on that great Fatherly love, we will inevitably see His personal expressions of that love in areas such as: generosity, acceptance, faithfulness, assistance, and even discipline. As scholars have come to understand that the fruit of the Spirit is "love" manifested in many ways, so the underlying (or perhaps best understood as the overwhelming) attribute of our Heavenly Father is LOVE.

LOVE

Most of us enjoyed the affection of our earthly fathers. Some were not as fortunate and were reared by men who found it difficult to express their affection, or didn't have their father's presence at all because of abandonment, divorce or death.

Even in those circumstances, there was a deep longing in the child's heart for the love of the father. Even in the worst of all experiences, there is innate within all children the desire to experience the love and affection of their father. I know, mine died when I was only eleven years old.

The Scriptures indicate that our Heavenly Father is extremely affectionate towards His children. I plan in the next few pages to escort us through some of the Biblical references and understanding of God's Fatherly affection. Before I do, I believe it would be helpful for us to do three things.

First, let us renew our minds by focusing on the word of God in respect to His love as discovered by the Apostle Paul and penned in the letter to the Romans.

"What then shall we say to these things? If God is for us, who can be against us? He who did not spare His own Son, but delivered Him up for us all, how shall He not with Him also freely give us all things? Who shall bring a charge against God's elect? It is God who justifies. Who is he who condemns?
It is Christ who died, and furthermore is also risen, who is even at the right hand of God, who also makes intercession for us. Who shall

separate us from the love of Christ? Shall tribulation, or distress, or persecution, or famine, or nakedness, or peril, or sword? As it is written: "For Your sake we are killed all day long; We are accounted as sheep for the slaughter Yet in all these things we are more than conquerors through Him who loved us. For I am persuaded that neither death nor life, nor angels nor principalities nor powers, nor things present nor things to come, nor height nor depth, nor any other created thing, shall be able to separate us from the love of God which is in Christ Jesus our Lord."

Romans 8:31-39

NOTHING (Not-A-Thing) shall <u>ever</u> be able to separate us from the love of God, our Father. You can NEVER be separated from His love. Paul basically covers everything that might come into your mind as having the power to separate you from God's love. He says things above or beneath, and everything in between. You are secure in His love regardless of where the pressures come from. I understand that it seems redundant to look at Scripture before we look at Scripture, but my purpose in doing this is to help us focus on both the security and the importance of understanding and living in the awesome shadow of His great love for us. This passage illustrates those characteristics so wonderfully. Keeping in mind the wonderful, unchanging love of God for us is essential.

<u>Secondly</u>, consider in keeping with that great Scripture the words to the gospel hymn by Fredrick Martin Lehman, "The Love of God." Actually, consider going to YouTube and entering in the title of this song and listen to The Gaither Vocal Band's beautiful 2013

version of it as you read it. Let the Spirit of God encourage you and minister to you as you prepare to see what the Scriptures say about the great love.

THE LOVE OF GOD[1]

Frederick Martin Lehman

Verse 1

The love of God is greater far
Than tongue or pen can ever tell;
It goes beyond the highest star,
And reaches to the lowest hell;
The guilty pair, bowed down with care,
God gave His Son to win;
His erring child He reconciled,
And pardoned from his sin.

Verse 2

When years of time shall pass away,
And earthly thrones and kingdoms fall,
When men, who here refuse to pray,
On rocks and hills and mountains call,
God's love so sure, shall still endure,
All measureless and strong;
Redeeming grace to Adam's race—
The saints' and angels' song.

Verse 3

Could we with ink the ocean fill,
And were the skies of parchment made,
Were every stalk on earth a quill,
And every man a scribe by trade,

To write the love of God above,
Would drain the ocean dry.
Nor could the scroll contain the whole,
Though stretched from sky to sky.

Refrain
O love of God, how rich and pure!
How measureless and strong!
It shall forevermore endure
The saints' and angels' song.

Thirdly, let us remember that God is Love. God is defined many ways in Scripture. His virtues, attributes and personality are numerous and technically indescribable. Yet in 1 John 4:8 Father God is described as love (Agape). There is a difference between saying that God feels love and that God IS love. Love is more than a part of Him, it IS Him. That means that all true love has its foundation, motivation and source in Him. With that in mind let us examine more of this word picture from a Scriptural stand point.

THE PRODIGAL

During His dialogue recorded in Luke 15:11-32, Jesus peels back the curtain (veil) and allows us an insider view of the Father's great love for us when He tells the story of the prodigal son. After the contemptuous son had disrespected his father, ruined his family's good name in another country, squandered his father's riches and broken faith with his father's God by living sinfully and feeding the swine, this now repentant young man fearfully returns to his offended father.

What is he to expect? One might expect the father to have a very judgmental attitude towards the sinful actions of the boy. Others think the dad might display an unforgiving attitude towards the rebellious and dishonorable son. You know a kind of, "You are dead to me" type of mind-set.

The way in which some churches and pastors depict God would justify one as believing God is waiting for us to sin so that He can "whack" us over our heads with a "gospel club." We take on the very role that God has given Jesus, and Jesus has postponed until the end of the age, that of Judge.

The father's attitude, however, proves to be quite different from most people's predictions. Jesus explains that the father sees the son coming from a far off (it makes you wonder if the father had not been looking daily for the return of his son) and runs to him, hugs him, loves on him accepts him back into fellowship with the family and throws a party. That's Jesus' picture of the Heavenly Father's love.

Perhaps it is our own misconceptions that have kept many from following our loving Father. In a sense of righteousness (usually our own) we begin to judge others or to desire that they pay for their sins and mistakes. Jesus has already paid the price and our heavenly Father is standing ready to forgive.

Too often the church (you and I) have acted like the prodigal's older brother and passed judgment on those whom the Father has accepted into His family, or renewed fellowship with (those members which are backslidden). Whomever God is willing to accept and forgive, **we must as well**. PERIOD!

I know this may come as a surprise to some in the church, but we have not been charged with the protection of the "family line." Our heavenly Father is more than capable of determining who has met the requirements of "faith in Christ" and should be admitted into His family. We are only to rejoice in our selection. Perhaps it would be helpful if we were to consider this, there may be others who would not approve of our inclusion in the family. OUCH!

Thank God it is not up to any other finite, imperfect, carnal person to decide. Our Father in heaven has retained that privilege and prerogative for Himself. And, I might add, He is more than capable of doing a magnificent job without my (our) help.

THE GOSPEL OF JOHN

In perhaps one of the most quoted and recognizable verses in all of Scripture (John 3:16) God's purpose for giving His Son, Jesus, to die for us was the product of His great love for the world. His driving force was love. His love for the world was the motivation for planning an acceptable remedy for the spiritual condition that was causing them to perish. He goes on in the next verse (17) to make sure we understand that He, Jesus, was not sent here to condemn us, but to save us.

John also records an important declaration of God's Fatherly love for the disciples during His upper room discourse the night He was to be betrayed. In chapter 16 verses 26 and 27 Jesus says,

"In that day you will ask in My name, and I do
not say to you that I shall pray the Father for you;
*for **THE FATHER HIMSELF LOVES YOU**,*
because you have loved Me, and have believed
that I came forth from God."
John 16:26-27(emphasis mine)

What an awesome declaration! The Father Himself loves you! (John 5:22, 27). Father does not judge, but has given that duty to the Son. The Son did not come to judge, but will at the last dreadful day.

APOSTLE PAUL

The Apostle Paul declares much about the love of Father God. In the 5th verse of Romans 5 he explains that since the Holy Spirit has been given to us, the Spirit has poured into our hearts the very love of God. The 8th verse describes how God shows His great love regarding us,

*"But God demonstrates His own **love** toward us, in that*
while we were still sinners, Christ died for us."
Romans 5:8 *(emphasis mine)*

That is amazing. God loves us before we love Him. He reaches out to us before we reach out to Him. He allows His only Son, Jesus, to die so that we may live.

In his 2nd letter to the church at Corinth Paul states that God "Loves" a cheerful giver in 9:7. There is a connection between loving and giving. Once again, remember that in John 3:16 God so loved that He "Gave."

Paul also reminds the church at Ephesus of the great love of God in 2:4-7,

> *"But God, who is rich in mercy, because of **HIS**
> **GREAT LOVE WITH WHICH HE LOVED US,***
> *even when we were dead in trespasses, made us*
> *alive together with Christ (by grace you have been*
> *saved), and raised us up together, and made us*
> *sit together in the heavenly places in Christ*
> *Jesus, that in the ages to come He might show the*
> *exceeding riches of His grace in His kindness*
> *toward us in Christ Jesus."*
> Ephesians 2:4-7 (emphasis mine)

His love has always had a purpose. And even in these verses we see the objective of His great love. His love made us alive, raised us up and sat us down with Christ in heavenly places so that He may show the exceeding riches of His grace. His entire purpose exudes love and affection.

1 JOHN

To further understand God as a Father who loves us, we must delve into the first Epistle of John. The Apostle John, through all four of his works, was the author that God chose more than any other to express His great love. This little book is filled with references to the amazing love of God, our Father, and the subsequent affect of that love being that we should emulate that Godly, Fatherly love in our relationship with all mankind. Let's walk through it together.

In 2:5 we are told that by keeping God's word, the love of God is (teliŏ'o) complete, consummated, consecrated, finished, fulfilled or made perfect in us. The word of God has a cleansing and completing component to it. We are also told by the Apostle Paul that we are cleansed by the washing of the word. Psalm 119 is filled with the rewards of studying, meditating, loving and keeping the commands, law or word of God.

Then in the same second chapter, verse 15, John lets us know that if we love the world more than we love Father God, then His love is not in us. This brings to remembrance the first of the Ten Commandments which demands preeminence of God above all other god's or loves.

The next chapter (3:1) begins by marveling at the great love the Father has given to us in that we are called His children. Again, He is the Father and we are the children <u>because of</u> the great love He has given to us.

Chapter four has more references to our Heavenly Father's love than any other section of Scripture. Dissecting this passage of God's word will create a deeper appreciation for this love and help us understand our Father's capacity for selfless and unconditional love.

> "*Beloved, let us love one another, for **LOVE IS OF GOD**; and everyone who loves is born of God and knows God. He who does not love does not know God, for **GOD IS LOVE**.*"
> 1 John 4:7-8 (emphasis mine)

Here we can see the correlation that exists between our loving each other and our loving God. There are a couple of statements that really stand out. First, "love is of God." It comes from Him. We cannot truly love without His love being poured out into our spirits (ref. Romans 5:5). Secondly, "for God is love." God not only gives it, or pours it out; He is the actual source of all love. He IS love. Our Heavenly Father IS love and is affectionate toward we who are His children.

> "In this **THE LOVE OF GOD WAS MANIFESTED** toward us, that God has sent His only begotten Son into the world, that we might live through Him."
> 1 John 4:9 (emphasis mine)

Love must be expressed (manifested) in order to be effective. Real love should not, dare I say cannot, be contained. Love seeks an expression. Authentic love must be shown and this verse tells us with no reservation how the love of God our Father was manifested toward us. God expressed His love by sending Jesus, His only begotten Son into the world so that we might have life through Him.

> "In this is love, not that we loved God, but that **HE LOVED US** and sent His Son to be the propitiation for our sins."
> 1 John 4:10 (emphasis mine)

The verse furthers the previous thought that all love proceeds from God and that He alone is the source of it. He loved us before we could ever love Him. And not only was His Son, Jesus sent, but He was sent with a purpose and for a reason, to be the propitiation for our sins. We have no reason or basis to gloat about our love for God, but rather that because of His great love for us in sending his Son, Jesus the Christ to die for us, and poured out in our hearts by His Holy Spirit, we are able to love Him.

> *"Beloved, if **GOD SO LOVED US**,*
> *we also ought to love one another."*
> 1 John 4: 11 (emphasis mine)

Here the Apostle of love lays out the call for us to love one another.   Not based on our worthiness or loveliness, but as a response to our Father's love for us. Both our worthiness and loveliness, if subjected to human judgment, would be up for continual review and thus our sense of real love from one another would be tepid at best. This love is the only NEW commandment that Jesus gave to His disciples (John 13:34). Here we find the motivation for that love.   Even the means by which the world will know that we are followers of Christ is rooted in the fact that we love each other in the power of God's love (John 13:35).

> *"No one has seen God at any time. If we love one*
> *another, God abides in us, and **HIS LOVE** has*
> *been perfected in us."*
> 1 John 4:12 (emphasis mine)

Once more we find the concept of our Heavenly Father's great love working in us to mature us, to help us grow up in the faith.   Our love for one another is indicative of His abiding in us.   To abide is to dwell or tabernacle. His great love is what causes the glory of God to be manifested in our lives.

> *"By this we know that we abide in Him, and He in*
> *us, because He has given us of His Spirit.   And we*

have seen and testify that the Father has sent the
Son as Savior of the world. Whoever confesses
that Jesus is the Son of God, God abides in him,
and he in God. And we have known and believed
THE LOVE THAT GOD HAS FOR US. GOD
IS LOVE, AND HE WHO ABIDES IN LOVE
ABIDES IN GOD, AND GOD IN HIM."
1 John 4:13-16 (emphasis mine)

John makes a case for the correlation of abiding in God and He in us with love. Since God is Love (again in verse 16), abiding in Him and His abiding in us and Christ, and giving us His Spirit we see a strong cord of inseparable love being woven between all parties.

"LOVE HAS BEEN PERFECTED AMONG
US *in this: that we may have boldness in the*
Day of Judgment; because as He is, so are we
in this world."
1 John 4:17 (emphasis mine)

Part of knowing our spiritual life is maturing in that we realize that the great love that our Father in heaven has for us, protects us when that great and fateful Day of Judgment comes. There is no eternal judgment for His children

*"There is **NO FEAR IN LOVE; BUT PERFECT***
***LOVE CASTS OUT FEAR**, because fear*
*involves torment. But **HE WHO FEARS HAS***
NOT BEEN MADE PERFECT IN LOVE."
1 John 4:18 (emphasis mine)

Continuing that sentiment, John says when we realize how perfectly God loves us there should be no fear at all. Fear is impossible if we truly understand the breadth and scope of the love of our Heavenly Father. The presence of fear reveals our lack of trust. Paul deals with fear in 2 Timothy 1:7 and says that God has not given the fearful spirit to us. Fear and faith are incompatible. If you have true faith and trust in the overwhelming Fatherly love of God, then you have no fear. Many people, even those who profess Jesus as their Savior, have such dread for the appearing of Jesus at His second coming. If they are truly His child, the fear has no place. His children should understand the great love He has for us and that all things are prepared for us out of His great love. There is no need to fear, He is in control.

"We __LOVE__ Him because __HE FIRST LOVED__ us."
1 John 4:19 (emphasis mine)

This little verse is filled with such vitally important information. We learn that we are only able to love God based on His love for us. His love shed in and on our hearts gives us the ability and the motivation to love Him in return. We could not love Him in our own strength. We cannot motivate ourselves to love Him properly or consistently. It is because of His selfless love for us and in us that we are made capable of experiencing and expressing love for our Heavenly Father.

"If someone says, 'I love God,' and hates his brother, he is a liar; for he who does not love his brother whom he has seen, how can he love God whom he has not seen?

And this commandment we have from Him: that
**<u>HE WHO LOVES GOD MUST LOVE HIS
BROTHER ALSO</u>**."
1 John 4:20-21 (emphasis mine)

Out of that infinite and unchanging love flow several other characteristics of our Heavenly Father. Gaining insight into His love opens the door to see how wonderfully He has provided for us a growing and deepening relationship as we learn to trust in His love and flee from fear.

Because of His great love for us, we can see His generosity at work in our lives. He is faithful in all areas of our lives. He is faithful to us and to His word regarding us.

He accepts us because of the finished work of His Son, Jesus. We do not have to perform to a certain standard for us to be accepted by our Father. There is no way for us to be acceptable because of our own actions, no matter how great we think they are. Our own righteousness is but filthy rags. We are only accepted before God because of the substitutionary work of Jesus Christ. His work is perfect and when applied to our lives, makes us perfect and acceptable to our Father in Heaven (Hebrews 10:14).

As we go through our daily lives, trying to live in a manner that is pleasing to God and a witness to the world of His great love, often we need help. He promises to never leave us and to not forsake us. He won't run away. He won't seclude Himself to some corner of the galaxy and hope you make it through somehow and endure to the end. NO! That's not the love of a Father.

He is there to reach down with His strong arm of love and lift you up and carry you. He wants you to succeed and live in peace and harmony. He wants to bring His kingdom to earth, and you are a prince/princess in His kingdom.

Yes, God is our Father. We have that type of relationship with the God of the universe. We gain insight into that relationship each time we dwell upon the privilege we have to call Him, Daddy. There is much Biblical evidence that we are to focus our relationship on His Fatherly attributes.

I remember back in April of 1997 when I had a special guest speaker come to my church. Jack Frost (yes that was really his name) shared several days on the topic of the Father's Love. There was so much revelation to my spirit during that conference, but I will always remember the statement, "We see God through the lens of our earthly fathers." It helped me both personally and professionally. I now began to realize why many in my congregation were struggling.

The concept is that the way we view God (the paradigm we use) is naturally determined by the type of relationship (or lack of the same) that we have had with our human father. Well, why is that so revelatory? It is because all fathers are human, and therefore have sinned and fallen short of the glory of our heavenly father. We are poor, inadequate representations of His perfect love. We leave people with an imperfect paradigm of a perfect God.

6 MAJOR FATHER TYPES

I actually found my handwritten set of notes taken at the April 1997 Father's Heart Conference in Monroe,

NC, at what was then New Life Christian Fellowship. During the session on April 21, (Wow, I just realized, 17 years later, that date is my father's birthday) Jack shared with us the following six major types or classifications of fathers.

1. Performance Oriented Father
2. Passive Father
3. Absentee Father
4. Abusive Father
5. Authoritarian Father
6. Good Father[2]

As I remember these classifications, a couple of things are very evident. First, this is not an exhaustive list. These are not the only types of fathers that one will come across in their studies or travels. They are just the major types that Jack, myself and others have noticed when sharing this truth.

Secondly, these types do not necessarily stand alone. Some people, maybe even most people, are a combination of these types. Very rarely can you pigeonhole people into one specific category in anything. As I have studied personality traits over the last 3 decades, I have always found the teacher/author declaring the same caveat in regard to the combination of more than one type. Sometimes a father may exhibit the traits of one type and then show traits of another, or they may demonstrate the behavior of more than one at the same time. Now, I will attempt to recreate those sermon notes for you to enjoy and glean from your own life experience as you understand what lens you use to view your heavenly Father.

1. PERFORMANCE ORIENTED FATHER

A performance oriented father is only pleased when we do "it" right, whatever the "it" is. I remember Jack speaking of his earthly father becoming upset because Jack didn't hit the tennis ball right (his dad was a tennis instructor with dreams that his boys would be tennis stars). He hit it into the net and that was terrible. When he failed at tennis, he felt his father's disappointment and anger rather than encouragement and love.

With this type of father there is no room for failure. There are stringent demands without a balanced love. If you don't perform right, you don't feel loved. If you do perform right, that feeling of love lasts only until you mess up. You have to earn the love. You have to work to keep the relationship.

Countless people have lived this way and transfer that view upon God. There are many Christians who treat God as a performance oriented Father. They see Him as One who has stringent demands (rules or commandments). He gives no room for failure in their eyes, and their relationship (though begun in faith) can only be maintained or cultivated based on their obedience or ability to perform right.

2. PASSIVE FATHER

This type is nearly the opposite of the performance oriented father. The passive father makes no great demands at all. Often he is a workaholic. Mostly he is unable to express emotion. He can't love. More often than not, he is "not home", even when he is home. He is emotionally detached. He may work, provide and even be a "good man" in regard to his morals and business dealings, but his interaction with his family is basically nonexistent.

Those who have been reared under the influence of a passive father will no doubt see God, the Father through that lens. When God is spoken of in paternal terms, they will automatically correlate their earthly experience and think of God as a passive father. They will treat Him as one who doesn't love and is detached from them emotionally. Even when they pray or go to church, they consider that He is not really concerned about them. He has "too much to do." I have noticed in our culture today, that when a prayer is included in a television show, they more often than not begin like this, "Lord, I know You are too busy up there to care about little old me, but I could sure use Your help here." Invariably there is the concept that is perpetuated that He (God) is too busy with other things like running the universe (working) to care for us or our problems, tests or temptations.

3. ABSENTEE FATHER

An absentee father is where the dad is actually not physically available to the child. Usually, this type is either the result of death, divorce, imprisonment or abandonment. Over more than 3 decades of ministry I have seen all of those situations. I personally can relate to some of them. I was only eleven years old when I came home from school on Halloween, 1972, to be told that my father has passed away. One day I had him, the next he was gone forever. In much the same way, divorce has taken a great toll on the family unit in our world. It is just as prevalent in church/Christian circles as in non-believing ones. The hurting adults usually hurt one another, and often use the children as tools of control in that hurt. The children are hurt by it and often have the same feeling I had as the father was there each and every day, and now he is gone. When a father breaks the law, he is confined to prison and cannot be in the lives of his children as well. Then there are those who just leave their children and they don't ever see them again. A hole is left in their soul as their need for a father is left unmet.

This is a very prevalent view of God as Father. That He really doesn't care and is off somewhere else doing something else with someone else. He just started the earth spinning and then has moved on to other important things in the universe. When difficult times happen in life, as they do with everyone, there is no understanding that they can run to their Heavenly Father for aid, strength or direction. They feel all alone without a real connection to God.

4. ABUSIVE FATHER

Regretfully, there have been a myriad of testimonies that children have been subjected to abuse by their father. Often we find on the news channels some form of criminal abuse that has taken place in young children's lives. Over the years, I have been able to speak with those who have memories of that paternal abuse and have seen firsthand the difficulty this makes for the abused in relating to God as Father.

This abuse can take many forms. Some recount the physical abuse of beatings and lack of proper nutrition. Others can remember the sexual abuse and the shattered trust that type of sin creates. Still others are able to tell of the impact verbal abuse had on their lives. The Scripture says,

"Death and life are in the power of the tongue."
Prov. 18:21

To some of us, it is incomprehensible to think of a father abusing his child in these ways, but to the victims of such abuse, it is not only a reality, it is also the only real memory of a father that they have to understand.

As a victim of abuse is told to view God as their Heavenly Father, it can create real problems. They may struggle to believe that God really loves them unconditionally. They would certainly have real trust issues and that may hamper their growth in faith. Even the use of the word, "Love" may be tainted by the act of sexual abuse and make it difficult for the victim to open up to God.

If this is indicative of your past, understand that God is not angry with you. He really loves you with no strings attached. He doesn't want to hurt you, abuse, or take advantage of you. He desires to love you into health and a real relationship with Him. The type of relationship you always dreamed of having with your earthly father, is more closely related to God's love for you than the actual abuse you encountered.

5. AUTHORITARIAN FATHER

An authoritarian father lives by the law. He is the law! Often in this scenario, the family is encumbered with lists of do's and don'ts. Much like the performance oriented father, love and acceptance are equated with living by the rules of the dad. An authoritarian father will major on truth, yet minor on life. Obedience is everything. Dad said it, which makes it the law, so I had better do it or risk not being (or at least not feeling) loved. This concept has been expressed and even taught in some of our churches today. God is the, "Law Giver" and we had better keep that law or be punished to an eternal damnation to the lake of fire. Now, I'm not talking about unbelievers here, I am referring to people who have accepted Jesus as their personal Savior and by grace have the right to be called the children of God. He is viewed or at least portrayed as so authoritarian that His saved, sanctified, filled and called must look out for this tyrant from heaven that is looking over their shoulder every minute of every day just waiting on them to break a rule so they can be tossed from the family. Wow, that would not give any child a sense of security or love.

6. GOOD FATHERS

There are many good fathers, men who have made the commitments to keep God as the center of their lives and to live a godly, holy life before their children. They are focused on building a safe place for their kids to grow and expand their interests while keeping their thoughts on biblical values. They rarely, if ever, show their anger. They give their children room to fail and are there to pick them up when they do. They don't give their love in increments or because the child has performed up to a certain standard. Love, they believe, is deserved by all children as an innate fact of being their child.

Herein can lay a very fine line as we seek to understand how a person may use the lens of an earthly father to understand their Heavenly Father. Subtle issues may arise that can still undermine our perception of Father God. No matter how "good" we may be as fathers, we can never be perfect. We are human and all of our best intentions and actions are less than flawless. To compare even the best of human Christian dads to our Heavenly Father is to reduce the omnipotent, omniscient, God of the universe to a mere human expression of His infallible and inconceivable love for His children. Basically, the premise of this type of father figure is that even at our best we fall short of being a perfect and adequate lens for God.

This does not negate the necessity for fathers to express their unconditional love and to strive to live a life that is virtuous and godly before their children. It merely helps us understand that there may still be some father issues in a person's view of God as a Heavenly Father when they have had a great example of a loving, earthly father to use as a lens of comparison.

The Scriptures reveal exactly how Father God feels about us and the power of His love which is greater, stronger, and mightier than any or all of these father issues. The proper lens to learn to utilize for establishing our personal view of God as Father then, is His own words as He has recorded them for us in the Bible.

The following pages are an attempt to strengthen the Scriptural view we should have as children of our Heavenly Father and how He loves us unconditionally. It is another item from Jack Frost's teaching on the Father's Heart. It was printed and distributed in the form of a bookmark so that we might keep the truth of our Heavenly Father's unconditional (Agape) love before us at all times.

Though Jack has gone on to his eternal reward, the ministry that he and his wife, Tricia Frost, were commissioned by God to proclaim (Shiloh Place Ministry) is still making an impact on the body of Christ and this and other resources can be found through their ministry website:

http://www.shilohplace.org.

I Am Loved By The Father[3]

Jeremiah 31:3

He has loved me with an everlasting love.
I have never not been loved.

John 3:16

God loves me so much that He gave His only Son to die for me so I might have life.

John 16:27

The Father loves me so much He wants to express His love to me in a feeling sort of way.

John 17:23

 The Father loves me just as much as He loves His Son Jesus. (also v. 26)

Ephesians 2:4-6

 Even when I have sinned, the Father loves me and asks me to sit beside Him with Christ.

Ephesians 3:19

 The Father wants to fill me to overflowing with His love.

1 John. 3:1

 God has extended His love to me and called me His child.

I Am Accepted By The Father

John 1:12

 I am called a child of God.

John 15:15

 I am called Christ's friend.

Romans 5:1

 In Christ it is just as if I had never sinned.

1 Corinthians 6:19

 I belong to the Father.

1 Corinthians 12:27

 I am a member of Christ's body.

Ephesians 1:5

> I have been adopted by Father God.

Colossians 2:10

> I am complete in Christ.

I Am Secure In The Father

Romans 8:1, 2

> I am free forever from condemnation.

Romans 8:31

> The Father will always be there for me.

Romans 8:35

> Troubles will not separate me from God's love.

Colossians 3:3

> I am hidden with Christ in the Father.

Philemon 3:20

> I am a citizen of heaven.

2 Timothy 1:7

> I have not been given a spirit of fear but of power, love, and a sound mind.

Hebrews 4:16

> I can find grace and mercy in my time of need.

1 John 4:18

> His perfect love casts out all of my fear.

1 John 5:18
>   I belong to God, and the evil one has no right to touch me.

I Have Purpose In The Father

Matthew 5:13
>   I am the salt and the light of the earth. (v.14)

John 15:16
>   I have been chosen to bear fruit.

Acts 1:8
>   I am a witness of God to the world.

2 Corinthians 5:18
>   I am a minister of reconciliation for God.

2 Corinthians 5:20
>   I am God's ambassador to the world.

Philippians 4:13
>   I can do all things in Christ

God Is Not Ashamed Of Me

Hebrews 2:11
>   Jesus is not ashamed to call me His brother.

Hebrews 11:16
>   God is not ashamed to be my God.

God Does Not Judge Me

John 3:16-18
> God didn't send His Son to die for me so that I might be judged by Him. When I believe in Him, I am not judged.

John 5:22
> The Father does not judge me.

John 12:47
> When I hear Jesus' words and do not keep them, He does not judge me, for He came to save me, not to condemn me.

God Has Forgiven Me

Jeremiah 31:34
> He has forgiven my iniquity and remembers my sins no more.

Micah 7:18
> The Father so delights in loving me that He has put all my sins under His feet and cast them into the depths of the sea.

Colossians 1:14
> God has redeemed me and forgiven all my sin.

1 John 1:9
> God forgives and cleanses me from all my sin.

This change of perspective will alter our relationship with Almighty God. He wants to be viewed as our Father. He desires that we treat Him with the love and respect of a father. His longing is that we put off our outer façade and put on the innocence of a child as we worship, pray and relate to Him daily. This will radically change your daily walk with God and increase your love and fruitfulness as you act in response to His love rather than respond in fear of judgment. In our profound wisdom and intellectual capacity, we try to dissect everything and tend to make it more difficult. Robert Foster's words aid us in this new perspective as we close out this chapter.

> "We should never make prayer too complicated. We are prone to do so once we understand that prayer is something we must learn. It is also easy to yield to this temptation because the more complicated we make prayer, the more dependent people are upon us to learn how to do it. But Jesus taught us to come like children to a father. Openness, honesty, and trust mark the communication of children with their father. The reason God answers prayer is because His children ask. Further, there is an intimacy between parents and children that has room for both seriousness and laughter."[4]

This Father of ours...is also positionally the great, awesome, powerful Sovereign ruler of all.

-Dr. Lonnie E. Riley-

CHAPTER TWO

GAINING INSIGHT INTO HIS

SOVEREIGNTY:

"In Heaven"

Now we come to this positional statement, after we have considered the great and mighty love of God that exudes from His person. Beyond what you and I might consider understandable or appropriate, in our humanness we find that we have limits to our love. We are unable, or at least unwilling to concede that God in His great mercy has forged an agape love, one that has no limits, and one that is self sacrificing. It is also one that He calls us to emulate as He has filled (poured into) us through His Spirit. After understanding this great love, as in a Father's love and we begin to think about our Father, we move to the next phrase, or next portion of the phrase in this classic example of prayer given by Jesus.

There is a shift from "Our Father" to "in Heaven." This statement is not a vain or feeble attempt to restrict God in time, or even in place, but that this place that we have come to know of as "heaven" is the focus of the presence of God. We have been taught and as the Scriptures have revealed this place, heaven, as in the first heaven, that above us, the skies; the second heaven, the area beyond our atmosphere into space, and then the third heaven, that place where God is. That is not to say that He is not or incapable of being somewhere else, or that He is not everywhere else, for the psalmist is plain in letting us know that there is no way I can escape from His Presence. Even into the grave, into Sheol, He is there. So there is an omnipresent capacity of God. But there has always seemed to be a saturation point or a clear manifestation in particular from where the presence of God emanates or finds it's "beginning" per say.

There was a time according to the Scriptures of the Old Testament that the presence of God resided between the Cherubim of the mercy seat which was above the Ark of the Covenant. There God's presence was made visible. Did that mean that God was now no longer omnipresent? No! It just meant that His physical manifestation, the Shekinah Glory of God, was revealed and/or concentrated there. God is everywhere, in everything, and everything is revealed through Him.

As we move from the concept of Heavenly Father we now use this next statement as a transition or step into the contentious realm of the sovereignty of God. If

He is in heaven, high and exalted above all, then this statement should help us focus on the fact that He is the King of the Universe. This Father of ours, though relational as that term implies, is also positionally the great, awesome, powerful Sovereign ruler of all (everything).

Now, this has been an area of much debate and controversy. Over the millennia there seems to be two extreme schools of thought that have developed and these two camps have almost always butted heads. There is the thought that holds to the sovereignty of God as being the fact that God controls everything and then there is the camp that believes that God has nearly abdicated His control.

In the first camp God seems to be a strange mix. He seems to be a potentate that is arbitrary, He loves who He loves, He hurts who He wants to hurt, and He sends sickness where he wants to send sickness. He just seems to be a capricious God that at certain times one can understand His great love and then at other times one cannot understand the "why" of certain circumstances. Why would this happen to this person and not to that one? Too often leaders have offered an unintelligent response, without doing the work, without finding the balance of God's attributes, just saying, "It was God's will", or that God is sovereign, God is in control, God can do what He wants to do, how He wants to do it and with whom or to whom He wants to do it.

Next we find the other edge of the spectrum, or the other swing of the pendulum, in those that would say that God has basically abdicated His sovereignty. That He is, or was, God of all, Potentate, Supreme, but that He has now relinquished that strength, that potency and though He is still powerful, there are things that are more powerful. Maybe not theologically, but experientially we are saying, if we are not careful, that the love of God has caused the power of God to be of no effect. Again, we find no balance.

Well, what is this balance? Is it now true that everything is ok with God? That it really doesn't matter, so we don't have to worry about the wrath of God anymore? There is no concern over the judgment of God? That we don't have to follow the words of Scripture, "Be ye holy for I am holy?" Are we not supposed to be a particular people, set apart, sanctified? How are we to bring together these two areas? How can we understand both of these premises of theology and put them into a context that helps us understand the greater picture of the God Who is the object and the recipient of this prayer and of this communication?

Now, just in case you are already looking at the concordance of your bible, let me help you out. Nowhere in the King James Version of the Bible do we see or read the word sovereign. It is a concept, but it is not a word in the Authorized Version that any translator used. Now, is there a reason why it was not used? Why would there be? Let's think about it for a second. We are talking about a version that has some known discrepancies that have been touched to a degree because they understood it was going to be given to, or laid before the King of England, who in his own right was the sovereign King of England. Don't forget, King James was the potentate of that country. The one whose will would be done.

Though there should not have been, we cannot guarantee that there was not some type of human delineation from the things and the teachings of scripture in regard to the sovereignty of God, and the potency and the supremeness of God, that may have been watered down or inoculated so that these subjects of the sovereign king of England were not placed in harm's way themselves. It is a unique and thoughtful proposition that may require a little more study, a little more research which is not the object of this publication. For our purpose in this setting it is safe to assume the concept is revealed and developed throughout Scripture and as newer versions have been developed we do find the word, sovereign. It is actually used several times in the New International Version.

If God is sovereign (and we hold that He is), how do we find or relate this sovereignty effectual and yet not predominant? Those are two of the largest issues. If it is effectual in the fact that God is sovereign, then, God is always sovereign, everything is done according to the power, the will, the sovereignty and the oversight or direct intervention of God. If it is effectual, does that mean that it is intended to be the overwhelming or overbearing attribute of God?

For if God is love, as the Scriptures state and as we studied in the previous chapter, how does that love relate to the sovereignty of God? Does the sovereignty of God fall under the characteristic of love or does the characteristic of love bow before the sovereignty of God? Is there a hierarchy in the attributes of God, or is there a unique mystery? Perhaps there is a mysterious dimension regarding the fact that all the attributes of God are equal, balanced and effective. They stand alone, yet they stand together.

Let's look at one area and show the different process of thought in regard to sickness/healing. If God is totally sovereign, and it is His will that people become sick and He does that in order to teach them a lesson, then how does that relate to the love of God? And if that is His will, how can a devout follower of God pray for a healing that would counter His divine will? Maybe the prayer for healing is a plea for a manifestation of the mercy of God or His forgiveness. If God is merciful and removes the sickness He sent, is His mercy more powerful than His will? Is our confession greater than His power? Even closer to the heart of the matter is, if God designs that a person be sick because of the need for a lesson or in order to punish him/her, then to go to the medical doctor and begin a course of treatment or to pray for healing is to try to thwart the will and purpose of God that brought the sickness upon them in the first place.

But I do have these statements to make. I have no grandiose visions of being the scholar that breaks forth the divisions long held between men and women of God, those that are on one side or the other in regard to the sovereignty of God. I do want to communicate to the universal church that sometimes the way in which we treat God is inappropriate. Even in my home I remember, and my siblings confirm, there was a protocol concerning how we approached our loving father. It is so with God as well. We love to speak of His love. We enjoy the concept that He is a loving God and our Heavenly Father as we focused in the previous chapter, however, in the midst of all this, as we focus only on the love, we do ourselves, the church and the world a disservice by neglecting to teach and live in the shadow of His sovereignty. We serve God. We are loved by God. A sovereign God. The God of the Universe. The Creator of all things. When we pray, we are still praying not to an impotent being beyond the clouds, but we are communicating to a powerful, omnipresent, all powerful, merciful, loving ruler, king of the universe Who is our

Father.   There is a balance to be maintained and
boundaries to be observed.

As we study this concept of the sovereignty of God,
I am taking the liberty of walking down to the coast
where I live. I live a block away from the Atlantic Ocean
and I am overcome anew with the vastness of it. As far
as I can see there is water. Our planet is approximately
2/3 water. I gaze at this body of water and I think about
water in the Scripture. I think how the Spirit of the Lord
hovered over the deep, those waters.

Eventually, God uses water to bring forth His
judgment on those first humans. Saving only Noah, his
wife, Shem, Ham, Japheth (his sons) as well as their
wives.   Those eight God chooses, perhaps in His
sovereignty, yet not only in His sovereignty, but also in
His love, in His plan and also because of the word that is
used in the Scriptures for the very first time, Noah found
"Grace" in the eyes of the Lord. So there were many
attributes at play in this decision. After the deluge, God
promised to never flood the entire earth again. Is that
because of mercy, love, design or just because He is
sovereign and omnipotent?

You will often see that there are times when there
is a lack of water (droughts) in the Scriptures. We see the
Children of Israel needing water and God being the
Provider of such, even through a rock. We read that God
uses His power to split the water and allow the children
of Israel to pass through the Red Sea, yet He uses that
same power and that same water to destroy the Egyptian
army. God in His love gives water to His people, God in
His judgment says that the way Moses (whose very name
reflects that he was drawn out of the Nile waters)
provided water, the attitude with which he is credited by
God, was enough to keep him, the great prophet of God,

the great leader God raised up, from going into the land of promise.

One of the two new sacraments of the new church is showing one's obedience by being baptized. Baptism represents a dying to the old life and the rising to newness of life through the realms, the means of water. Eventually, there will be a river that flows from the very throne of God.

So I sit here and I look at all this water. More water than land. If something were to shift on the axis of our planet and suddenly the fishbowl of our existence were tilted in a different area, quickly and without any hesitation, I would be covered by the salt water that I now see stopping just yards from my feet. What is preventing this ocean from consuming me? What is stopping this salt water from contaminating this beach, these buildings, these people, these roads, this city or even this state? What is it that is preventing it? Is it a plan God put forth? Is it His sovereignty that He continually keeps a barrier that stops it from crossing? What motivates that sovereignty to do that? Is it grace? Is it love? Is it pity? Is it just that He has given His word, so it is His immutability? Huh?

Really consider what the motivating, mitigating factors in these things are. Must there just be one? Is it not possible that the sovereignty of God, the love of God, the mercy of God, the holiness of God, the omniscience of God, the omnipresence of God, the power of God, the grace and all the other attributes of God are all unified in this respect?

It is done by the power of God and to fully understand God, we must understand these attributes. In order for God to make Himself known to us in the dispensations of time, at certain times and events one characteristic or one attribute seems to be dominant for a season or for an entire dispensation or one attribute leads into the revelation of the other. So that we understand perhaps to a greater measure both the former and the latter.

For example, the Scripture teaches that the wages of sin is death. That is the wrath of God, the plan of God, part of the power of God and the holiness of God, that the wages, the earning, something that happens because of sin, yet, there is a gift of God. God is a giver and that gift is eternal life. That is provided because of the grace, love and mercy of God. Herein is love that God sent His one and only Son for us. So His love, the magnitude of His love, is demonstrated through a deeper understanding of his sovereignty. One magnifies the extent of the greatest of the other. And to allow, does not mean to abdicate. To place laws into effect does not mean to limit Him. His power is not limited just because He made the laws effectual.

That is a miracle. The power of God, motivated by other merciful, compassionate, loving attributes of God, crossing the "laws" of nature (put in place by God) will constitute the event we have labeled as miraculous. He has chosen in His sovereignty to put things in place and in order because of His omniscience, because He knows the best way for these things to come out. Those best ways will produce the holy, loving relationship He desires to have with His children.

GOD IS SOVEREIGN

If we will allow God to open the eyes of our heart, we will gain insight to the fact that the concentration of His manifested presence is focused in a place we refer to as heaven. He is not only in that place, but is also both the Creator and Ruler of it as well.

Just as communication has changed in the 5+ decades of my life, so has the attitude toward God Himself as well as what is sanctified, set apart and holy. The mind-set of many has been to humanize God. The Scriptures are very clear that He is far above us in thought and power. He is to be worshipped, not treated as though He is part of our "gang." I read somewhere years ago that, "God made man in his own image and man returned the compliment." Humans know that they can't stand before a Holy God, so in their practical theology (that which they practice daily) we have the tendency to not revere Him as Pure and Holy. We have humanized God to the extent that we no longer fear or respect Him.

When we begin to keep God in high esteem and understand that He is sovereign, our love and awe of Him will have a powerful basis point. But I'm getting ahead of myself. What does it really mean to be sovereign? When we look up the various definitions of the word, we find statements like, superlative in quality, of the most exalted kind, of an unqualified nature, having undisputed ascendancy and possessed of supreme power.[1]

Truly, God is all of this and more. In order to properly focus and partially comprehend His sovereignty, we will delve into these statements and try to understand how they are applicable to God.

SUPERLATIVE IN QUALITY

Superlative is not a word that has been given much colloquial use in recent years. Most understand it's meaning as to be above, or higher than its comparisons. Though God has no real comparisons, He is definitely above all in the universe in both the physical and spiritual dimensions. He is without equal, exceptional, matchless and supreme.

To be superlative in quality is to render Him as excellent in every way. There is nothing wrong or out of place in regards to Him. He is not sinful, nor does He allow sin into His presence. His thoughts are above our thoughts. His ways exceed ours.

Both His thoughts and actions are superior and excellent. Who can know the mind of God? How can finite man even pretend to grasp His thoughts? Now, without a true understanding of His thoughts, we cannot attribute to Him a motive for His actions. He does or refrains from doing based on His thought process that we freely admit is beyond our limitations.

He is our Sovereign. We must take the position, by faith, that whatever He does, allows, or refrains from doing is for both our personal good and the advancement of His Kingdom and is eminently greater than our feeble notions or ideas. Our selfish wants and desires are not the foundations of His decision making process. He loves us, and knows what is best for us as well as what is profitable to His kingdom.

OF THE MOST EXALTED KIND

He is exalted above all in the universe. He is on the throne of the universe, high and exalted above all the earth. As such, He is worthy of our praise, adoration and tribute. In ancient times, a conquered foe would pay tribute to their new sovereign for several reasons.

First, they paid because it was part of the agreement made between the parties in negotiating the surrender. Second, they paid and continued to pay so that there would not be a renewed attack on their country. Third, the payment placed them under the care and protection of the new monarch.

We pay tribute, as those in historical times would pay tribute to their king. Our tribute is offered because we love Him for His great mercy and love. Our tribute is not monetary; it is that in all things we live our life so that we bring honor and blessing to Him.

"Yours, O Lord, is the kingdom; You are exalted as head over all. Wealth and honor come from You; You are the ruler of all things. In Your hands are strength and power to exalt and give strength to all"
1 Chronicles 29:11, 12, (NIV)[2]

In recent years a fresh look at an exalted God has permeated our genre of music with such title as, "I Exalt Thee" and "How Great Is Our God." These bring our focus back to the ascendancy of our God and help us develop a fresh appreciation and awe for the Mighty One we serve.

OF AN UNQUALIFIED NATURE

When we use the term, unqualified, we are not using it in the sense of without qualifications or incompetent, rather we are using it in the sense of unable to be qualified. The nature of God is vast. It is ever revealing.

As soon as the Children of Israel understood one aspect of the nature of God, another facet of His nature would be revealed. Sometimes that new feature or characteristic would complement what they already understood or had just learned about God. At other times, the new revelation would seem to be opposed to another aspect of God. Even today we have those who focus on legalism over grace, or mercy above accountability.

Understanding that God's nature is unable to be qualified, simply means that we cannot put Him in our own convenient box and expect Him to always act or respond the same way. Through the Scriptures God is revealed in many ways. The most prominent choice of His revelation is through the use of compound names. He may be known as "The God that heals" and/or "The God that provides." This knowledge is expressed in differing additions to the name for God. This concept will be developed much more in our next chapter as we consider the phrase, "Hallowed be Thy Name."

HAVING UNDISPUTED ASCENDANCY

Now here is a word with which most of us are familiar. UNDISPUTED. In the realm of sports it is always the hope for the outcome to be undisputed, meaning of course that there can be no disputing (argument, disagreement, difference of opinion or quarrel over) the final results.

Every four years the world places each country's prize athletes in competition with one another at the Olympics. There are many rules and protocols that have to be both adhered to and enforced for there to be a successful ending to the games. Over the last few decades, there seems to have always been some type of dispute over qualification, technique, drug enhancement . . . the list could go on and on. There have been many disqualifications and even some cause for others to relinquish their title and medal. This leaves a bitter taste in the mouth of spectators and gives the offender and his country a proverbial black eye on the world stage.

There was a time in my younger years (I really don't like having to qualify it that way) when the heavy weight boxing belt was divided between the professional entities and there was no agreement on who was the real champion. In the mid '80's, a series of unification bouts between the rival champions was conducted in order to unify the belt. This resulted in Mike Tyson being proclaimed the "Undisputed Heavy Weight Champion of the World."

Now, this does not always mean that there are no detractors. There are always those who concoct some alternate reality and try to dismiss the results, even in sports where the winner should be obvious.

In declaring that God has undisputed ascendancy, we are affirming the Word of God as true in its claim. We can find within the writings of Scripture that God is often revealed as being high and lifted up, above all powers and thrones.

"For You, Lord, are most high above all the earth;
You are exalted far above all gods."
Psalm 97:9

Even in the record of the fall of Lucifer we find his statement as a testimony to God's ascendancy. He says he will "ascend into heaven," "Exalt his throne," "ascend above the clouds," and be like the "Most High."

"How you are fallen from heaven,
O Lucifer, son of the morning!
How you are cut down to the ground,
You who weakened the nations!
For you have said in your heart:
'I will ascend into heaven,
I will exalt my throne above the stars of God;
I will also sit on the mount of the congregation
On the farthest sides of the north;
I will ascend above the heights of the clouds,
I will be like the Most High.'
Yet you shall be brought down to Sheol,
To the lowest depths of the Pit."
Isaiah 14:12-15

Yes, there may be detractors and doubters. There may even be so called "scholars" who will argue against

God's undisputed ascendancy, but the reality is that God has proclaimed it, and to disclaim it is both heresy and idiocy. To put it bluntly and clearly so as to not allow any misunderstanding, to take a stand against the Sovereign God of the universe is for all practical purposes an act of treason. And in most, if not all countries in our world, that is punishable by death (Romans 6:23).

POSSESSED OF SUPREME POWER

Most Americans understand the concept of Supreme. One of the three branches of our government is the judicial branch which finds it's culmination in the Supreme Court of the United States. The Supreme Court has the final word on the legality of an issue and has the power to strike down anything it deems unconstitutional. There is no other legal remedy once this court has ruled. There is nowhere else to litigate in order to topple their ruling.

The word, "Omnipotent" is the .25 cent word theologians use to describe the all encompassing, supreme power of our Sovereign Lord. He has both the capacity and the will to stretch forth His mighty arm and act on behalf of His plan. He has shown His inclination to exert the great power even in creation. With just a word, He is able to create both the seen and visible realm out of unseen and invisible matter.

As one reviews the testimony of Scripture, as alluded to above, we see the hand of God creating everything from nothing to destroying everything in a flood; opening barren wombs, producing water from a rock and delivering manna from the sky. He stops the sun from setting, moves nation against nation, and even closes the mouths of lions and protects His messengers from being consumed by fire. There is nothing that is impossible with our mighty God. He is able to go way beyond our thoughts, dreams and plans. The Scriptures even quote Him as saying such.

> *"Is anything too hard for the Lord? At the appointed time I will return to you, according to the time of life, and Sarah shall have a son."*
> Genesis 18:14

> *"Behold, I am the Lord, the God of all flesh. Is there anything too hard for Me?*
> Jeremiah 32:27

Before we leave this topic allow me to encapsulate my theory of the sovereignty of God.

GOD IS IN CONTROL!

There is nothing, absolutely not-a-thing that happens in the entire universe that is outside of God's influence and authority. He is King of all kings and Lord of all lords and as such has NO limitations. He is Alpha and Omega (the beginning and the end), He is present everywhere so that everyone can know Him. He is above all things and before all things. He created everything (visible, invisible, heavenly and earthly) and holds it all together.

He knows everything (past, present and future). Nothing is too hard for Him, for He has ALL power and authority to use it. He answers to no one as He is LORD Most High. All others must eventually answer to Him. There is no limit to His sovereignty, yet He has chosen in His sovereignty to create man as a free moral agent with the freedom of choice of whether to obey or disobey the Sovereign King of the Universe. He does not control each person's will. We each have the freedom to choose whether or not we will participate in His grand design for the universe.

God's sovereignty is but one of His attributes. It is not the overwhelming attribute to which all others must kneel, but rather (as also is the case of His love) it permeates all of the other attributes. Though at times we may only see one of His characteristics at work in any given circumstance, they are all still part of Who He is and they collectively make Him God.

CHAPTER THREE

GAINING INSIGHT INTO HIS

CHARACTER:

"Hallowed be Your Name."

In church, sometimes we use words that have little or no real meaning to the ordinary person, and we can alienate them if we are not careful. They can zone out and not focus back in when we utilize what many have called "Christianese." Some of those statements that make perfect sense to we who are believers, can cause confusion and misunderstanding in those who are seeking God. "Have you found Jesus?"

"Have you been washed in the blood?" "I want to be under the spout where the glory comes out." "Are you sold out for Jesus?" "The old man is dead." "Give God your first fruits." And, "Do you feel convicted?"

Hallowed, is not a word we use much today. The average person might hear it and think of October 31st, Halloween. Some may equate it with something without a core or center as in a hollowed out tree, as a sound that a wolf might make toward the moon (howling).

The basic meaning of the Greek word is to be or make holy, to consecrate, to set apart or sanctify.[1] It comes from the root word used for the term, *Saint* in other portions of the New Testament. And saints are those that are God's elect and are understood to be set apart for God's use, consecrated and made Holy by the infilling of God's Holy Spirit.

Using that as our reference point, we believe that Jesus is teaching that the actual name of our Father in Heaven is holy, separated, pure and to be revered and treated as such. If you are familiar with the Ten Commandments given to Moses on Mount Sinai, this will remind you of number four:

> *"You shall not take the name of the Lord your*
> *God in vain, for the Lord will not hold him*
> *guiltless who takes His name in vain."*
> Exodus 20:7

I was reared in an environment where the Name and Word of God were revered highly and it was unacceptable to speak derogatory of either one. As I have grown in my theological studies, I have deepened my respect for both, with a new and distinct understanding of this commandment, the statement in the prayer and the actual Name of God as given to Moses at the burning bush.

Let me now endeavor to explain why I am equating this with gaining insight into God's character.

What is in a name? What does it mean? Allot of us want to know who we are and where we came from. There are several websites available today to assist you in creating a family tree by finding information about your ancestors. There is a flea market near my home in Myrtle Beach that is open seven days a week during the tourist season. It is not your normal flea market, it is really little stores that are kept up by individuals that are not willing to purchase or lease a storefront location, instead they rent space in this old mall. There are several places that have little certificates with people's names on them followed by the meaning of those names. I just find it very intriguing that there are people who are actually making a living by telling people what their names mean and offering that meaning for sale on a certificate.

On my 50th birthday, besides the usual, playful gifts mocking my age and senility, I also received a large framed history of the name "Riley" along with a copy of my family crest. It is very meaningful to me and hangs in a very prominent place in our home. It tells of our Irish (or Scottish) roots and even mentions some notable people from our lineage. Most people love hearing what their names mean.

During the summer of 2013, Kim and I enjoyed our first season at the beach as much as we could. We went to the beach often, but we spent more time actually in our pool. Kim does not feel safe in the ocean where she can't see what is around her (especially since there are shark sightings daily). The pool was a great place to meet our new neighbors. There are only a handful of people who live in our community year round, the rest of the units were occupied on a weekly basis by people from all over the nation. Kim and I enjoyed meeting everyone, but I have a tendency to become "Uncle Lonnie" to all the little ones.

One week we had a couple of elementary age girls who enjoyed playing around us. Their names were Sophie and Grace. While swimming one day, I asked them if they knew what their names meant. Neither of them had a clue. I took the time to tell them the ancient Greek meanings of their names. They loved knowing that so much that they ran to their parents and exclaimed who their name revealed them to be. Sophia means "Wise" and Grace means a "Gift." I referred to them that way the rest of the week and they began to reflect the meaning in their demeanor. They pranced around making sure everyone knew of their wisdom and that they were as special as a Christmas or birthday gift. Yes, it was very cute.

In biblical times, names had meaning as well. Consider the first man, Adam, His name means "red man." Eve's name means, "Life." As the progression of Scripture develops, we see many names that have distinct meaning. I will highlight a few for us to prime our memories.

During the time of the three patriarchs the meaning of names described the person or their destiny. Abram came from the Ur of the Chaldeans and settled in Canaan. God struck a covenant with him and changed his name to Abraham, meaning, "Father of a multitude." This was prophetic since as of yet he had no children and he was advanced in age.

When the promised child was born, Abraham was instructed to name him, Isaac, meaning "laughter" because Sarah (whose name had also been changed to mean Princess) had chuckled at the prophecy.

Isaac had twins and the second born was named Jacob, meaning "The supplanter," or "deceiver" recognizing his deceitful nature. However, once he returned to Canaan, he wrestled with The Angel of the Lord the night before he was to meet his indignant brother, Esau (rough). As the wrestling match wore on, Jacob was able to hold tightly the Angel who demanded to be let loose. Jacob would not relent without a blessing from the Angel. The Angel demanded that Jacob confess his name, and once he did, God gave him a new name, "Israel," meaning prince with God. God's people would become known as, "The children of Israel" or the nation of "Israel." It is so even today.

Moses' name means, "Drawn forth," named so by the princess of Egypt that drew him out of the Nile. Joshua means, "Jehovah is salvation." On and on it goes. Each king of Israel and Judah had telling meaning to their names. Even at the simplest levels of naming one might be known as Ben- with the father's name placed after it. For example, Ben-hadad, the king of Syria during the reign of Ahab, means, "Son of Hadad." Simple, yet meaningful.

As we jump into the New Testament we see meaning to certain names as well. Jesus means, "Jehovah Saves" and Immanuel means, "God with us." Simon's name is changed to Peter, "A rock" and Saul's name is changed to Paul, "Little."

The beauty of the Scriptures is that they reveal God to us. There is a pulling back of the curtain around the spiritual world and revelation takes place. From the beginning of Scripture until the end of the book of Revelation, we come to understand God, albeit incrementally. One of the major ways that He is revealed to us is through the recording of His actions.

The people of the Bible would use compound names for God based on His actions and/or character. Each of the names of God has a specific meaning or reveals aspects of the nature, character and attributes of God.

The experiences of the people of God as they grew to know, understand and relate to their God helped them understand Who He was. What kind of God they served. As they understood His personality or disposition they added to the name to reveal those traits. In the same way they would relate to His integrity and temperament and add some type of description to His name.

When they were blessed to have a new revelation of some part of God's character, they would often add that characteristic as a compound to His name. Much the way today we might say of a man, "He is a loving father." In this example we already know he is a father, but we compound it with loving after seeing him interact with his children. Next we might say that the same man is a "Strict father." He is no less a father, but we see a little deeper into his personality or disposition. One trait does not negate the previous one, but rather may compliment or expound upon it and it may just reveal a completely different aspect of the man that is totally without reliance on the other traits. Consider this; the strictness of the father may reflect his great love for his children and/or the love of the father may be the motivating force behind his strictness. The more additions to the term, "father" that we create, the clearer our understanding of the type of father he is. Other traits (names) we might add to a father are: Good, bad, sorry, strong, or faithful.

So it is in Scripture with God. We don't always see it in our English versions. I will attempt to uncover some of the names of God so that we may understand some of His nature. This is not intended to be an exhaustive listing or study of the many meanings and nuances of the translations available. We will merely break the surface; there are plenty of books out there that will dissect all of the implications within God's many titles and the significance they hold to Israel, the Church and the world in general. We will focus our attention on the three more notable names of El, Adonai, and JHVH.

EL

The word El comes from a root word meaning "might, strength, power." This basic form is used over 250 times in the Old Testament. The name, "El," was used of any deity. The gentiles used it often as they referred to their false gods. Sometimes it is translated as "Mighty" when referring to angles or even to men. When used of the true God of Israel, "El" is almost always qualified by additional words that further define the meaning that distinguish Him from false gods. Let's look at these "compound" names and see how we might *GAIN INSIGHT* into God's character through them.

El Elyon: Translated as "The Most High God." It reveals God the Supreme Sovereign, the Strongest of the strong. This is the name used in Abraham's encounter with Melchizedek king of Salem in Genesis 14:18-20. In

Psalm 9:2, the Psalmist vows to sing praises to "El Elyon." There are some instances where God is just called "Elyon."

El Roi: We find the use of this name for God when Hagar, Sarah's handmaid from Egypt, runs from the cruel treatment of her jealous mistress in Genesis 16:13. When she is visited by the Angel of the LORD, she uses this compound for God which is translated as, "You-Are-the-God-Who-Sees."

El Shaddai: Though the root understanding of this name is, "The All Sufficient God," most English versions translate it as, "God Almighty." Over the centuries there has been some differing opinions surrounding the etymology of "Shaddai." When the Septuagint (the Greek translation of the Old Testament) was translated, the thought was that Shaddai delineated from the verb "Shadad" which means "to overpower" or "to destroy.

The Latin Vulgate continued the thought by translating it as "Omnipotens" (where we get our word Omnipotent.) Basically it was saying that God is so overpowering that He is considered "Almighty." The blessing Jacob gives in Genesis 49:25, however, reveals that Shaddai might be related instead to the word for breasts (shadaim). This would indicate that sufficiency and nourishment come from God. God first uses this Name when He refers to multiplying Abraham's offspring (Gen. 17:2). Used almost exclusively in reference to the three patriarchs (Abraham, Isaac, and Jacob), El Shaddai was the primary name by which God was known to them (according to Exodus 6:2-3).

El Olam: The Everlasting God is the way it is translated in Genesis 21:33. This speaks of the infinity of God. Its basic meaning is, "God of eternity; God the everlasting; God forever." (Vines 98) We understand this to mean that He is without beginning or ending. This is a difficult concept for us to internalize since we celebrate birthdays (beginnings) and mourn at funerals (endings).

El Kanno: This is used by God to describe Himself in the 2nd of the Ten Commandments as a Jealous God. Some of the other instances cause us to see Him as a passionate bridegroom who lovingly watches over His bride.

El Rachum (El malei Rachamim): As the root of the word "Rechem" means womb, it denotes both the compassion and mercy of God.

El Hanne'eman: This opens our eyes to God's faithfulness, translated in Deut. 7:9 as, "The faithful God."

El Haggadol: "Gadol" means great, grand or awesome specifically in reference to God. Moses used this compound of El in Deuteronomy 10:17 during his appeal to Israel to follow after God wholly and to repent of their stiff-necked behavior.

El De'ot: In calling on the omniscience of God, Hannah used this name for God during her prayer when she brought Samuel to Eli as a young child to serve in the house of the LORD (1 Samuel 2:3). It means, "God of Knowledge."

El Hakkavod: The Hebrew term for, "Glory" is kavod. It carries the implications of weightiness and honor. It is the main word used to describe God's glory in the tabernacle or temple. When the Ark of the Covenant was stolen during Eli's days as Priest, his daughter-in-law named her new born child, "Ichabod" meaning, "The Glory has departed." This name reveals the glorious nature of God as, "The God of Glory."

El Sali: The Psalmist refers to, "The God of my Strength" in Psalm 42:9. It literally means that God is my rock.

El Yeshuatenu: Uniquely, this name is from the word meaning salvation, victory or deliverance. He is known as, "The God of our Salvation." The uniqueness is in the similarity of the Jewish Name for Jesus, "Yeshua." Closely related to that is, "The God of my Salvation", El Yeshuati.

El Yisrael: It is easily seen that the compound here is Israel. This is the Name given as, "The God of Israel."

El Hakkadosh: Kaddosh carries the meanings of clean, holy, set apart or one of a kind. Often in Scripture God is pictured as being Holy. Isaiah said the cherubim were singing, "Holy, Holy, Holy" that is, "Kaddosh, Kaddosh, Kaddosh." This compound is rendered as, "The Holy God."

Immanuel: Most of us are somewhat familiar with this name. It is used in the Christmas story as meaning, "God with us." And that is a correct translation. Actually,

Immanu is a plural preposition and El is placed at the end of the name. Literally it is, "With us God."

El Echad: The One God. (Malachi 2:10)
The meaning of Echad is one. And it makes us think of its use in the Shemah:

> *"Hear, O Israel:*
> *The LORD our God is one LORD;"*
> Deuteronomy 6:4

Elohim: The first instance where God is mentioned in the Bible reads as follows,

> *"In the beginning God created the heavens and*
> *the earth."*
> Genesis 1:1

The Hebrew word used for God is Elohim. This is the plural form of God and means "Creator" or "Judge."

Eli: Though this form is actually a proper name of the Priest who took Samuel in and taught him the ways of God, it is also part of one of the sayings of Jesus while He was on the cross.

> *"And about the ninth hour Jesus cried out with a*
> *loud voice, saying, "Eli, Eli, lama sabachthani?"*
> *that is, "My God, My God, why have You forsaken*
> *Me?"*
> Matthew 27:46

The addition of the "i" at the end makes it possessive thus meaning, "My God."

YHVH

Now we come to an area of no little dispute. This Name has confounded people for thousands of years. Some scholars have endeavored to break the code while many have fearfully chosen to leave it alone in a spirit if reverence and awe. It has been pronounced as Jehovah, Yahweh or Yahveh. Yet these translations are but educated guesses that are less than foolproof.

The tetragrammaton, four letters, of Y (yod), H (Hey), V (Vav) and H (Hey) are the consonants of the actual Name of God as given to Moses at the burning bush. When he was "negotiating" over God's call on his life to become the agent of God in delivering the Israelites, he asked for God's name. God replied, "Ehye asher ehyeh" translated in the King James Version as, "I AM THAT I AM." It comes from the verb, "To exist, or to be."

Because of the strong admonition of God to not take His Name in vain in the Ten Commandments, the children of Israel would not even attempt to say it, less they violate the command unwittingly and be held guilty. Only 10 times a year would the Kohen Gadol (High Priest) utter the Name and that was only during performing his duties on Yom Kippur.

In an attempt to ensure that the Name was not taken in vain, the Scribes (Masoretes) inserted the vowels from the word Adonai (my Lord) into the tetragrammaton to create Jehovah. Later it was conceived that the scribes may have inverted the vowels of Adonai and placed them in YHVH creating Yahweh or Yahveh.

The bottom line is that we don't know the correct pronunciation. The vowel pointing system of today was not invented until around 600 A.D. Therefore ancient Hebrew was purely consonantal, with no way of knowing the vowels intended between the consonants of the Name. Much of the language at that time was verbally passed down from generation to generation and used so often that there was no dispute on the way a word should be pronounced. But since there was no use of the Name in general and only 10 in specific, once a year, there is simply no way to confirm the actual proper pronunciation of this Name.

When an Israelite is reading the Torah and comes upon the Name, they will substitute the word Adonai (my Lord) in its place. When not reading Torah or the Siddur, most observant Jewish people will refer to the sacred name simply as "Hashem" meaning "the Name."

This Name appears over 6,800 times in the Scriptures. In the KJV, and the subsequent NKJV, the actual Name is rendered as LORD (all caps.) When the actual use of Adonai (my Lord) is used in conjunction with YHVH, then the Name is translated as GOD (also all caps.)

Since we will be studying Adonai next, in order to keep confusion at bay as we look at some of the compounds of the Name, I will utilize the tetragrammaton YHVH to signify the personal Name of God prior to the addition of the compound. Again, we are not attempting to create an exhaustive listing of all the compounds associated with YHVH, but to open our eyes to the characteristics of God as revealed in some of these names.

YHVH Elohim: Actually a compound of two of the names of God. This is translated as, "The LORD God."

YHVH Yir'eh (Jireh): "The LORD sees" is used by Abraham when speaking to Isaac on Mount Moriah. Isaac asked where the sacrifice was (not knowing he was the intended sacrifice) and Abraham answered with this compound. It has developed that God not only sees our needs, but will provide for them, so that it often is used as "Jehovah Jireh", "God will provide." We often sing this song,

> *"Jehovah Jireh, my Provider, His grace is sufficient for me. Jehovah Jireh, my Provider, His grace is sufficient for me. My God shall supply all my needs according to His riches in glory. He shall give His angels charge over me; Jehovah Jireh cares for me, for me, for me. Jehovah Jireh cares for me."*

YHVH Nissi: Meaning, "The LORD is my Banner" this compound stresses that God is our rallying point and our means of victory; the One who fights for His people.

YHVH Shalom: "The LORD of Peace." Shalom actually refers to more than just the absence of strife. It speaks of wholeness in body, soul and spirit. Your entire welfare is reflected when one speaks of shalom. It intimates health, prosperity, favor, safety and that all is well. Shalom is also used as a salutation.

YHVH Tseva'ot (Sabbaoth): "The LORD of armies (hosts)." A military figure portraying God as the commander of the armies of heaven.

YHVH Ro'i: "The LORD my Shepherd." This is used as the beginning of the 23rd Psalm. The very term "shepherd" creates a loving, caring, providing and protecting image of God that has provided strength and comfort for His followers that has transcended the two covenants.

YHVH Rophe':   Exodus 15:26 first reveals this compound of the Name meaning, "The LORD Who heals you." It was in connection with a promise from God that none of the diseases He placed on the Egyptians would fall on the Israelites if they would heed the voice of God and obey Him.

ADONAI

This name is the plural of Adon and means lord or master. It carries the concept of ownership in 1 Kings 16:24. It is often used in the Scriptures, and as mentioned earlier, was the word of choice to utilize instead of YHVH when the Torah was being read.

There are compounds associated with Adonai, mostly in conjunction with the other names of God creating a more majestic name, i.e. "The Lord GOD" or "The Lord GOD of Hosts."

JESUS

When Jesus shared this model of prayer, He was addressing young Hebrew men that had just begun their mentoring relationship (discipleship) under His tutelage. He broke spiritual ground in creating the paradigm shift of calling God our Father. Yet He also created a balance that included a continual respecting, honoring, and revering of God's Name.

Jesus would later expose another aspect in successful prayer to His followers. This new revelation would be brought to light during the intimate conversations that took place the night before His crucifixion and it would change the prayers of His disciples forever. They (and we) are now told to pray in His (Jesus') name! Recall these statements from Scripture.

*"And whatever you ask **IN MY NAME**, that I will do, that the Father may be glorified in the Son. If you ask anything **IN MY NAME**, I will do it."*
John 14:13-14 (emphasis mine)

*"You did not choose Me, but I chose you and appointed you that you should go and bear fruit, and that your fruit should remain, that whatever you ask the Father **IN MY NAME** He may give you."*
John 15:16 (emphasis mine)

*"And in that day you will ask Me nothing. Most assuredly, I say to you, whatever you ask the Father **IN MY NAME** He will give you. Until now you have asked nothing **IN MY NAME**. Ask, and you will receive, that your joy may be full."*
John 16:23-24 (emphasis mine)

*"Therefore God also has highly exalted Him and given Him the name which is above every name, that at the **NAME OF JESUS** every knee should*

*bow, of those in heaven, and of those on earth,
and of those under the earth, and that every
tongue should confess that Jesus Christ is Lord,
to the glory of God the Father."*
Philippians 2:9-11 (emphasis mine)

ANOTHER THOUGHT

Now, so that we do not become too highly exalted
in our own self-righteous keeping of the commandment
regarding the Name of God, let's remember how God
Himself expanded the interpretation of the command in
Malachi 1:6-2:6. Especially consider this statement:

*"To you priests who despise My name. Yet you
say, 'In what way have we despised Your name?"*
Malachi 1:6

I'm sure they were more than confident that they had
not spoken the personal name of God. Most likely they
were devout enough to have either used Adonai as a
replacement when reading or Hashem (the Name) when
speaking. How did God say they had despised His name?
God desires that His name be great among the Gentiles,
that incense be offered in His Name, and that His name
be revered. How were the priests profaning God's name?
He outlines it for them, for they were:

1. Offering defiled food on His altar. (1:7)
2. Offering blind sacrifices, the lame and sick.
   (1:8)

3. Offering the stolen, the lame, and the sick. (1:13)

Remember that according to the sacrificial law (Word of God), a sacrifice must have no blemish. It was to be perfect. They profaned His name by offering to God that which is less than He desires, asks, or commands is evil (1:8). He counsels them to offer something that way to their Governor and see how that makes him feel and how he reacts towards them. It was more than just the speaking of the Name in a wrong way, God deepened the meaning to cover our way of life lived before the world as we carry His name. Later in Malachi God makes a grand promise,

> *"But to you who fear My name*
> *The Sun of Righteousness shall arise*
> *With healing in His wings*
> *And you shall go out*
> *And grow fat like stall-fed calves.*
> *You shall trample the wicked, for they shall be*
> *ashes under the soles of your feet*
> *On the day that I do this."*
> *Says the LORD of hosts."*
> Malachi 4:2-3

We do well to understand and continually contemplate that both our speech and our conduct can glorify or despise the Name of our Lord. Not only those within the availability of our company and access to our personal life see this, but God is taking note of how we "Hallow" His name in word and deed.

CONCLUSION

According to this prayer, we must keep in mind that we are to revere (keep holy, separate and pure) the Name of Our Father, Who is in heaven.

That Name opens our eyes and helps us to GAIN insight into His magnificent character. What a wonderful, matchless, glorious God we serve! In succinct fashion, let's review that according to His names (His character) revealed in Scripture He is:

Sovereign, yet He sees me; He is all sufficient, almighty and everlasting; He is jealous, yet compassionate, merciful and faithful; He is awesome, omniscient and glorious; the God of my strength, the God of our salvation and the God of Israel. He is Creator, Holy, With Us and My Personal God. He is my Lord, my Provider, my Banner and my Peace. He is my Commander, my Shepherd and my Healer.

He is YHVH; everything I may ever need!

And Jesus went about all Galilee, teaching in their synagogues, preaching the gospel of the kingdom, and healing all kinds of sickness and all kinds of disease among the people.

-Matt.4:23-

CHAPTER FOUR

GAINING INSIGHT INTO HIS

KINGDOM:

"Your Kingdom Come"

I n chapter two we explored the premise of God's sovereignty. Our primary intent was to understand the foundational principle that God is in control. In this chapter we want to *GAIN INSIGHT* into the Kingdom that our Sovereign rules. The topic of the Kingdom of God is too complex for even one volume to cover let alone one chapter, so we must set the parameters we will use in discussing it.

As we delve into this field of study we will dissect the concept of the Kingdom in the following way:

1. It is established.
2. This Kingdom is not a democracy.
3. The Kingdom is not a religion.
4. It is in us now.
5. It will come on the earth.

IT IS ESTABLISHED

It is important that we begin this understanding with a realization that this prayer is not asking for the Kingdom of God to be established. It is already so. God is the ruler of an already established Kingdom. This kingdom originated from Him as the "self-existing one or self-sufficient one." He is the creator of all things both visible and invisible and He is independent from both. They are reliant upon Him, but He is not dependent upon either or both of them.

First, God fashioned the invisible world of powers and angels. He created the domain or realm of His invisible kingdom and called it "heaven." Because of His great love and desire to share that love, He spoke and the visible cosmos was created. At the center or heart of that creation was God's crowning event, the production of one who was constructed in God's likeness and commissioned to reign over this newly created visible plain. Adam.

Through the temptation and fall of mankind, the authority to rule over God's visible realm was relinquished or abdicated. By virtue of their "bowing" to the temptation and "yielding" to the tempter, they in effect surrendered the dominion of the visible realm of God's kingdom to satan.

The Old Testament is the story of God's plan to bring about the restoration of His original design that mankind be in relationship with Him and do His will and bidding as His ambassadors to the created visible realm. This is to be accomplished by the sending of a new "Second" Adam, in Jesus Christ. One Who was able to assume the authority of God, while human, and assert Himself over satan and eventually take control over the abdicated kingdom (Matthew 28:18).

In order to accomplish this, without crossing the laws and borders He set in place, God chose a man (Abraham) to create a people or nation (Israel) through which He would send this Second Adam. Through the ups and downs of this nation's faith, God led them and prepared the way for the eventual revealing of the promised Messiah, Jesus, who is the Second Adam.

John the Baptist was the prophesied forerunner of Jesus with the responsibility of proclaiming the coming of God's Messiah to the nation of Israel. While ministering at the Jordan River, John's vibrant and sometimes poignant call to faith, repentance and baptism was laced with these hopeful and life-giving words,

*"Repent, for the **KINGDOM OF HEAVEN** is at hand!"*
Matt. 3:1 (emphasis mine)

Interestingly, Jesus, as He began His earthly ministry, reiterated the same message,

> *"Repent, for the **KINGDOM OF HEAVEN** is at hand."*
> Matthew 4:17 (emphasis mine)

Part of Jesus' ministry as it developed and grew was to continue the proclamation of the good news of the kingdom.

> *"And Jesus went about all Galilee, teaching in their synagogues, preaching the **GOSPEL OF THE KINGDOM**, and healing all kinds of sickness and all kinds of disease among the people."*
> Matt.4:23 (emphasis mine)

In the Sermon on the Mount, Jesus takes us through what we have come to know as the Beatitudes. He pronounces that certain attitudes and actions are rewarded with a specific blessing. It is fascinating that the only reward that is repeated in the list is the promise of the kingdom. And even more interesting is the use of the word "is" instead of a promise such as, "shall be at the end of the age." It is available now, not at the end of time. It is a present reality and possibility for the children of Father God.

> *"Blessed are the poor in spirit,*
> *For theirs is the **KINGDOM OF HEAVEN**."*
> Matt. 5:3 (emphasis mine)

> *"Blessed are those who are persecuted for righteousness' sake, For theirs is the **KINGDOM OF HEAVEN**."*
> Matt. 5:10 (emphasis mine)

As Jesus teaches further in that message on the mountain, He explains that we are not to worry, but rather to have faith in God's protection and provision for us. As God takes care of birds and flowers He will also take care of us, His children. These creatures do not "toil or spin" (labor or stress), because they just instinctively know that God sustains them. Jesus motivates us to keep our priority on seeking the kingdom of God and allow the Father's great love for us to manifest in His taking care of our needs.

*"Seek first the **KINGDOM OF GOD** and His righteousness, and all these things shall be added unto you."*
Matt. 6:33 (emphasis mine)

Though time and space will not permit that I comment on each instance of Scripture where the Kingdom of God is mentioned, I will take the time to list many of them for you to read and understand how important it is in the overall message of the New Testament. I have emphasized the Kingdom reference in each verse.

*"Not everyone who says to Me, 'Lord, Lord,' shall enter the **KINGDOM OF HEAVEN**, but he who does the will of My Father in heaven"* Matt. 7:21

*"And as you go, preach, saying, 'The **KINGDOM OF HEAVEN** is at hand.'"* Matt. 10:7

*"But if I cast out demons by the Spirit of God, surely the **KINGDOM OF GOD** has come upon you"* Matt. 12: 28

"but He said to them, 'I must preach the
KINGDOM OF GOD to the other cities also,
because for this purpose I have been sent.'"
Luke 4:43

"Now it came to pass, afterward, that He went
through every city and village, preaching and
bringing the glad tidings of the **KINGDOM OF
GOD**. And the twelve were with Him,"
Luke 8:1

"Then He called His twelve disciples together and
gave them power and authority over all demons,
and to cure diseases. He sent them to preach the
KINGDOM OF GOD and to heal the sick."
Luke 9:1

"Now when He was asked by the Pharisees when
the **KINGDOM OF GOD** would come, He
answered them and said, 'The **KINGDOM OF
GOD** does not come with observation; nor will
they say, 'See here!' or 'See there!' For indeed, the
KINGDOM OF GOD is within you.'"
Luke 17: 20

"Jesus answered and said to him, 'Most
assuredly, I say to you, unless one is born again,
he cannot see the **KINGDOM OF GOD**.'"
John 3:3

"Jesus answered, 'Most assuredly, I say to you,
unless one is born of water and the Spirit, he
cannot enter the **KINGDOM OF GOD**.'"
John 3:5

"Jesus answered, 'MY KINGDOM is not of this world. If MY KINGDOM were of this world, My servants would fight, so that I should not be delivered to the Jews; but now MY KINGDOM is not from here.'" John 18: 36

"to whom He also presented Himself alive after His suffering by many infallible proofs, being seen by them during forty days and speaking of the things pertaining to the KINGDOM OF GOD" Acts 1: 3

"Therefore, when they had come together, they asked Him, saying, 'Lord, will You at this time restore THE KINGDOM to Israel?'" Acts 1: 6

"But when they believed Philip as he preached the things concerning the KINGDOM OF GOD and the name of Jesus Christ, both men and women were baptized." Acts 8: 12

"And he went into the synagogue and spoke boldly for three months, reasoning and persuading concerning the things of the KINGDOM OF GOD." Acts 19: 8

"So when they had appointed him a day, many came to him at his lodging, to whom he explained and solemnly testified of the KINGDOM OF GOD, persuading them concerning Jesus from both the Law of Moses and the Prophets, from morning till evening." Acts 28: 23

*"Then Paul dwelt two whole years in his own
rented house, and received all who came to him,
preaching the **KINGDOM OF GOD** and teaching
the things which concern the Lord Jesus Christ
with all confidence, no one forbidding him."*
Acts 28: 30-31

*"for the **KINGDOM OF GOD** is not eating and
drinking, but righteousness and peace and joy in
the Holy Spirit."* Romans 14:17

*"For the **KINGDOM OF GOD** is not in word but
in power."* 1 Corinthians 4:20

*"He has delivered us from the power of darkness
and conveyed us into the **KINGDOM OF THE
SON OF HIS LOVE**,"* Colossians 1:13

The problem we usually have with this line of
thinking is that we have not seen it; therefore we do not
consider it as confirmed. Regretfully, unless most of
those in our churches today can actually visually verify
something, they have little understanding of the spiritual
realm.

This Kingdom is not visible to our human eye at
this time. It is a spiritual realm. God is a Spirit and we
must understand that His Empire is spiritual. Now, that
does not make it less real or without consequence. God
has chosen in His great wisdom to keep us from believing
based only on what we can see. He has built a Kingdom
based on faith.

There have been times in human history when the
curtain between the Kingdom and our visual reality is
lifted and there has been the ability to peer into or even

enter into the other realm. Sometimes it was God in the form of a Christophany (Old Testament manifestations of the pre-incarnate Christ) or one of His Kingdom's representatives (usually in the form of an angel) that pierced the curtain and invaded our world. Such times so surprised those around that they were told to, "Fear not." Possibly because they believed that to see any form or representative of the Sovereign God meant certain death.

Yet there have been some extraordinary times when a person has been given the privilege of gazing into the Kingdom. One such instance that readily comes to mind is the story of Elisha and his servant in 2 Kings 6. The king of Syria was frustrated that his battle plans were not working and as he sought answers was told of Elisha living in Dothan. The king sent a mighty entourage of horses and chariots as well as a "great army" to surround the city. The servant of Elisha was afraid and asked him what they should do. The prophet asked God to open the eyes of the servant and He did. The servant was able to see, in the spirit realm, that there were fiery chariots all around to protect and support them.

Jesus revealed to His disciples that His unique method of ministering was to look above "the line" and do what He saw the Father doing. The concept of living above the line is one where we recognize that there is a "line" separating the spirit world and the material/earthly world, and we have a choice how we live.

Jesus tells us in the following verses about His reliance on the Father's influence in the spirit world (above the line) and brought that into the material world as He ministered to those around him (below the line.) This is how Jesus was bringing the Kingdom of God to the world.

"Then Jesus answered and said to them, 'Most assuredly, I say to you, the Son can do nothing of Himself, but what He sees the Father do; for whatever He does, the Son also does in like manner.'"
John 5:19

"For I have come down from heaven, not to do My own will, but the will of Him who sent Me."
John 6:38

"For I have not spoken on My own authority; but the Father who sent Me gave Me a command, what I should say and what I should speak."
John 12:49

"Do you not believe that I am in the Father, and the Father in Me? The words that I speak to you I do not speak on My own authority; but the Father who dwells in Me does the works."
John 14:10

According to His word, Jesus was able to use His senses beyond the "line" and brought what He experienced into the world to build God's kingdom. He said that He only did what He *saw* the Father doing. In like manner, He said what He heard the Father saying and with the Father's authority and according to the Father's will. It was all done as Jesus was fulfilling His own words, "The Kingdom of Heaven (God) is at hand."

Everything has actually always been about the Kingdom. When God created Adam and blessed him with

Eve as his helper, he told them to take dominion (reign, authority, rulership) over the earth.

As the late Dr. Myles Munroe of Bahamas Faith Ministries International states,

> "The Book of Genesis opens with God's activity in the creation of the physical world that would be the environment for the manifestation of His eternal purpose. His intention was to establish His Kingdom in that physical world, without having to come visibly into that world Himself. The purposes of the invisible God would be served by a visible creation that was the result of His creative genius. His plan would be carried out by creating from His own spirit being a family of offspring who would be just like Him, created in His exact image. As His representative they would release, establish, and implement His invisible Kingdom in the visible, natural world. This is His original purpose for creating man. It was not an accident. It was not a fluke. It came about through the planning and preparation of the great God of heaven who, through His love and wisdom, constructed this awesome plan. Man was right there in the center of the plan."[1]

In the end, it will be all about the final restoration of the physical Kingdom of God on the earth per His initial desire and design. This spiritual Kingdom is established, and will come on the earth, and in us and for us, just as our Savior, Jesus, the Anointed Messiah of God revealed it would on that great day when we stand before Him:

"Then the King will say to those on His right
hand, 'Come, you blessed of My Father, inherit
the kingdom prepared for you from the
foundation of the world:'"
Matthew 25:34

THIS KINGDOM IS NOT A DEMOCRACY

This is a notion that is entirely foreign to our western culture and mindset. Everything in our American form of government has at its core the concept that the people actually rule through their elected representatives, as the Declaration of Independence so clearly declares:

> "We hold these truths to be self-evident, that all men are created equal, that they are endowed by their Creator with certain unalienable Rights, that among these are Life, Liberty and the pursuit of Happiness.--That to secure these rights, Governments are instituted among Men, deriving their just powers from the consent of the governed," [2]

Most Americans will also remember reading, or at least hearing, the famous words that marked the climax of President Abraham Lincoln's memorable Gettysburg Address:

"that this nation, under God, shall have a new birth of freedom—and that government of the people, by the people, for the people, shall not perish from the earth."[3]

Oh how those sentiments make us well up in pride for our great cause and the wonderful promise of our nation. The depth of those resounding cords of both freedom and self-reliance vibrate in our souls, and justly so. Many have risen from object poverty to the heights of success and riches only because they were free to do so in accordance with their own plans, hard work and free will. However, when we speak of the Kingdom of God, we must not translate our human experiment in democracy as His chosen form of government.

As per chapter two, we must always remember that God is Sovereign. He is the ruler of this kingdom. He was not elected to the post, nor will His term expire. He is the King of the Universe and will remain so for all eternity. We, His children, in an attempt to understand all of His motives and decisions, often quarrel at the most and "agree to disagree" at the least as to how He governs. Our reasoning does not negate the fact that He does govern all things and that His Kingdom is established.

Though we cast our vote by the label of Christianity we aspire to (Baptist, Lutheran, Methodist, Pentecostal, Presbyterian, Independent etc.) that vote does not encapsulate our Sovereign King to our belief, form or structure. For example, if we decide from our own limited understanding of the purposes and plans of God on which position is the correct one in regards to the second coming of Christ, our decision has no bearing or weight on God's plan. We do not get to vote.

We cannot assemble a "Supreme Court" of our faith and decide to dismantle the truth of God. Well, I speak out of turn. We can assemble whatever court we want and decide whatever we desire, but it ultimately has no effect whatsoever on Him, His plans or His eternal kingdom. He is the Sovereign King of this Kingdom and all events will proceed as He has planned and foreordained that they should with or without our vote.

We are accustomed to forming Political Action Committees or organizing Town Hall meetings to lobby our legislative bodies or force them to change the rules and laws of the land. This is not only inappropriate in relation to our Sovereign Lord, it is ALWAYS ineffective. He alone is in charge and His kingdom does not bow to our desire or capitulate to our demands.

The bottom line in this thought is that though we may interject our own thoughts and opinions, they ultimately mean nothing in the decision or implementation process of our King. We may even grow our following (His church) and teach them what we think about His kingdom, but it remains His kingdom and it is ruled His way regardless of our thoughts, desires, theological presuppositions or even the size of our following.

Remember, His thoughts (which are higher) and His ways (which are greater) will continue to rule and guide the universe. We are part of His established kingdom. We are not citizens of a spiritual democracy, but rather we are servant leaders of our great Father the King of everything.

His word is Absolute and not negotiable. He rules, period. We submit, period.

To protest His policies or to fight for "consensus and compromise" is ridiculous and borders on a sick, prideful insanity on our part. All things (and people) find their greatest fulfillment in their understanding of their place in the plan or purpose for which it (they) were created. The Sovereign King of all has lovingly intended a position for each person that brings out their best gifts and develops them to the full potential He placed within them.

THE KINGDOM IS NOT A RELIGION

Let us now step way out of our comfort zone and understand that mankind has created something (as we seemingly always do) out of God's provision that merely reflects His purpose. I understand that Jesus told the disciples that He would build His "church" and that the gates of hell would not be able to stand against it. Our next task is to try to understand if He was speaking about what we now relate to as Church, or if He has revealed a different purpose or plan from what we now know and experience.

But before we "go there", I must ask you to shed some of your thoughts and allow the Holy Spirit of God to open the eyes of your heart to see what He has desired the church to be. Again, it's not what we want, but what He wants. It really doesn't matter what we think, it only matters what the Sovereign King of the Kingdom desires, thinks, plans and purposes for His church to be.

In his book, *Rediscovering The Kingdom*, Myles Munroe also offers this narrative regarding the establishment of religion instead of the Kingdom.

"From the very beginning, God's plan for mankind centered in the fact that God desired to have a personal relationship with man and vice versa. *It was never God's plan to establish a religion.* As stated earlier, religion is a result of man's response to a deep spiritual vacuum in the recesses of his soul, for something he cannot describe or identify. The word *religion* denotes belief systems, creeds, and adherence to faith or convictions. These systems are manifested in the development of an array of traditions, rituals and cultural practices that extend from the simple to the very complicated. Every civilization throughout history cultivated forms of religion that sustained their viability as social entities and served as an outlet to address the mystical questions of life and death.

For many, religion has been and continues to be a tireless preoccupation distracting them from the unresolved fears of the human heart. The need for religion in some form is a universal phenomenon and is inherent in the human spirit. All humankind, left to themselves, will inevitably develop some form of religious practices. In many incidences, this can take the shape of systems of philosophies, theories, ideologies, a set of principles or documented convictions. Whatever the form takes, the purpose is the same – the attempt to satisfy the indescribable spiritual craving in the spirit of mankind.

It is interesting to note that in the ancient writings of the Hebrew prophet and patriarch Moses, who chronicles the creation narrative of the physical universe and mankind, we do not find the establishment of a formal religious system or code of traditions for man to follow or practice."[4]

When God created all that there is and placed His prized creation (man) in the center of it, He commissioned man to take dominion (rule) over it all and to populate it with his offspring. There is not mention, not even a hint, that God wanted the formalization of a religion. His desire was (and still is) a special, intimate relationship with mankind.

Because of the fall, humanity has been searching for a way to have that initial life that was present in Adam and Eve. We have tried all types of things and programs. When they fail, we find other ways to fill the voids of our life and preoccupy our minds hoping that we will nullify the emptiness. Religion is really a search for God. The Kingdom of God is not a search for Him, He is the King. Those in the Kingdom are not searching any longer. They are in a real and right relationship with the King. Once again, the words of Dr. Munroe may assist us through this new thought pattern.

"The Kingdom is not a religion because religion is man's search for God. With the Kingdom the search is over; God has revealed himself to man and sent His Son to set us free from our sins and restore us to Himself. The kingdom is not a religion but a relationship, an intimate communion in which we enter into a deeply personal relationship with the living Christ. Of all the faith systems in the world, the Kingdom alone is effective because it alone has the blood of Christ, which takes away the sin of man. It alone has the Spirit of God dwelling in the lives of believers. It alone can restore us to righteousness and holiness.

The blood of Jesus is critical. No matter how often we go to church, no matter how active we are, no matter how many times we receive communion, no matter how much money we give in the offering, and no matter how much time we spend helping the poor or the sick, unless we have confessed Jesus Christ as our Savior and Lord and allowed His blood to cover and cleanse us, we are still lost and are aliens from the Kingdom. Good works won't cut it. Sound theology won't cut it. Correct doctrine won't cut it. Only the blood of Jesus can cleanse us of sin and make us righteous and holy again. Good works, sound theology, and correct doctrine are byproducts of a growing life in the Spirit. But apart from the blood of Jesus they have no power.

Jesus came to reintroduce the Kingdom of God to mankind and restore us to righteousness and holiness. He accomplished this by dying on the cross, where His shed blood had the power to cover and wash away our sin. Because of our sins, we were spiritually dead, slaves to our sin and hostage to satan and his kingdom of darkness. By His death on the cross, Jesus paid the ransom to free us from satan's grip. He became our substitute so that we could go free. Jesus became sin for us so that we could become the righteousness of God (see 2 Cor. 5:21). His dead body lay in the tomb for three days, cold and lifeless. Death could not hold Him. On the morning of that third day, He rose from the dead. Jesus' resurrection guarantees that all who have been washed clean of sin by His blood will also share in His life – eternal life."[5]

IT IS IN US NOW

Here is the crux of the matter. The Kingdom of God has been since before the foundations of the earth and will ultimately be in control for all eternity, but it also is within us NOW! It is not in some far off land or a vague mystical place on the other side of the universe: it is in us now!

Jesus, when speaking in answer to a query by the Pharisees regarding when the kingdom of God would come, rolled back the curtain that was blocking their perception and said,

> *"The kingdom of God does not come with observation; nor will they say, 'See here!' or 'See there!' For indeed, the kingdom of God is within you."*
> Luke 17:20b-21

In the Kingdom Dynamics portion of my study Bible, (The New Spirit Filled Life Bible) the commentators penned a strikingly profound understanding of this revelation of Jesus' statement that, "The kingdom of God is within you." Here is that explanation.

"Fundamental to NT truth is that the kingdom of God is the spiritual reality and dynamic available to each person who receives Jesus Christ as Savior and Lord. To receive Him – the King – is to receive His kingly rule, not only in your life and over your affairs, but through your life and by your service and love. "The kingdom of God is within you," Jesus said.

This is never to be construed as possible if we operate independently of God's power and grace.   The possibility of reinstatement to rulership is brought about only through the forgiveness of sins and full redemption in Christ through the Cross.   The Bible never suggests either 1) that there exists in man a divine spark, which may be fanned to flame by noble human efforts, or 2) that godlikeness is somehow resident in man's potential, as though human beings are or may become "gods."   To the contrary, man is lost in darkness and alienated from God (Eph. 4:18; 2:12).

However, full salvation brings restored relationship to God and a full potential for his kingdom's ruling "within us" as we walk with Him. Jesus has sent the Holy Spirit to cause the anointing of His Messiahship to be transmitted to us (Is. 61:1-3; Luke 4:18; John 1:16; 1 John 2:20, 27; 4:17). So it is, and on these terms only, that a human being can say, 'The Kingdom of God is within me.'"[6]

The thought that enters my mind, is that wherever the King is, there is the kingdom. If that is so, then the Christian holds the presence of the King within, thus the kingdom is within us. That means the Kingdom of God is at hand as we yield to the sovereignty of God.

IT WILL COME ON THE EARTH

At the end of Jesus' earthly ministry, after His resurrection from the dead, He spends 40 days in intimate conversation with His apostles. He reveals more about the kingdom of God to them in the shadow of His sacrificial atonement and being made alive by the power of God.

> *" The former account I made, O Theophilus, of all that Jesus began both to do and teach, until the day in which He was taken up, after He through the Holy Spirit had given commandments to the apostles whom He had chosen, to whom He also presented Himself alive after His suffering by many infallible proofs, being seen by them during forty days and speaking of the things pertaining to the kingdom of God."*
> Acts 1:1-3

He tries to encourage His disciples one last time. He says things that would make the average Israelite's head spin. You (disciples) are going to be baptized with God's Spirit in a few days. I am sure their minds must have raced back in their memories as they remembered Old Testament saints who experienced this same outpouring. Moses, Samson, Samuel and David all did.

So did Elijah, Elisha, Isaiah, Ezekiel and Daniel. They are being promised by the Messiah that they would be named among a select few (at this time in history) that have had this awesome experience.

> *"And being assembled together with them, He commanded them not to depart from Jerusalem, but to wait for the Promise of the Father, "which," He said, "you have heard from Me; for John truly baptized with water, but you shall be baptized with the Holy Spirit not many days from now."*
> Acts 1:4-5

They are still caught up in the mindset of the physical kingdom of God being manifested. I guess they assumed the power that would be associated with the outpouring of the Holy Spirit of God was what would be needed to conquer the Romans and subdue the various sects of Judaism.

Quickly and without hesitation Jesus lays that to rest. In the same breath He explains the purpose for the promised infilling of the Holy Spirit was for power to be His witnesses. Interestingly enough, the Greek word for witness, *"martus,"* can also be translated as martyr. Now, that's another paradigm shift! Here is that dialogue between Jesus and the Apostles just prior to the ascension.

> *"Therefore, when they had come together, they asked Him, saying, "Lord, will You at this time restore the kingdom to Israel?" And He said to them, "It is not for you to know times or seasons*

which the Father has put in His own authority.
But you shall receive power when the Holy Spirit
has come upon you; and you shall be witnesses to
Me in Jerusalem, and in all Judea and Samaria,
and to the end of the earth."
Acts 1:6-8

Though many preachers, pastors and orators of the past have taken issue with this question of the apostles, I find it a most natural (and familiar) inquiry. There are those who delicately reprimand these giants of the early Church for their lack of spiritual perception or understanding, and attribute the motivation for the question to "unsanctified selfishness." I tend to disagree. It seems that regardless of the spiritual maturity of an individual, church or even the dispensation in which one lives, there has always been a proclivity to seek to understand with some degree of accuracy the answer to this question. Even in the shadow of apocalyptic writings of the Apostles' John and Paul, we still find our ranks divided in regard to the course of final events.

Within the study of theology there is a subdivision in which the emphasis is placed on last things, or "the end times." This branch of theology is known as *Eschatology*. According to the dictionary,

"Eschatology is defined as, 'a branch of theology concerned with the final events in the history of the world or of humankind; a belief concerning death, the end of the world, or the ultimate destiny of humankind; *specifically*: any of various Christian doctrines concerning the Second Coming, the resurrection of the dead, or the Last Judgment. In Christianity, the end times are thought to have begun with the life and ministry of Jesus, the messiah who will return to establish the Kingdom of God.'"[7]

Regardless of which side of the eschatological position you align yourself, this study of last things always ends with the beautiful picture of the New Jerusalem coming down (Rev. 21:1 & 2) and bringing the presence of God to dwell among us all (Rev. 21:3). The Kingdom of God is established on the earth forever. He will rule and all who have become His children will be with Him throughout all eternity. The attributes of God will be displayed via the way of life of His children. According to the Apostle John,

> *"And God will wipe away every tear from their*
> *eyes; there shall be no more death, nor sorrow,*
> *nor crying. There shall be no more pain, for the*
> *former things have passed away."*
> Revelation 21:4

Basically this is telling us that as the Scriptures begin with mankind in a perfect garden on a perfect Earth, so it will end. Originally, mankind had no sickness, pain or death. These things are going to "pass away" and we will finally experience the loving physical rule of God on Earth. The first humans were not worried about "making it to heaven", because God gave them the entire earth to take dominion over. God will cause that to happen in eternity.

> *"Then the King will say to those on His right*
> *hand, 'Come, you blessed of My Father, inherit*

the kingdom prepared for you from the
foundation of the world:'"
Matthew 25:34

Heaven, as we hear often declared, is the place where the presence of God is centrally manifested. For the time being, it is where all saints will go after death. Once the culmination of all things comes to fruition, God will make His abode among mankind in the New Jerusalem and will literally bring heaven to Earth.

The actual kingdom of God that is prayed for will come to completion and all of the prophecies that have given the church hope will be fulfilled. The actual, literal Kingdom of our Lord and of His Christ will come forever.

"Then the seventh angel sounded: And there were
loud voices in heaven, saying, "The kingdoms of
this world have become the kingdoms of our Lord
and of His Christ, and He shall reign forever and
ever!"
Revelation 11:15

Let's continue to both pray and work to bring about God's glorious kingdom on earth. He has a plan in motion, and when the time is right, He will implement the final stages of that plan and bring His kingdom here. As we lead unbelievers to the Cross of Jesus, they not only find forgiveness for their sins, but they also relinquish control of their life and accept Him as their King (Lord) and enter into His kingdom.

Praying for
God's will to be
done in our
individual lives is
not always easy,
and is often very
difficult.

-Dr. Lonnie E. Riley-

CHAPTER FIVE

GAINING INSIGHT INTO HIS

WILL:

"Your will be done on Earth as it is in Heaven"

Jesus brings together much of what we have studied thus far in a statement He made near the end of the Sermon on the Mount regarding obedience to God's will. He plainly explains that only the ones who are obedient to God's will are going to enter the Kingdom (Matthew 7:21). So it would seem advantageous for each of us to know and do God's will.

That being assumed, so much has been said and done in the name of "the will of God" that it is enough to make even the most sincere and dedicated Christian question someone's intentions when uttering those words. It is especially questionable when someone (specifically a spiritual leader) labels their demands of you as being God's will for YOUR life and of course, even more so when it could help them succeed or get what they want. I believe that the overwhelming majority of pastors and spiritual leaders truly want to know God's will and to express it to their flock. But like the old saying goes, "One bad apple will spoil the whole bushel." History is littered with gruesome things that have been done under the pretext of accomplishing God's will.

Allow me to remind you that according to those in control the Crusades were the will of God. Consider these ancient words regarding God's will and the Crusades:

> "According to the teaching of Augustine, the greatest Christian theologian, the Crusades were "just" wars — not because they were devoid of *"the real evils in war,"* which he said were the *"love of violence, revengeful cruelty, fierce and implacable enmity, wild resistance, and the lust of power, and such like."* Far from it, as the Crusaders' own histories tell. They were to be considered "just" for the most fundamental

reason of all: that they were waged at the command of God! In Augustine's own words:

How much more must the man be blameless who carries on war on the authority of God, of whom everyone who serves Him knows that He can never require what is wrong?

And who better to declare a war just than the Pope himself, the Vicar of Christ on earth? In the Roman Catholic Church, a *vicar* is a priest who acts for another higher-ranking clergyman. The Vicar of Christ acts for Christ. On that fateful day in November, over nine hundred years ago, after Pope Urban II promised the Crusaders *"remission of their sins"* and *"the assurance of the reward of imperishable glory in the kingdom of heaven"* for waging war, they all cried out in unison, *"It is the will of God!"*

In response, Pope Urban told them that Christ *was* in their midst and God in their spirits. Therefore, when they attacked the enemy, it was the will of God.

Most beloved brethren, to-day is manifest in you what the Lord says in the Gospel, "Where two or three are gathered together in my name, there am I in the midst of them;" for unless God had been present in your spirits, all of you would not have uttered the same cry; since, although the cry issued from numerous mouths, yet the origin of the cry was one. Therefore I say to you that God, who implanted this in your breasts, has drawn it forth from you. Let that then be your war cry in combats, because it is given to you by God. When an armed attack is made upon the enemy, let this one cry be raised by all the soldiers of God: "It is the will of God! It is the will of God!"

Being thus equipped with the boundless confidence of doing God's will, the Crusaders set off for the east. They were a new kind of pilgrim, no longer humble and lowly, but great and mighty. At the end of their pilgrimage they attacked the "enemy" in the holy city of Jerusalem, raising the cry, "It is the will of God!" Or more simply put, "God wills it!"[1]

In retrospect, the church is ashamed of its actions and has confessed that those military expeditions were sinful and wrong (Pope John Paul II, 2000). They have created a blithe on the name of the Church and distrust in the mind of countless nations and would be followers (for good reason).

I have a problem equating God's will with some of the injustices done in the world, plagues that have fallen on nations, disasters (both natural and man-made) and the sorrows faced by so many, even those who carefully and selflessly follow His commands. Remember that even Adolf Hitler wrote in *Mein Kampf* of his anti-Semitic ways as doing the work (will) of God.

"Therefore, I believe today that I am acting in the sense of the Almighty Creator: By warding off the Jews I am fighting for the Lord's work."[2]

I have found that if someone really wants to do a thing, no matter how wrong or even sinful it is, they can always find a justification for it if they look hard enough. We can even find a "Scriptural" foundation for our acts if we take verses out of context or follow human reasoning and apply it by reducing God to our thoughts, concerns, plans or will.

Often, many Christians believe that the will of God is going to be something we dislike. As I grew up, we did not have the tasty, flavored, sugary types of medicine offered to kids today. Medicine tasted nasty. I can remember having to hold my nose to take a spoonful of it. Many believers equate that concept to God's will for their life. "I won't like it, though I know it's good for me." Sort of like going to the dentist, we know we should, but it is unpleasant.

Now here is the rub. We claim that our God is Sovereign and in control of everything. How do we equate all of this? Are we just playing games? Is it just a bunch of semantics? Is it true that God is "still on the throne", but He is not in control of certain aspects of the universe or world? As Christians who are trying to "make God more palatable" are we denying His sovereignty in order to make Him appear more friendly, loving and merciful? I know at times I still struggle coming to grips with the purpose of God in situations that have affected my life.

As an 11 year old boy my life was changed forever on October 31, 1972. I was made fatherless as a blood clot traveled through my dad's veins and lodged between his lungs, suffocating him. I was thrust into this category without warning or preparation and had to endure all the personal, family, church and societal repercussions associated with fatherlessness. Was such a dramatic and life-changing event God's will?

My young nephew was driving his fiancé and unborn child home late one rainy December evening in South Georgia. No one truly knows what transpired, just the results. His little truck slid off the pavement, rolled off the shoulder and flipped onto the side of the road. She laid unconscious, the baby dead and my nephew fighting a losing battle for his life. A life with such promise, potential and hope was snuffed out in a moment's time. They were to be married on my birthday and I was anticipating performing the ceremony.

He was a person who had influenced many with his smile, good nature and forgiveness; yet he would never light up another Thanksgiving meal or Christmas morning with his grin. Are we, as a family supposed to take comfort in the fact that this was God's will? It really makes you wonder what kind of God we serve when we equate the terrible things to Him.

In over 50 years of life, 30 plus years of ministry and 3 years serving as a funeral assistant and apprentice funeral director, embalmer and crematory operator, I have seen more than my fair share of hurt, loss and torment.

Many times I have heard the uneducated and less than comforting words, "It was God's will." Then the same people turn around and tell the survivors to "Trust in the LORD", "Lean on Him, and He will help you through with the power of His Holy Spirit." All true words mind you, but hard to believe when you just attributed the loss, the hurt, or the torment to the same God you are admonished to trust!

As one studies the topic of God's will it can quickly become a miry subject much like quick sand. The more you think and struggle, the deeper you seem to fall into it and the harder it is to get yourself out. I know. I've been there. Perhaps you will concur that sometimes all we need is someone who understands the nature of this quicksand to throw us a rope and gently guide us to solid ground. Perhaps that's why I'm writing this, and possibly it is for you that I have specifically been challenged to write. Hmmm. Does that make both my writing and your reading "The will of God?" OK, I will stop with the brain teasers (for now). As we delve into this topic our outline will cover the following areas:

1. Definition.
2. How is God's will done in heaven?
3. Is God's will always done?
4. Final thoughts.

DEFINITION

Perhaps it will do us well to understand this concept by setting a firm definition of what we mean when we talk about the will of God. Looking the word up gives us the following thoughts:

Something desired; *especially*: a choice or determination of one having authority or power.
The part of a summons expressing a royal command.
Mental powers manifested as wishing, choosing, desiring, or intending.
A disposition to act according to principles or ends.[3]

Now let's look beyond just our English thoughts of "will" and see what was thought of according to the Greek word used in the prayer. The word "Thelema" in Greek is usually translated as desire, pleasure, or will. It has intrinsic meanings of determination, choice (specifically purpose or decree) or an inclination.[4]

Whatever it is that can be called God's desire or pleasure, could certainly be called His will. So also could that which He determines, chooses or is inclined to make or cause to happen. One of the concepts that comes to mind when we speak of someone's will is the legal document that is used to show the personal wishes of a deceased person. We often call it the "Last Will And Testament." Interestingly, two words pop out at me in that last statement, "Will" and "Testament."

Thinking along that line, I believe that God's will can be found in His testaments (Old and New), or the Bible. God's corporate and individual will is revealed in the Holy Scriptures. If it is not revealed explicitly, it has to conform to what is explicitly written. God does not contradict His Word. That being said, there are several distinct and definitive Scriptures that shine light on specific things that are a part of God's will.

Initially, let's assume that the submissive attitude of King David should be that of all the subjects of the Kingdom.

> *"I delight to do Your will, O my God,*
> *And Your law is within my heart."*
> Psalm 40:8

Again we find a correlation between doing God's will and His word (law). We are left to presuppose that the existence of the law (Scripture) within his heart creates both a desire and willingness to perform God's will. We see the New Testament parallel in Paul's writing to the church in Ephesus,

> *"Therefore do not be unwise, but understand what the will of the Lord is."*
> Ephesians 5:17

Jesus' death was part of God's will. Consider these verses that explain that God planned the fact that Jesus would die a substitutionary death for us, making Him the propitiation for our sin.

> *"who gave himself for our sins to rescue us from the present evil age, according to the will of our God and Father,"*
> Galatians 1:4 (NIV)

> *"They did what your power and will had decided beforehand should happen."*
> Acts 4:28 (NIV)

> *"This man was handed over to you by God's set purpose and foreknowledge; and you, with the help of wicked men, put him to death by nailing him to the cross."*
> Acts 2:23 (NIV)

Our salvation was part of God's will. The driving force of God's agape love made it a focus of His divine will that we should be saved and adopted into His family. He even reiterates it in the negative that it is not His will that people perish.

"he predestined us to be adopted as his sons through Jesus Christ, in accordance with his pleasure and will"
Ephesians 1:5 (NIV)

"For this is good and acceptable in the sight of God our Savior, who desires all men to be saved and to come to the knowledge of the truth."
1 Timothy 2:3-4

'The Lord is not slack concerning His promise, as some count slackness, but is longsuffering toward us, not willing that any should perish but that all should come to repentance."
2 Peter 3:9

Our spiritual growth is part of God's will. We were not rescued by God to just sit and wait our turn to ride to heaven. God intends that we grow and mature. He wants us to enjoy our new life in Christ and to reflect His image in the earth so that others will be drawn to Him.

"Be assured that from the first day we heard of you, we haven't stopped praying for you, asking God to give you wise minds and spirits attuned to his will, and so acquire a thorough understanding of the ways in which God works."
Colossians 1:9 (MSG)

"For this is the will of God, your sanctification: that you should abstain from sexual immorality;"
1 Thessalonians 4:3

*"Do not be conformed to this world (this age),
[fashioned after and adapted to its external,
superficial customs], but be transformed
(changed) by the [entire] renewal of your mind [by
its new ideals and its new attitude], so that you
may prove [for yourselves] what is the good and
acceptable and perfect will of God, even the thing
which is good and acceptable and perfect [in His
sight for you]."*
Romans 12:2 (AMP)

As we study God's word, we will see God's will being revealed on a much more individual level with certain people. Noah, Abraham, Joseph, Moses, Samuel, David and Daniel are a few from the Old Testament. Mary, Joseph, John the Baptist, the 12 apostles, Paul and a host of others are examples in the New Testament.

As we think of His will we must consider that there are several aspects of God's will that may help us understand some of the intricacies of attributing everything or anything to His will. Let's look at three distinctive facets of God's will in the Bible.

THE SOVEREIGN WILL OF GOD

This aspect of God's will recognizes that whatever He purposes, plans or declares is His ultimate will. Sometimes we refer to it as His hidden will based on His declaration that His thoughts and ways are higher than ours and more than we can comprehend. The focus of this facet of God's will, is that He ordains everything that comes to pass. There is nothing that happens outside of God's sovereign will. This is a tenet that is supported throughout the whole of Scripture. Both Old and New Testaments corroborate the idea of God's sovereign will.

"I know that You can do everything,
And that no purpose of Yours can be withheld
from You."
Job 42:2

In Him also we have obtained an inheritance,
being predestined according to the purpose of
Him who works all things according to the
counsel of His will,
Ephesians 1:11

These verses let us know that in the grand scheme of things, nothing happens that is beyond God's control. It is sovereign and can never be frustrated. Now, this does not mean that God "causes" everything to happen. It only helps us understand that because He is sovereign, He must at least permit or allow things to happen. Because He always has the power to stop things from happening, there must logically be at least a passive permission for things to happen based on His entire plan.

Though portions of the sovereign will of God may be revealed, as in the case of Daniel in the development and fall of nations, the overall picture is hidden. Even in the realms of eschatology, there is so much symbolism or description of things foreign to the writer, that it leaves room for uncertainty. This is partially the reason for such wide extremes regarding the second coming of Jesus.

THE KNOWN
WILL OF GOD

Though at times the sovereign will of God seems hidden to us, at least until after it has happened, the known will of God is that which is revealed to us mainly through the Scriptures.

This perceptive will of God, as some have described it, is the revealed will that declares what we should or should not do. Things like don't steal, love your neighbor, repent and be holy.

Mostly this is made known through the canonical books of the Bible; it can also be more subjective. Abraham knew God's will prior to their being any written testament at all. We can know it by perceiving the voice of God through His Holy Spirit into our conscience. There are also verbal gifts of the Holy Spirit where He empowers another person with knowledge of God's will.

Though these subjective areas are real and can be very powerful in directing our path, we must always remember that God will not contradict Himself. If He reveals that His will is that we not steal, we cannot believe any spirit or person who declares it is God's will that we steal. Balance is always secured by testing that which is revealed by the known, written, preserved, inerrant word of God. It makes no sense for God to have inspired the Bible only to contradict it.

How then do we relate the sovereign will of God and our disobedience to the known will of God? Simply this, we are accountable when we disobey. We have the power and ability to disobey God's commands, but we certainly do not have the right to do so. We can't just claim that our sin fulfills God's sovereign will so we are justified in sinning. NO.

Think of both Judas and the Romans. Both were instruments that God utilized to fulfill His sovereign will, right? But that does not justify their sins. They were no less evil or treacherous, and they were held accountable for their rejection of Christ. Even though in His sovereign will God allows or permits sin to happen, we are still accountable to Him for that sin!

THE PERSONAL WILL OF GOD

This facet of God's will describes what is pleasing to Him in our individual lives, including the direction we should take in all areas of our existence. Some refer to it as God's "call" upon their life. I know that I believed that God had placed a call of full time ministry on my life and that has affected nearly every decision that I have made since that awareness.

This can become a very strange and dangerous preoccupation for people. Often this causes them to be open to suggestion by their own personal soulish parts (intellect, emotions and volition). I have seen this first hand. There was a tremendous amount of pressure placed on this facet of spirituality in the High School and Bible College I attended. Everyone seemed to be on a quest to "find" God's will for their lives. Some were to be pastors, or missionaries while others to be teachers or nurses. The only other "calling" I can remember that was ever mentioned was to be called by God to go back to the two schools as workers or teachers. Those who testified to knowing what God's will was for the rest of their lives were perceived as the most spiritual and looked up to as leaders on the campus.

Now, I am not saying that God cannot or will not make a person's professional calling known, but I find it extremely off point to create an atmosphere of determining one's spiritual growth and maturity based on having such a calling. As I look back over these nearly 40 years I see where many people said they were called during their school years, and it all changed once they moved to other jobs or schooling. God reveals His will for our lives in His timing.

Noah was over 500 years old before he was called to build the ark (Gen.5:32). Abram had already turned 75 when God called him to leave Haran (Gen.12:4). Moses was about 80 years old when he met God at the burning bush and received his call to deliver Israel from Egypt and lead them to the Promised Land. (Deduced from Deut. 3:2 where he is 120 at death and had been in the desert 40 years). David was only a young teenager when Samuel anointed him as the next king of Israel (1 Samuel 16:11-13). We could go on throughout Biblical history of both the New and Old Testaments and find differences regarding when someone knew of God's will for their life.

It is my pastoral judgment that we should make living according to God's known will the chief aim or purpose for our lives (Romans 12:1-2). That being said, to know the will of God, we should immerse ourselves in the written Word of God. We should saturate our minds with Scripture and pray that the Holy Spirit will renew our minds through it so that we are able to fulfill those verses and "prove what is the good, acceptable and perfect will of God."

HOW IS GOD'S WILL DONE IN HEAVEN?

As we saw in the previous chapter, God's Kingdom is established. That Kingdom is spiritual, but it is alive and well everywhere the King is enthroned.

In terms of "visual" reality, the Kingdom will one day come to the earth. As we move next to the concept of God's will being done, let us see the actual qualifiers that the word of God uses in asking us to pray in this fashion.

Interestingly enough, this prayer is not asking us to pray that God's will be done in heaven. He is the Sovereign King of that sphere. Everything God commands, desires, purposes or decrees is done in His presence. Jesus does not teach His disciples to pray that God's will be done in heaven. That would be a totally unnecessary and inappropriate request. No, this section leads us to ask for the will of our Father, the Sovereign I Am of the Kingdom that is coming, to be accomplished in the same way, fashion and attitude it is completed in heaven.

That means the next area of our study into this concept is to understand *HOW* God's will is done. The reason for this is found in the prayer itself. We are told to pray that God's will be done on earth (where we live) **AS** it is in heaven. In order to effectively pray that God's will be done on earth, we must first have a clear understanding of how God's will is done in heaven. Then we can make the proper application to our lives and His divine will on earth. Think for a moment. How is God's will done in Heaven? When the Angels, Cherubim and Seraphim understand what the will of God is, how do they respond? Do they react the way most Christians on earth react?

I believe that God's known will in heaven is done:
1. Immediately
2. Without hesitation
3. Unquestioned
4. Instantaneously
5. Flawlessly
6. Completely
7. Perfectly
8. Totally

Now, let that sink in for a moment.

Ok, let's imagine what the earth (again, where we each live, work and play) would look like if we did His will in that way. Is that even possible? You tell me. Can a believer whose past has been forgiven, who has been in-filled with the very essence of the 3rd person of the divine Trinity as their Source of power and who has the mind of Christ Jesus able to do God's will the way it is done in heaven?

I say a resounding YES!!

I believe that God also knows that it is possible and is the very reason Jesus encourages us to pray that it happen. Why pray for something that is impossible to happen? God has designed that it can happen. What is keeping it from developing and coming to fruition? We are.

We have allowed ourselves to stifle what God intends for us. We are not really walking in the kind of obedience that it will require in order to see His will done on earth in the same fashion it is accomplished in heaven. Think about what we know and understand heaven to be like by answering these questions.

Is there any bickering or gossip?
Does God allow racial division?
Is there sickness or poverty?
Are there denominations?
Is there any unforgiveness?
Who receives all the praise and glory?

IS GOD'S WILL ALWAYS DONE ON EARTH?

I know it can be hard to admit, but the answer is NO. The will of the Supreme Sovereign of the universe is not always done on earth. We know that both historically and experientially.

Historically we would have to say that it was God's will that the fall of man occurred and infected the entire human race with a sinful nature. We can think of nation after nation that has gone through slavery, murder and faced annihilation. The deaths that resulted from Hitler's camps and other such atrocities would have to be labeled as God's will if it were always done on earth.

Biblical history would also have hurtful and sinful acts be considered God's will. It would require that we say it was God's will for Abraham to lie, Moses to murder or David to commit adultery. We must recognize that God, in His sovereign wisdom, has given to all of humanity a "will" as well. And that will is free to choose. God so designed it that we can decide to disobey the will of the very One who designed, created and devised free will.

We mentioned earlier that God's will is that none should perish and that all would come to repentance. We know from this world that we live in that there are thousands who die without such a relationship with God. His will is not done.

FINAL THOUGHTS

Praying for God's will always begins with us, or it should. As I consider how we know and follow the will of God in our lives, I am reminded of something else Dr. Charles Allen wrote:

> "How can I know the will of God for my life? Many will never know, because God does not reveal Himself to triflers. No one can walk into His holy presence on hurrying feet. If you merely pray, 'Lord, this is my will, I hope you will approve,' you are wasting your breath. Only those who sincerely want God's will, and have faith enough in Him to dedicate themselves to His will, can ever know it. To pray, 'Lord, show me Thy will. If I like it I will accept it,' is a futile prayer. You must accept it before you know it. Whether or not you can do that depends on what opinion you have of God."[6]

Praying for God's will to be done in our individual lives is not always easy, and is often very difficult. Consider that the very Disciples that were taught this prayer didn't really understand it in the garden called Gethsemane where Jesus asked them to pray with Him and was eventually betrayed by Judas Iscariot. No doubt they struggled with it when He was being stripped and beaten outside the Roman courtyard. While they watched Him die a humiliating death on the cross, observed as He was carried to Joseph of Arimathea's tomb and placed in a cold grave they had no comprehension of God's will.

Even Jesus spent an evening in prayer agonizing over this in Gethsemane. The struggle He endured created such stress that He was sweating and the sweat was mixed with blood. The crux of that prayer was asking for the "cup" to pass from Him, but He always ended by surrendering His own will and submitting to God's.

The Apostle Paul struggled as well. He even compares it to dying every day. He prayed 3 times for a thorn in the flesh (a messenger of satan) to be removed from him and the answer was, "NO!" God reminded Paul that His strength was perfected in Paul's weakness. Paul had to put his own will to death each day and submit himself fresh and new to the will of God.

In order for God's will to be done on earth as it is in heaven, the first thing is to have God's will done in our lives, then branch out from there. It begins with each of us. As we learn to do His will, our obedience will extend to our point of influence. It will affect our family, our friends, our employment and even our church. We must understand that it is not our job or responsibility to see that others are obeying God's will for their lives. We are not to judge. We are to show them what it looks like to live in such a way that the world knows we are following the will of God.

I understand that this type of commitment is not easy and that we may not always understand His sovereign will. That's when faith is necessary. Faith in a loving God. Faith in His wisdom. Faith that His plan for us is much better than our plan for ourselves. Faith that He will guide us and never leave or forsake us in the process.

Whether you shrink from God's will or see it as what is best for us depends on the advantage point you choose to view it from. Kim and I were recently introduced to a unique woman with 10 children. At first glance everything seems rather normal, but as she begins to share with us, we see it differently. Sue (not her real name) married, but was unable to have children. They adopted 3 special needs kids. Her husband died in their 30's. Eventually she marries a gentleman with children from two previous marriages (one ended in death, the other divorce). Now she is the mother of ten.

She was questioning us regarding why these little ones were abandoned, why she couldn't have children, why they lost their new father (her husband), and on and on she went. Though it is nearly impossible to give her all the answers she is looking for, we pried a little more regarding the children. It turns out they are doing well, serving God and living on their own. Based on the situation they came from, there is little hope they would have accepted Jesus and done so well. We also found out that they are being used to encourage and witness to other kids who have gone through extreme loss or abandonment.

Truly we are able to see (sometimes by looking backward) how God is fulfilling the promise He made through the Apostle Paul:

"And we know that all things work together for
good to those who love God, to those who are the
called according to His purpose."
Romans 8:28

We must also remember that God's will was to give us "free will" so that we can make decisions that affect our life. Sometimes it is not God who leads us through deep valleys and dark waters. And sometimes it isn't even satan who we can credit for our problems. It can be our own ignorance or folly that has brought us down that path.

Though we have that free will, God's will is still at play in our lives, and has been since before we were born. Consider the fact that none of us decided which century we would live in or to what country we would belong. Neither did we have any say in who our parents were. We were not free to choose our sex, physical appearance or the color of our skin. All of these were decided by God.

Finally, many of us really desire to know His will and to walk in His ways. There just seems to be some real questions regarding how to know God is revealing His will to us with certainty. Let me close this chapter with information that I have found to be of great comfort and instruction when pursuing God's will:

10 Ways God Reveals His Will For Us:

1. He speaks to us through the Holy Spirit right to our heart, so be listening.
2. He allows us to be restless because He wants to show us something, so ask Him.
3. He gives us confirmation on His Word through others, so talk it out with someone.

4. He gives us unexpected favor and surprises us with a special blessing, so keep seeking.
5. He may want to give us something else so He answers with a no, so be grateful.
6. He may want to give us a setback to change our path, so pray for that plain path.
7. He may want us to spend more time in Praise and Worship, so let's appreciate Him.
8. He may want us to experience disappointment to get our attention, so be aware.
9. He may want us to go through defeat to get us to study His Word more, so be thankful.
10. He may let us have hardships with finances or tragedy, so we know we need to lean on Him only.[7]

The Christian life is one of constant and consistent expansion.

-Dr. Lonnie E. Riley-

SECTION TWO

SECOND
"G"

GROWTH

"In this manner, therefore, pray:
Our Father in heaven, Hallowed be Your name.
Your kingdom come.
Your will be done on earth as it is in heaven.
Give us this day our daily bread.
And forgive us our debts, as we forgive our debtors.
And do not lead us into temptation,
but deliver us from the evil one.
For Yours is the kingdom and the power and the
glory forever. Amen"
Matthew 6:9-13

CHAPTER SIX

WE GROW IN

FAITH:

"Give Us This Day Our Daily Bread"

This is the natural subdivision of this prayer. It is both evident and dramatic when we stop and actually take the time to realize how the wording changes. It is apparent in the pronouns that are used. In the first section we focus on God by using the pronoun, "You" in reference to Him (Our Father in Heaven). We say "Your name," "Your kingdom," and "Your will." But here it changes. In the next few requests we focus on "us" and "our." It seems important, fitting and proper that we focus on God *before* we focus on ourselves. We gain a proper view of the Person to whom we are speaking before we make requests for ourselves. It is the best way. A renewed understanding of God, His role as our Father, His majesty and sovereignty, the unique names He has revealed in order to show His nature, and the fact that we are part of His kingdom and desiring His will instead of our own, readies us to pray for our own needs while understanding the importance of submitting to Him.

This division also leads to the second "G" in the 4G's of communication we are associating with the Lord's Prayer, "*GROWTH*". We must all realize that our relationship with God is meant to continually grow. I have heard it said from many pulpits across the nation (and have even said this many times myself), "If you aren't growing, you're dying."

The Christian life is one of constant and consistent expansion. If we allow ourselves, we can learn from and thereby grow because of everything that transpires in our life. Both the good and the bad, the pleasant and the difficult, even the exciting or the painful can be areas that God can use to help us grow.

Spiritual growth is a necessity. We are expected to grow both individually and collectively. The Scriptures validate such claims. Consider what the Apostles Paul and Peter had to say in their writings concerning growth.

*"but, speaking the truth in love, may **GROW** up in all things into Him who is the head—Christ— from whom the whole body, joined and knit together by what every joint supplies, according to the effective working by which every part does its share, causes **GROWTH** of the body for the edifying of itself in love."*
Ephesians 4:15-16 (emphasis mine)

*"We are bound to thank God always for you, brethren, as it is fitting, because your faith **GROWS** exceedingly, and the love of every one of you all abounds toward each other,"*
2 Thessalonians 1:3 (emphasis mine)

*"as newborn babes, desire the pure milk of the word, that you may **GROW** thereby,"*
1 Peter 2:2 (emphasis mine)

*"but **GROW** in the grace and knowledge of our Lord and Savior Jesus Christ. To Him be the glory both now and forever. Amen."*
2 Peter 3:18 (emphasis mine)

Clearly these early church leaders saw the need for growth in our spiritual lives. Our Heavenly Father thought it was of such importance that He inspired them to write about it. They mention areas of growth like, "Love," "Grace," "Knowledge," "Word," and "Faith."

Faith is the actual focus in this section of the prayer. In order to truly surrender to God and ask Him to "Give us this day our daily bread," requires an act of supreme faith. Faith is an integral part of spiritual growth. We must have faith in Christ in order to become a Christian in the first place. The writer of the book of Hebrews makes it even clearer when he states that, "without faith it is impossible to please God" (Hebrews 11:6).

Much has been written about this phrase in the prayer. There have been many who seem to think that something deeper or more spiritual is being implied here. I am not totally opposed to seeing some of the deeper concepts or even the spiritual concepts that can be developed from these words, and I will share some of that with you in this chapter, but part of my hermeneutic (method of biblical interpretation) is to first and foremost look at, accept and follow the plain meaning of the Scripture before trying to spiritualize it or develop some analogy from it.

IT MEANS WHAT IT SAYS!

The easiest and most direct interpretation of this passage is to just take it at face value. It means what it actually says. We are to exercise our faith daily in relying on God for our sustenance or needs in this life. Dr. Allen explains it this way,

"The God who made our bodies is concerned about the needs of our bodies and He is anxious for us to talk with Him about our physical needs."[1]

Not only as Creator, but also as our Heavenly Father is His concern for our needs evident. In just a mere 10 verses after the conclusion of this prayer, Jesus gives further details about the Father's provision and the faith we need to develop.

*"Therefore I say to you, **DO NOT WORRY** (have faith) about your life, what you will eat or what you will drink; nor about your body, what you will put on. Is not life more than food and the body more than clothing? Look at the birds of the air, for they neither sow nor reap nor gather into barns; yet your heavenly Father feeds them. **ARE YOU NOT OF MORE VALUE THAN THEY**? Which of you by worrying can add one cubit to his stature? So why do you worry about clothing? Consider the lilies of the field, how they grow: they neither toil nor spin; and yet I say to you that even Solomon in all his glory was not arrayed like one of these. Now if God so clothes the grass of the field, which today is, and tomorrow is thrown into the oven, will He not much more clothe you, **O YOU OF LITTLE Faith**? Therefore do not worry, saying, 'What shall we eat?' or 'What shall we drink?' or 'What shall we wear?' For after all these things the Gentiles seek. **FOR YOUR HEAVENLY FATHER KNOWS THAT YOU NEED ALL THESE THINGS**. But seek first the **KINGDOM OF GOD** (remember, Your Kingdom Come?) and His*

*righteousness, and **ALL THESE THINGS
SHALL BE ADDED TO YOU**. Therefore **DO
NOT WORRY*** (He says it again) *about
tomorrow, for tomorrow will worry about its own
things. Sufficient for the day is its own trouble."*
Matthew 6:25-34 (emphasis mine)

At another point in this Sermon on the Mount, Jesus
makes it abundantly clear that God is interested in giving
His children their needs by drawing on the love and
compassion an earthly father has for his children.

*"If you then, being evil, know how to give good
gifts to your children, how much more will your
Father who is in heaven give good things to those
who ask Him!"*
Matthew 7:11

I have three sons, 2 biological and 1 step-son.
They are each precious to me. I have a different personal
relationship with each one.   We talk about different
things. I advise them differently when they are making
decisions. They each decide whether they want to ask my
advice, listen to it or follow it. There is hardly anything
that is the same in these relationships except the fact
that all three of them see me as their father. They know
that if it is within my earthly powers, I will do anything
for them.   Sometimes it helps to understand the word
picture that God is painting for us in the Scriptures by
remembering how it applies to our lives. Robert Foster
puts it clearly in the eyes of a child.

"Jesus taught us to pray for daily bread. Have
you ever noticed that children ask for lunch

money in utter confidence that it will be provided. They have no need to stash away today's sandwiches for fear none will be available tomorrow. As far as they are concerned, there is an endless supply of sandwiches. Children do not find it difficult or complicated to talk to their parents, nor do they feel embarrassed to bring the simplest need to their attention. Neither should we hesitate to bring the simplest request confidently to the Father."[2]

In his book, *Trevor's Song*, T. A. Beam recounts a dramatic event that took place in his family. They have a farm and as their children grow they are expected to help with the daily chores. Sometimes that requires that the oldest children will be responsible for running some automated equipment that can be dangerous. The book tells of his eight year old son, Trevor, being seriously injured by one of those machines.

At first Trevor's survival was in question as he was air lifted from the farm to the trauma center. Then, once they were sure that he would live, the doctors actually asked permission to amputate one of his legs. After prayer and understanding God's promises to them, they refused the advice of the doctors for the amputation and saw God intervene miraculously as the leg healed.

It was a long and arduous process, but God used the medical community to bring total healing to this boy. After months in the hospital, the doctors consented to let them take Trevor home and care for him there. They set the next day as his release day. It happened that on that particular day a serious winter storm hit. Wind, snow, sleet and ice all slammed the city. Knowing little Trevor's excitement about going home that morning, the nurses tried to prepare Trevor that his father (Troy) would probably not be able to make it through the weather to pick him up. After a quick look of concern, Trevor just smiled back at the nurses and exclaimed with a grin, "You don't know my daddy."

Troy indeed came and Trevor was able to go home and continue his healing. Today he is a fully healed young man. Running and playing like any other child. Eventually, Troy would come to see that his faith at such a crucial time had also spoken to many around him; doctors, nurses and others taking care of his son. Without actually saying so, his actions proclaimed to the world the words of his little boy, "You don't know my daddy." Let's look at Troy's own words:

> "He was drawn to those words. There was something about them that echoed in his spirit, something that was far larger and greater than himself. They reminded me of my own heavenly Father, he whispered silently to himself. *That's it – this is about my heavenly Father! I'm learning on a whole new level that I can depend on His Word absolutely, whether it is the written Word that God has given us or the living Word He revealed in His Son, Jesus Christ.*

Troy's thoughts took him to familiar Bible passages he had known and quoted since childhood.

And [Jesus]said, Verily I say unto you, Except ye be converted, and become as little children, ye shall not enter the kingdom of heaven
Matthew 18:3

It was enough to make a man rethink his whole life! Troy talked to himself softly, "What would happen if we would just believe the Word of God the way young children implicitly believe what they are told?"

Then it dawned in on him. *If we could have the faith in our heavenly Father that Trevor has in his earthly daddy,* Troy reasoned, *wouldn't we all be receiving a lot more blessings in life? Wouldn't we experience joy and peace such as we have never known before? Wouldn't our world be a much better place?"*[3]

What a great story the Beams have to tell of faith and God's willingness to answer prayer. The testimony of Trevor's healing is moving. Just as stirring is the truth Troy shares in helping all of God's children, when the necessities of life hit hard, to boldly say with a "secret" understand and a wide grin, "You don't know my Daddy!"

The main focus here is that, before we begin to see the "types" or "spiritualization" of a passage, we should first interpret the obvious and natural. God is truly concerned about our needs and wants us to develop our faith in Him to the point of relying on both His *ability* to provide and on his *willingness* to provide. There is a big difference.

Most people who are believers will readily admit that He is able. They can wax long about the omnipotence of God. He can do anything. There is nothing too hard for God. He can overcome any obstacle. He can provide whatever we need.

The root of the matter is the gap in our thinking that God is able and our believing that He is willing. It is one thing to speak about how powerful God is. It is another thing to have faith that God is willing to use that power on our behalf.

I know earlier we are taught to pray that His will be done. I can't tell you the many times I have heard people pray for something with great faith and then nullify that faith with the statement, "If it is Your will." There are no more faith destroying words we can utter in our prayer life than those.

I am sure you are saying, "Dr. Riley, are you *trying* to confuse me?"

I assure you, that is not my intention. It can seem a little confusing at times and the last thing we need is to be confused in our prayer life. Let's see if we can clear this up. Imagine you and I are engaged in a conversation. In this scene, you need something and I have what you need. Let's see if this makes it any clearer.

You: Hi, Lonnie. I am so glad to be able to talk with you today. By the way, I loved your last book.

Me: Thank you very much. I'm glad it is helpful. What can I do for you today?

You: I am in a real bind, sir. I am $100.00 short on my rent this month and the landlord is breathing down my back. I just had some unexpected bills. I had to get my car fixed so I could go to work and have some money to pay him. He says that I have to pay it today or he will begin eviction procedures. I'm really up a creek and could use some help.

Me: That is a real bind. I am sorry to hear about your troubles. You know, I really like you and I'm glad that you came to me. I want to help you out. Open that desk drawer for me. In the back is a little box. Do you see it? Good. Open the box and you will find $100.00. Take that and pay the rest of your rent.

You: Wow that really is $100.00. You really do have it. I really do need that amount to take care of my rent. I am so scared that I'm going to be kicked out on the street and lose my job and not be able to eat or anything. I could sure use this $100.00 if you don't mind giving it to me.

Me: Like I said, you can have it. Use it to pay your rent. Don't worry about all the, "what ifs" that could happen without paying the rent. Take that money and pay it.

You: I know that the money is yours and you can do whatever you want to with it. That's exactly the amount I need. If you don't mind, I could sure use it, but only if it's ok with you.

Me: What else do you want me to do? I've told you where it is. I've said you can have it. Do you want me to go pay your rent for you? Take the money out of the box and go pay your rent!

You: Thank you so much for your kindness. I appreciate all that you have ever done for me, Lonnie, and I know you will come through for me this time. "If it's your will," please find a way in your mercy and love to give me that $100.00.

I could go on and on. This does seem a little absurd and stretched to the limit, or does it? We have

God's will revealed in His word. If He has already committed to something and said that is what He wants to do, why do we add the "if it's Your will" caveat to the end of our conversation? We already know it is His will because He said, and even had it written down, so we could know it. It shows NO faith to pray that way when His will is already revealed. It is actually the opposite of faith. We are not showing faith in His word, His ability, or His love for His children.

Sometimes the best way to grow in our faith is to take God at His word and watch as He fulfills it. 2 Peter 1:3 should strengthen our faith that God has given us everything we need for both *life* and godliness. He is concerned about our lives and has made provision (YHVH Yir'eh) for life as well as our godliness. In order to build our faith in His willingness to do what He is able, Peter goes on to remind the church that God has given us, *"exceedingly great and precious promises."* If He promises, He "wills" to do it. And if it IS His will, we don't have to pray "IF," but rather a strong, "YES" or "AMEN" (meaning, so be it).

> *"For all the promises of God in Him are Yes, and*
> *in Him Amen, to the glory of God through us."*
> 2 Corinthians 1:20

Just as I had the $100.00 you needed (the ability), I also wanted to give it to you (the willingness). But the more you kept on, the less I believed you understood and had faith that I either meant what I said or that the money was really mine to give.

> *"And it happened when He was in a certain city,*
> *that behold, a man who was full of leprosy saw*

Jesus; and he fell on his face and implored Him,
saying, '__LORD, IF YOU ARE WILLING, YOU__
__CAN MAKE ME CLEAN__.' Then He put out His
hand and touched him, saying, '__I AM WILLING;__
be cleansed.' Immediately the leprosy left him."
Luke 5:12-13

We can easily see these two concepts working in tandem in this verse. The man comes to Jesus and makes the bold statement that He can be healed if Jesus will do it. He did not know what Jesus' will was. It wasn't written down in a miraculously preserved book that he could read. So he makes the simple statement that oozes with faith in Jesus' ability. Then, without any hesitation, we see the response of Jesus in saying that He wills it. Right then and there, the leprous man was healed. The *will* and the *ability* were activated by *faith* and it brought about the miracle.

Faith in **both** His ability and willingness is what is needed to see the answer to prayer. This means that each of us must take some time to search God's word and understand what His will is regarding what we are facing. Once you know what He has already said about it, you don't have to tack on that faith killing addendum to your prayer. You already know it's His will. Just believe Him to bring His will to pass and you will receive it.

"And whatever things you ask in prayer,
believing, you will receive."
Matthew 21:22

Earlier, we studied that this prayer includes that we see His will done on earth like it is in heaven, right?

How His will is done in heaven is exactly how He wants it completed on earth. We are just asking for the earth to line up with His already revealed will. Remember how His word (His will) is done? It is done:

Immediately
Without hesitation
Unquestioned
Instantaneously
Flawlessly
Completely
Perfectly
Totally

There you have it! As I have heard it said many times, "God said it, I believe it, and that settles it!"

OTHER CONCEPTS

Besides the above mentioned literal and historic way of interpreting this passage, there are other interesting concepts that come into play. It is always interesting to see the alternate meanings of a passage and realize how the Spirit of the Word can make it applicable to whatever He wishes. This is not the way we build theological tenets, but it is a way the Holy Spirit will sometimes encourage believers, and even churches, through difficulties and challenges. Here are some alternate ways of viewing the meanings behind this passage.

In the Gospel of John there are seven "I AM" statements that Jesus makes in order to reveal certain aspects of Himself and His ministry.

THE SEVEN "I AM" STATEMENTS OF CHRIST

1.   I Am The Bread Of Life:

"And Jesus said to them, 'I am the bread of life. He who comes to Me shall never hunger, and he who believes in Me shall never thirst'" John 6:35

2.   I Am The Light Of The World:

"Then Jesus spoke to them again, saying, 'I am the light of the world. He who follows Me shall not walk in darkness, but have the light of life.'"
John 8:12

3.   I Am The Door:

"I am the door. If anyone enters by Me, he will be saved, and will go in and out and find pasture."
John 10:9

4.   Good Shepherd:

"I am the good shepherd. The good shepherd gives His life for the sheep." John 10:11

5. Resurrection and Life:

"Jesus said to her, 'I am the resurrection and the life. He who believes in Me, though he may die, he shall live.'" John 11:25

6. Way, Truth and Life:

"Jesus said to him, 'I am the way, the truth, and the life. No one comes to the Father except through Me.'" John 14:6

7. True Vine:

"I am the true vine, and My Father is the vinedresser." John 15:1

Part of the uniqueness of these titles is that they begin with, "I AM." If you remember from the chapter on "Hallowed by Your Name," you will recognize this as the meaning of the name of God, YHVH (Jehovah), which was given to Moses on the mountain where he saw the burning bush. In essence, with each declaration Jesus is ascribing Deity to Himself.

Let's look at the first "I Am" and consider how it relates to this verse. Jesus develops this word picture in several verses of the 6th chapter of John:

*"Then Jesus said to them, 'Most assuredly, I say to you, Moses did not give you the **BREAD** from heaven, but My Father gives you the true **BREAD** from heaven. For the **BREAD** of God is He who comes down from heaven and gives life to the world."*

Then they said to Him, 'Lord, give us this
BREAD *always.'*
And Jesus said to them, 'I am the ***BREAD*** *of life.*
He who comes to Me shall never hunger, and he
who believes in Me shall never thirst. But I said
to you that you have seen Me and yet do not
believe. All that the Father gives Me will come to
Me, and the one who comes to Me I will by no
means cast out. For I have come down from
heaven, not to do My own will, but the will of
Him who sent Me. This is the will of the Father
who sent Me, that of all He has given Me I should
lose nothing, but should raise it up at the last
day. And this is the will of Him who sent Me,
that everyone who sees the Son and believes in
Him may have everlasting life; and I will raise
him up at the last day.'
The Jews then complained about Him, because
He said, 'I am the ***BREAD*** *which came down*
from heaven.' And they said, 'Is not this Jesus,
the son of Joseph, whose father and mother we
know? How is it then that He says, 'I have come
down from heaven?'
Jesus therefore answered and said to them, 'Do
not murmur among yourselves. No one can come
to Me unless the Father who sent Me draws him;
and I will raise him up at the last day. ⁴⁵ It is
written in the prophets, 'And they shall all be
taught by God.' Therefore everyone who has
heard and learned from the Father comes to Me.
Not that anyone has seen the Father, except He
who is from God; He has seen the Father. Most
assuredly, I say to you, he who believes in Me has
everlasting life. I am the ***BREAD*** *of life. Your*

*fathers ate the manna in the wilderness, and are dead. This is the **BREAD** which comes down from heaven, that one may eat of it and not die. I am the living **BREAD** which came down from heaven. If anyone eats of this **BREAD**, he will live forever; and the bread that I shall give is My flesh, which I shall give for the life of the world.' The Jews therefore quarreled among themselves, saying, 'How can this Man give us His flesh to eat?' Then Jesus said to them, 'Most assuredly, I say to you, unless you eat the flesh of the Son of Man and drink His blood, you have no life in you. Whoever eats My flesh and drinks My blood has eternal life, and I will raise him up at the last day. For My flesh is food indeed, and My blood is drink indeed. He who eats My flesh and drinks My blood abides in Me, and I in him. As the living Father sent Me, and I live because of the Father, so he who feeds on Me will live because of Me. This is the **BREAD** which came down from heaven—not as your fathers ate the manna, and are dead. He who eats this **BREAD** will live forever.'"*
John 6:32-58 (emphasis mine)

Jesus is the Bread. Now let me give you a quick Hebrew lesson. The Hebrew word for bread is, "Lechem." It is pronounced with a hard guttural "ch" when speaking Hebrew, but we English usually say, "Lehem." The word for "House" in Hebrew is, "Beit" which is pronounced like "Bait." Follow me here, if one wants to say the house of bread it would be, "Beit-Lechem." In English we have learned to say, "Bethlehem." Wow! Isn't it interesting that the One (Jesus) Who is the Bread of life was born in Bethlehem (the house of bread)?

As we follow the progression of the dialogue in John 6 quoted above we find two distinct parallels. One is related to the manna of the Old Testament and the other is associated with the institution of the Lord's Supper (Eucharist).

MANNA

Jesus speaks of being *the living* **BREAD** *which came down from heaven.* This is a reference to the "daily bread" that the Israelite nation received in the wilderness once they were emancipated from slavery in Egypt. Not only did God deliver them with a mighty hand (save them), He also miraculously provided for them "daily." The nation of Israel (some estimate to be nearly 3 million strong at that time) did not have to scrounge around in the desert hoping to find enough food for their families; instead, God sent them food. Jesus explained this to those present and equated His being sent by God to the manna God sent in the desert.

Let's take a quick review of the manna. The actual meaning of the word we translate as "manna' is, "What is it?" The children of Israel had no idea what this miraculous bread was. The manna appeared 6 out of 7 days. The first 5 days they were to gather enough for that one day. If they gathered more than enough, it would spoil over night. On the 6th day they were to gather enough for 2 days because the manna would not fall on the Sabbath. This, in the context of our prayer, could symbolize that Jesus is the daily bread (the manna). That He was sent from God to bring us life, everlasting life.

EUCHARIST

Not only does this refer to the past application of manna, but it also points to the eventual instituting of the Eucharist (Communion or Lord's Supper). Jesus referred to the eating of His flesh (v.51) and the fact that He was giving His flesh as the Bread the world needs to experience life. That is exactly how He presented it to the disciples on the Thursday before He was crucified on Friday. We have come to know it as, "The Last Supper." Jesus used this same analogy by equating His body with the bread:

> *"And as they were eating, Jesus took **BREAD**,*
> *blessed and broke it, and gave it to the disciples*
> *and said, 'Take, eat; this is **MY BODY**.'"*
> Matthew 26:26 (emphasis mine)

The Bread of Life sent down like manna from God is born in Bethlehem (the house of bread) so that He might be crucified and through Communion remind us that He is our daily Bread that will return for us one day. Hallelujah!

PASSOVER

There is another beautiful picture regarding Jesus as the Bread of Life. It is found, interestingly enough, in the Jewish Seder (Passover meal). My wife and I have hosted many Christian versions of the Passover Meal, explaining the tremendous symbolism found within it. One of the staples of this meal is matzo bread. In this meal, the host has a matzo Cover that has 3 sections for 3 pieces of matzo bread. At the appropriate time in the meal, the host removes the middle (second) piece of matzo, breaks it, places one half back in the cover and the other in a special cover. It is then hidden until after the 3rd cup. Then, whichever child finds it receives a reward or prize.

Jesus is our Matzo Bread (without leaven, or sin). He is the 2nd Person of the Trinity. He was broken for our sin and buried. On the 3rd day He arose and brings the gift of life to all who accept Him as a little child.

Thank God for our daily bread, both literally and spiritually! We are blessed. Remember what the Psalmist said,

"I have been young, and now am old; Yet I have not seen the righteous forsaken, nor his descendants begging bread."
Psalm 37:25

Faith in both His ability and willingness is what is needed to see the answer to prayer.

-Dr. Lonnie E. Riley-

CHAPTER SEVEN

WE GROW IN

GRACE:

"And Forgive Us Our Debts"

It is wonderful to be told by Jesus that we can come to our Father and actually request things from Him. Sometimes just realizing that we have permission keeps us from feeling guilty about it. There is an all too prevalent concept that God is extremely busy running the universe and that we are a bother when we request anything from Him.

Well, that is just not true. Jesus made it very clear that we are more than just permitted to ask. We are encouraged to boldly ask things of God and He is thrilled to intervene for us.

"Let us then approach God's throne of grace with confidence, so that we may receive mercy and find grace to help us in our time of need."
Hebrews 4:16 (NIV)

WE ALL NEED FORGIVENESS

Nothing could be truer than what is addressed in this next part of the prayer. We all need forgiveness. Somehow each human being understands this need and is in search for something or someone that will clear the slate and give them a second chance. The Scripture is clear in that we all have this need.

"for all have sinned and fall short of the glory of God,"
Romans 3:23

After the fall of Adam and Eve in the Garden of Eden, the sinful nature of Adam was passed down through spiritual genetics from generation to generation. We are actually born into sin. We are born spiritually dead in the very fallen image of our forefather, Adam. Consider the words of the Psalmist:

"Behold, I was brought forth in iniquity, and in sin my mother conceived me."
Psalm 51:5

Think about a little toddler who is caught with his hand in the cookie jar. He doesn't have to be taught to tell a lie when confronted about it. He will just do it. It is innate within his little soul to lie to protect himself. He doesn't know why he does it, he just does.

If that attitude is left unchecked by the influence of Godly parents, family members and a local body of believers, that child will by nature gravitate toward the sinful. We are all sinners and will continue down the path of sin into total depravity if left to our own devices.

Sin leads to guilt. When God came into the Garden of Eden after the fall, Adam and Eve had hidden themselves. They sewed garments out of fig leaves to hide their nakedness and hid in the brush from the presence of God. They were ashamed of their sin and felt the guilt that is associated with failure.

As the verse in Romans indicates, everyone has sinned. Each of us at some point has fallen short of what is expected by a holy God. It doesn't matter who you are, you have sinned at some point. Dr. Billy Graham has preached the gospel to more people than anyone in history. He has had millions respond to his evangelistic altar calls over the decades and was spiritual advisor to

Presidents. Even a man of such faith, character and power before God had to come to grips with his sinfulness before Almighty God.

Though the Pope is venerated before millions of Roman Catholics and leaders and other believers all across the globe, he also understood his sinfulness. They have each been to "confession" in order to receive forgiveness for their individual sins.

The most merciful and caring person of influence during my lifetime has been recognized by many as Mother Teresa of Calcutta. She was a selfless woman who followed the call to reach the slum children of Calcutta and those with leprosy. She touched millions with her compassion and even won the Nobel Peace Prize. Yet, all of her accomplishments couldn't erase the fact that she, too, had a sinful nature and had sinned and fallen short of God's glory.

Most of us can think of times when we would lie in bed at night and the sinful deeds of our life replayed in our heads like a movie. We question what would or could have happened "if only" we had made a different decision or turned onto a different path in our life.

The guilt and shame that accompanies that type of thinking can become unbearable. The weight of sin has no doubt caused many to become diagnosed with severe mental disorders. Though our minds are a masterpiece of creation they tend to bend, and in some extreme circumstances, may even break underneath the weight of guilt and un-forgiveness.

CREATED IN GOD'S IMAGE?

I have often heard it said by many well intentioned ministers and scholars that each of us is created in the image of God. I know that sounds good and gives us great comfort when we study self-help manuals, but I have to take this issue to task. As I have studied over my career, I keep bumping my head on this thought. I have ceased saying it in my writings or my messages because of my findings. My contention is that Adam and Eve were created in God's image. However, we were born in the fallen, sinful image of Adam. It is very clear in the creation narrative in the book of Genesis that God created man/woman in His own image.

"Then God said, 'Let Us make man in Our image,
__according to Our likeness__; let them have
dominion over the fish of the sea, over the birds of
the air, and over the cattle, over all the earth and
over every creeping thing that creeps on the earth.'
__So God created man in His own image; in__
__the image of God He created him__; male and
female He created them. Then God blessed them,
and God said to them, 'Be fruitful and multiply;
fill the earth and subdue it; have dominion over
the fish of the sea, over the birds of the air, and
over every living thing that moves on the earth.'"
Genesis 1:26-28 (emphasis mine)

After creating man in His image from the dust of the ground and woman (also in His image) from one of man's ribs, God blesses them and gives them the first great commission: 1) Be fruitful and multiply, 2) Fill and subdue the earth, 3) Take dominion over everything. The one commandment (not ten) was to never eat the fruit from the tree at the center of the garden, the tree of the knowledge of good and evil.

How awesome that must have been. There was an openness to everything around them, a simplicity to their life and mission, as well as a clarity to their relationship with their Creator. Bear in mind, God not only created them, He empowered them. In the 2nd chapter of Genesis we are told that Adam had the intellectual capacity to name all of the animals, fish and birds. They enjoyed a sinless world that had not been touched by the curse of the fall. Everything was beautiful and good. Not only that, they walked with God in the evening and enjoyed His presence as they began to fulfill the great commission given them.

Then it happened!

While strolling through the garden, or perhaps even while tending the garden, Eve enters into a conversation with a serpent that is possessed by satan. She succumbs to the temptation and eats the forbidden fruit. Next, she shares with her husband and Adam eats as well. The last half of Genesis chapter 3 details the punishment for their disobedience.

Something changed. Not just that the serpent would slither, Eve would experience pain in childbirth or that Adam would have to toil against the earth in order to eat. Something happened spiritually. These two precious and special people died spiritually. They sinned and broke covenant with their God.

They disobeyed and lost that unique relationship they had enjoyed with God. They were no longer in the image of God. Their sin changed them. God does not sin, nor is sin allowed in His presence. When Adam and Eve became sinners, they ceased to be in the image of God. They also terminated that close personal relationship they had enjoyed with their Creator.

Genesis chapter 4 shows the devolution of sin. The first generation born to Adam and Eve is touched by the heinous act of murder. Because of jealousy (sin) over an unacceptable sacrifice (sin) Cain murdered (sin) his brother, Able.

"Sin will take you farther than you want to go,
keep you longer than you want to stay, and cost
you more than you want to pay."
- Unknown

We begin to see the new nature at work in Adam's children. The LORD evidently instituted some form of sacrificial system by which sinful mankind could appease the wrath of a Holy God. We don't know the exact requirement of this sacrificial system like we do that which is given to Moses on Mt. Sinai. Many surmise that God established this sacrificial regiment after the fall when He covered them with the skin from animals. It is thought that when God killed the animals for the clothing, He ordained the sacrificial system. However it was instigated, evidently it was clear enough for God to let His displeasure be known to Cain.

This, in and of itself, is proof of the spiritual death being passed to the next generation. One sin led to the multiplication of several more in their child. Even more telling than that is the actually wording in Genesis 5.

> *"This is the book of the genealogy of Adam. In the*
> *day that God created man, **He made him in the***
> ***likeness of God.** He created them male and*
> *female, and blessed them and called them*
> *Mankind in the day they were created. And*
> *Adam lived one hundred and thirty years, and*
> ***begot a son in his own likeness, after his***
> ***image,** and named him Seth."*
> Genesis 5:1-3 (emphasis mine)

It is very clear in this passage of Scripture that there is a distinction regarding the likeness or image of Seth as opposed to Adam and Eve. Seth is not said to be made/created in the likeness or image of God, but the likeness or image of Adam.

That is interesting. Though Adam and Eve were made in the likeness of God, they fell. When sin entered into their spirits they were no longer like God. Mankind was no longer a reflection of His image. They were now disobedient, sinful creatures that had violated the command of a Holy and Righteous God. That, then, is the image of their offspring. That is the image that all of humanity has received at birth.

Romans 1:18-32 is the most graphic way that the Holy Spirit has Paul describe the depravity that man falls into as a result of the sinful nature handed down through Adam. That is why Romans 3:23 can unequivocally say, "All have sinned."

Paul also paints a shorter picture, but no less poignant when he writes to the Christians in Ephesus describing what those saints were like prior to being made alive in Christ Jesus. This is applicable to all of mankind because of Adam's nature being passed to us.

"And you He made alive, who were dead in
trespasses and sins, in which you once walked
according to the course of this world, according to
the prince of the power of the air, the spirit who
now works in the sons of disobedience, among
whom also we all once conducted ourselves in the
lusts of our flesh, fulfilling the desires of the flesh
and of the mind, and were by nature children of
wrath, just as the others."
Ephesians 2:1-3

Verses such as these just accentuate the dramatic results of the fall of our first ancestors. The continual plunge from Godliness and Holiness affects us all. Just going to church, giving to charity and living a moral life are not enough to repair the damage and stop the decline.

WHAT DO WE NEED?

This sinful nature that has been passed down has left an incredible void in the life of each descendant of Adam and Eve (all of humanity). When they were created their lives were full because of the inner presence of God. They not only had His unique company as they strolled along in the evenings, but they also possessed an intimate, internal filling of God. Their spirit was alive and communed at all times with the living God. The priority of spirit, soul and body were in place the way God designed it. Man is a spirit and as such communed with God and allowed God to influence his spirit. The spirit controlled the soul and the body.

All of this was lost as a result of the fall. Because of the curse upon humanity, God declares that we cannot live if we were to actually see His presence (Exodus 33:20). Historically, we see that whenever God begins to reveal Himself, the recipients of His visitation are naturally afraid and struck by their sinfulness.

Nearly every angelic visitation recorded in Scriptures begins with the salutation, "Fear not!" Even when the great prophet, Isaiah, saw a vision of God's train filling the temple, he recognized and verbalized his unworthiness because of his sin.

> *"In the year that King Uzziah died, **I saw the***
> ***Lord** sitting on a throne, high and lifted up, and*
> *the train of His robe filled the temple.*
> *So I said:*
> ***'Woe is me, for I am undone!***
> *Because I am a man of unclean lips,*
> *And I dwell in the midst of a people of unclean*
> *lips;*
> ***For my eyes have seen the King,***
> ***The LORD of hosts.'***
> *And he touched my mouth with it, and said:*
> *'Behold, this has touched your lips;*
> ***Your iniquity is taken away,***
> ***And your sin purged.'"***
> Isaiah 6:1, 5, & 7 (emphasis mine)

The great fear that he felt, even though he had been blessed with a view of God sitting on a throne, was directly related to his being unclean, specifically in the area of speech.

What is interesting here is the remedy applied to him by the angel. Not so much that a hot coal was used to touch his lips, but rather that by this action his iniquity and sin are taken care of, removed.

Besides the physical manifestation of God being suddenly intolerable to mankind, there was the emptiness, the hollowness or perhaps best described as the barren cavity in our souls which was created to hold the very presence of God. This void is what drives most of humanity to act and react the way they do. Our rebellious tendencies (part of the image we received from Adam) cause us to find other avenues to fulfill that which is lacking in our spirits.

I have heard people comment that humans have a "God-shaped hole" in their souls. Only He will fit in it. Everything else leaves us empty. Nothing we say, do or refrain from doing will help. No matter how much we give away, help others, read the Bible or even go to church; none of that will, in and of itself, fill this void caused by our sinfulness.

As I watch the world progress down the road toward demise, I see people frantically searching to fill that void. The pursuit for money seems to entice many. Their hopes are that given enough money they will find peace and acceptance. The old adage, "Money can't buy happiness" is not necessarily true. Some people are very happy once they reach the plateau of wealth, but they are not satisfied. The void in our lives is not in the shape of a dollar bill.

Others are using relationships in the same way. If they can just find the right person(s) to hang out with, be seen with or marry, they will be fine. Some are just looking to satisfy their sexual urges in an attempt to satiate the hunger within, but to no avail. Another person or a relationship with them is not the shape of the void in their life.

Some have just decided it is too painful to keep trying all the options so they check out. I don't mean they kill themselves, they just zone out. Often this is done with the aid of drugs or alcohol. There is an addiction that, though it doesn't fill the void, it does numb the person or remove them from the reality of feeling and understanding there is something missing.

All of these counterfeit answers and many more are preoccupying this godless world. Today, I am even more convinced than ever that the remedy offered by the very God that created man in His image is the only one lasting and satisfying antidote to our sin-sick nature.

The Remedy = Forgiveness

The simple cure for the problem of sin is complete and unequivocal forgiveness. A stroke of the brush that totally wipes out the sins of our life and thereby makes it possible for us to be restored to a real and vital relationship with our Creator is the easy, straightforward, uncomplicated answer. Sounds great doesn't it? Total forgiveness. Being able to lay your head down on your pillow at night and fall asleep knowing that your sins have been erased and you are in a close relationship with God Who is totally filling the void in your soul. Being able to walk with your head held high and your shoulders back because those sinful acts or thoughts are not held against you any longer. The slate has been wiped thoroughly clean without even the slightest smudge remaining.

Sign me up! I want that kind of forgiveness. What do I have to do? Hmm. There in is the next problem. What is there that you can do to make God forgive you? What is the formula for "working" this forgiveness angle with God so that He will wipe all my sins away?

You are probably waiting on me to tell you to go to church, or read so many verses or chapters in the Bible. Maybe you are expecting me to give you my address and ask you to give till it hurts. Well, let me ask you this. How many times of going to church is enough to obtain forgiveness? How many verses or chapters would you have to read? How much money would you have to give to get God in the mood to totally clean your slate? How would you know for sure that it was enough? What if you died and realized you were one Sunday short, one verse away, or ten cent less than God required? Bummer!!

There has to be a way to actually know for sure. There is no peace in hoping or guessing that we are forgiven. The remedy is to be forgiven and know it beyond a shadow of a doubt.

The main question then is to understand what is required to be the recipient of this type of forgiveness. The God of universe is at odds with us because of our sinfulness. How can He be loving and just at the same time? What is it that can justify our forgiveness and still meet the call of justice for our sinfulness? Because, remember God has proclaimed:

"For the wages of sin is death"
Romans 6:23a

If that is true and the wages of sin is death, then death is the only justifiable sentence for our sinfulness. How can God, in good conscience, forgive us when the eternal sentence upon us is death? God cannot be Just if

He looks the other way or lets the sins of some go unnoticed or just forgives them on a whim. The only way for the slate to be wiped clean is to pay the price. Death! The only way for us to avoid this death is to have an acceptable substitute stand in for us and receive our punishment.

In the Old Testament God instituted the sacrificial system for that purpose. People would offer an animal as a sacrifice for the debt their sins had incurred. The problem was that man continually sinned and had to continually offer sacrifices. What mankind needed was a sacrifice that would cover all of our sins (past, present and future). One that would not have to be made again and again on our behalf.

> "For such a High Priest was fitting for us, who is
> holy, harmless, undefiled, separate from sinners,
> and has become higher than the heavens; who
> does not need daily, as those high
> priests, to offer up sacrifices, first for His own
> sins and then for the people's, **FOR THIS HE
> DID ONCE FOR ALL WHEN HE OFFERED
> UP HIMSELF.**"
> Hebrews 7:26-27(emphasis mine)

> "But Christ came as High Priest of the good
> things to come, with the greater and more perfect
> tabernacle not made with hands, that is, not of
> this creation. Not with the blood of goats and
> calves, but **WITH HIS OWN BLOOD** He entered
> the Most Holy Place **ONCE FOR ALL, HAVING
> OBTAINED ETERNAL REDEMPTION.** For if
> the blood of bulls and goats and the ashes of a

> *heifer, sprinkling the unclean, sanctifies for the*
> *purifying of the flesh,*
> *how much more shall the blood of Christ, who*
> *through the eternal Spirit offered Himself without*
> *spot to God, **CLEANSE YOUR CONSCIENCE***
> *from dead works to serve the living God? And for*
> *this reason He is the Mediator of the new*
> *covenant, by means of death, for the redemption*
> *of the transgressions under the first covenant,*
> *that those who are called may receive the promise*
> *of the eternal inheritance."*
> Hebrews 9:11-15 (emphasis mine)

When Jesus Christ died on the cross of Calvary, He was in affect taking our place and paying our debt for our sinfulness. His death was to pay our debt and clear the way for His Father, God Almighty, to rightfully and justifiably forgive us of our sins and declare that we are pure before Him. Allowing Him to fill us with His Holy Spirit, thereby filling the "God Void" within us and allowing us to be considered one of His holy and accepted children (John 1:12).

By accepting the payment that Christ Jesus made for us as our own, we can become a child of the most holy God and renew our long lost fellowship with Him. Look at what the Scriptures say about those who have accepted the forgiveness of God the Father.

> *"**BLESSED** are those whose lawless deeds are*
> *forgiven, and whose sins are covered;"*
> Romans 4:7 (emphasis mine)

> *"There is therefore now **NO CONDEMNATION***
> *to those who are in Christ Jesus, who do not walk*

according to the flesh, but according to the Spirit."
Romans 8:1 (emphasis mine)

"In Him we have **REDEMPTION** *through His blood, the forgiveness of sins, according to the riches of His grace"*
Ephesians 1:7 (emphasis mine)

"in whom we have **REDEMPTION** *through His blood, the forgiveness of sins."*
Colossians 1:14 (emphasis mine)

"And you, being dead in your trespasses and the uncircumcision of your flesh, He has made **ALIVE** *together with Him, having forgiven you all trespasses,"*
Colossians 2:13 (emphasis mine)

"If we confess our sins, He is faithful and just to forgive us our sins and to **CLEANSE US** *from all unrighteousness."*
1 John 1:9 (emphasis mine)

This last verse in 1 John is one that many people have used in connection with evangelism. I have studied several different evangelistic models over the years and most of them use this verse when explaining to the unbeliever the need for repentance. Now I certainly believe in the need for repentance and the confession of our sins to God. I actually am in the camp of older ministers who think that the church today is not putting enough emphasis on both repentance and confession, so I don't want to be misunderstood on this topic.

The interpretation of this verse in 1 John 1:9 is lacking and needs to be developed a little more. First of all, we must understand to whom the Apostle is writing.

"The recipients of John's first letter were most likely the Christians in Ephesus and its surrounding area. They were the same Christians to whom Paul wrote his letter to the Ephesians. It also appears they were the same Christians to whom Peter wrote his first and second letters, namely those Christians in Pontus, Galatia, Cappadocia, Asia, and Bithynia. Some of the Christians would have been those of the churches John mentioned in Revelation 1:11: Ephesus, Smyrna, Pergamum, Thyatira, Sardis, Philadelphia, and Laodicea. The church of Colosse was within the vicinity of Asia Minor as well, which was the same Roman province in which the city of Ephesus was located. Colosse was not too distant from Laodicea, which is the city Paul mentioned in his letter to the Colossians (cf. Colossians 2:1). The church of Colosse was started by Epaphras, who apparently learned the gospel from Paul in Ephesus. It seems probable therefore, that John's first letter was also intended for the Christians in Colosse.

It appears relatively certain that John's first letter was a circular letter. He wrote it to strengthen and encourage the same Christians among whom Paul had labored on his first and third missionary journeys, and to whom Peter wrote from Rome. John was well known to those Christians, having ministered among them for many years. Thus John wrote to them with a bond of affection, addressing them as "little children", "children", and his "beloved"."[1]

Since this book is written to believers in Jesus by one of the original Apostles of Jesus, then the message of this verse is totally different. Let me dissect it for us.

IF: He is making a subjective argument here. If we confess gives the opportunity for there to be no confession. It also leaves the opening that there is no forgiveness or cleansing unless we choose to.

WE: Plural and inclusive. As John talks about this confession he is talking about Christians confessing and includes himself in the dialogue.

CONFESS: To admit. Think of a criminal who confesses to a crime. In the spiritual world we are criminal in our sinfulness and we must own up to our sins.

OUR: Again John uses both the plural and the possessive. Our sins. He is not saying that we must sin, but he understands that we may and that when we do (all of us), even Apostles, need to confess it to God.

SINS: It is also plural. This may be because of multiple sins of a person or the plurality of sins because of a group of people. "Sins" in this instance is the Greek word, *Hamartia* meaning:

"To be without a share in, to miss the mark, to err, be mistaken, to miss or wander from the path of uprightness and honor, to do or go wrong, to wander from the law of God, violate God's law, sin, that which is done wrong, sin, an offence, a violation of the divine law in thought or in act, collectively, the complex or aggregate of sins committed either by a single person or by many."[2]

This reveals the ability, or at least capability, of Christians to miss the mark before God and that they should confess it when they do.

_HE:_ The context suggests that the work of forgiveness of the confessed sin is the responsibility and privilege of God the Father.

_IS:_ God is described here as continually present. Not was or will be, but actually "is." It reminds me of God's answer to Moses' inquiry of God's name being translated, "I am."

FAITHFUL: This describes God as being trustworthy in the carrying out of His promise.

AND: A conjunction joining the two descriptions of God's action towards the confession of our sins.

JUST: The better translation here is righteous. He is correct and righteous in the action He intends to take as a response to our confession.

TO FORGIVE: God will carry out His promise to cancel our debt and apply the blood of Jesus to our sinfulness, thereby forgiving us of missing the mark.

US OUR SINS: This is an effort to keep the attention on exactly what God is forgiving. Notice also that the Apostle continues to use the plural and possessive wording so that all Christians who fall are included.

AND TO CLEANSE US: Not only is forgiveness promised by the righteousness and faithfulness of God, but also simultaneously He will cleanse us. To cleanse is to make clean. Though our sinfulness defiles us, His promise is to wipe the slate clean as well as to forgive us.

FROM ALL UNRIGHTEOUSNESS: The word ALL is one of my favorite words in Scripture. Here it is inclusive of both my sins and the unrighteousness that is in my soul. He is continually cleaning us up as we confess our sins to Him.

I am so thankful for His faithfulness toward all who call Him, Father. I know that we don't have to fall into sin, but the reality is that often we do. The great promise here is that as long as we will confess our failures and sins to Him, He will *always* clean us up and forgive us for the mess.

This section of the prayer is to encourage us to ask for God's forgiveness. The tenor of Scripture is that we can rest in the promise that when we do ask, He will be faithful to His promise and take care of it as only He is able.

CHAPTER EIGHT

WE GROW IN

MERCY:

"As We Forgive Our Debtors"

As? What in the world does that mean? Forgive us our debts (trespasses) **AS** we forgive our debtors (trespasses)? You've got to be kidding me, right? Do we really want God to forgive us the way we forgive others? Honestly, I don't know how confident I would be that I was forgiven. How about you? Does that breed confidence in your forgiveness?

Have you ever had a splinter in your finger? They hurt and are incredibly annoying. When my wife and I were starting our most recent church plant, we eventually took over an entire 6,000+ square foot building. It was a challenge since it wasn't built in the best way to effectively house a church. The very back section, nearly 2,500 square feet, had been used as a mechanics garage for a season, then an office for a landscaping company and finally another mechanic who also bought and sold used car parts. We went in there and took all interior walls, electrical and plumbing out and started over with a large shell. I did a lot of the work by myself at the beginning. Big mistake, but I thought, "Hey, a willing heart is all God needs."

Eventually I had several talented men come in and get us on track. Before they came on board, I was mainly doing demolition and cleanup. I remember once day as I was moving all the debris I had created to the trash pile that a thin little splinter slid violently into my index finger of my left hand. It hurt. It hurt so bad that I picked the board back up and threw it several yards past the debris pile. "That will show that board just who I am."

I didn't have the tools necessary to remove the splinter at the church, so I just manned up and kept working. I waited until I got home and had Kim help me remove the little "thorn in the flesh." We spent most of the evening digging that little guy out. I felt it several days even after it was removed.

A small splinter hurts a lot. "**_AS_**" is the splinter in this section of the prayer. We ask God to forgive us AS we forgive others. Nothing feels natural about that. I don't necessarily like it. I'm not good at forgiving. I struggle with it. What does that look like?

Can you forgive, but learn from the experience? Can you really forgive, but keep a person at a distance so that you aren't hurt anymore? What does real forgiveness look like toward others, and is that the AS we want God to use in forgiving us?

Out of this entire prayer and all the important aspects that are addressed in it, this is the only section that Jesus felt was problematic enough to address again and explain what is meant during the prayer.

> *"For if you forgive men their trespasses, your*
> *heavenly Father will also forgive you. But if you*
> *do not forgive men their trespasses, neither will*
> *your Father forgive your trespasses."*
> Matthew 6:14-15

This is a hard pill to swallow. If I don't forgive others, God will not forgive me? Yeah, but you don't know what they did to me! They treated me so bad. They talked about me. They lied, stole, or abandoned me. They took advantage of my faith and trust. They were my mentor and they betrayed me. On and on it can go. We have certain expectations of people and they, almost reliably, let us down. We have the "right" to get mad and put them in their place. Is it really our duty to forgive them? Will God actually withhold His forgiveness towards us if we don't forgive those who have sinned against us? I must confess, as a man I really, really don't like these words. If you have wronged me, my wife or my family, I don't really want to forgive you. If I do choose to forgive you, I don't want to give you the opportunity to hurt me or my family again. Can we be honest here? I bet you feel the same. What is God trying to do to us? How can anyone be expected to live up to this standard?

JUSTICE OR MERCY?

Think about it for a minute. Most of us cry loud and hard for judgment when a wrong is committed against us or our families. "Throw the book at them!" we cry. When we are the victim we're ready to pull out our over sized Authorized King James Version and with conviction dutifully quote,

> *"And if any mischief follow, then thou shalt give*
> *life for life, eye for eye, tooth for tooth, hand for*
> *hand, foot for foot, burning for burning, wound*
> *for wound, stripe for stripe"*
> Exodus 21:23-25 (AKJV)

But when we are the ones who have committed the wrong, we plead for mercy. We call it a mistake. We pull out the "violins" and play a pretty pity party before our judges. We throw ourselves on the "mercy of the court" and become theological experts on the New Covenant's emphasis on grace and love. Hey, we may even quote this part of the Lord's Prayer to those who would sit in judgment, right?

Thinking this way reminds me of the message of Jesus when they were talking about forgiveness in the 18th chapter of Matthew. There is a king who is trying to call in all the debts that are owed to his kingdom. One man owes ten thousand talents.

"The Talent is a Greek coin worth 6000 Drachmas. A drachma is a day's wage. In today's money it would be about $360,000 U.S."[1]

Knowing the actual value of a talent in today's value puts this into perspective. The amount this guy owed the king, based on the definition above, is $3.6 billion. Wow! You talk about someone in over their head and living beyond their means. This guy is an accident waiting to happen. The king threatens to sell the man, his wife, his kids and all his possessions in order to pay the debt. The man pleads for patience and mercy. In a moment of undeserved favor (Grace) the king relents and *forgives* the debt.

This guy, relieved, runs out and finds someone who owes him 100 danarii. A denarius was one day's pay, so 100 denarii were equal to 100 day's pay. If the average daily wage in our country is $200.00, this guy would have been in debt $20,000.00. That's a far cry from $3.6 billion. The man who owed the $20K also asked for mercy and patience, but received none! The creditor grabbed him by the throat (I guess trying to squeeze the proverbial turnip for blood) and then had him thrown in prison.

Someone tells the king about this incident and, as we say in southern Georgia, the king has a conniption fit. He orders the original man arrested. He explains how the man should have given mercy just as he had received mercy. Then the king has him taken to the torturers until he is able to pay the entire $3.6 billion.

This story clearly illustrates how we want mercy when we stand in judgment, but demand justice for those who hurt us. The real kicker here is what Jesus says immediately after telling this story.

*"So My heavenly Father also will do to you if
each of you, from his heart, does not forgive his
brother his trespasses."*
Matthew 18:35

Ouch! It sounds much like the deeper explanation Jesus gave after the Lord's Prayer. There must be some kind of forgiveness on our part and it is somehow related to the forgiveness we receive from our heavenly Father. Jesus deals with forgiveness, or the lack of the same, on several occasions. It always has a high priority in the Kingdom of God.

I can tell you from my ministerial experience that un-forgiveness has the potential to ruin a person's walk with the Lord. They are unable to totally trust Him and believe that they are forgiven since they harbor resentment and un-forgiveness in their heart. This will also impair their testimony to the world which we are commissioned to win for Jesus. Most people don't want the type of "religion" that holds grudges and judges others instead of forgiving them.

It is my experience that un-forgiveness debilitates more Christians than any other problem. This requirement may very well be the hardest of all the demands of Christianity. Perhaps it can be said that there are more questions and more anguish over this topic than any other. Why is it so hard? Why do so many followers of Jesus have such a difficult time forgiving others? Perhaps it has to do with faulty expectations regarding forgiveness and how we actually walk this out in our daily lives as disciples of Jesus.

FORGIVE AND FORGET

I have heard it said that God forgives and forgets. That sounds good. When I think of all the times I have failed, sinned and acted out, it sounds really good. Then we are told to be like Him and do the same. That sounds impossible, right? I mean, we are not God. We can't do the things God does.

Well, let's look at the premise. Does God forgive? Unequivocally from a Biblical, theological or even philosophical view we must answer, "YES." Now, does God forget? That's a different question and brings many of God's attributes into the discussion.

God is omniscient (all knowing) and to actually forget something would diminish His omniscience. If that happens, God would cease to be God. Ergo, God is totally unable to forget anything. All knowledge is His, both past, present and future.

Do you think that God forgave some of the great people of the faith? Abraham, Isaac, and Jacob all lied. Moses committed murder as well as he dishonored God in the desert. David committed murder and adultery. Peter denied that he knew Jesus. Did God forgive these? The record is clear that He did, but did He forget those sins? If God is the Author of the Scriptures as we believe, how could He possibly have inspired the writers to chronicle those sins if He had forgotten them? From that standpoint I have to say that God cannot forget anything and that includes our sins.

Now if God doesn't forget them, how can we expect to? He does not command that we forget, just that we forgive. If forgetting were part of the equation then surely He would have issued such a command as well.

We do understand from Scripture that God makes a choice, a conscience decision to not remember those things against us once we come to faith in Jesus. He does not hold those sins to our account, but rather places them in the "paid in full" column of His heavenly books once and for all (Hebrews 9:12). Jesus became our sins while on the cross and paid the eternal debt of death so that we might have abundant, eternal life. The actual sinful acts (past, present and future) that we commit are no longer held against us because of the grace (undeserved favor) of God. We covered this in the last chapter, but it bears repeating because of the correlation we have tried to impose on ourselves.

> *"For this reason I also suffer these things, but I am not ashamed; for I know whom I have believed and I am convinced that He is able to guard what I have entrusted to Him [a]until that day."*
> 2 Timothy 1:12 (NASB)

How, then are we going to come to grips with the "AS" portion of this prayer? "Forgive us our trespasses AS we forgive those who trespass against us."   I like to tackle these things the way I once heard was the best way to eat an elephant....one bite at a time. Well, I believe we have eliminated a major part of the problem by understanding that forgiving is not the same as forgetting and it is neither commanded nor implied in this verse. Once that expectation is removed, we are not constantly under another barrage of guilt and shame.

Next, let's tackle another theological concept, another "bite" if you will: Can we do anything at the same level as Almighty God? In our limited humanity are we able, in our own strength, to accomplish anything with the same intensity or on an equal plane as Him? I must consider the distinct reality that the answer is, "NO!" I do not know of one thing that we can do that is equivalent to the quality or quantity that God can do. Refer back to His nature as revealed in His names. Think further about His sovereignty. In what way are you His equal?

That being the case, we must understand that we are unable to forgive in the same way, shape or form as God. We can't do it in the same quality or quantity. That does not diminish our responsibility to forgive, but it does help us understand that we are not able to forgive as God does.

We are unable to forgive at the "divine" level. This is a significant lesson to learn. It is imperative that we understand that we can't just "wake up" one morning and decide to forgive and expect that it is done at the same eternal level as God forgives.

The only way we can truly forgive in the fashion that I believe our Heavenly Father desires us to forgive is to stop trying. We cannot do it. It is impossible for us to do it in our own strength. We can only do this when we allow God to love and forgive through us.

We must have His love poured out in our spirits. We must see the other person through His eyes of love, not our eyes of pain. The Holy Spirit pours the love of God into our hearts and enables us to forgive with the power of God's love.

"Therefore, having been justified by faith, we have peace with God through our Lord Jesus Christ, through whom also we have access by faith into this grace in which we stand, and rejoice in hope

of the glory of God. And not only that, but we
also glory in tribulations, knowing that
tribulation produces perseverance; and
perseverance, character; and character, hope.
Now hope does not disappoint, because the love of
God has been poured out in our hearts by the
Holy Spirit who was given to us."
Romans 5:1-5

I was in a meeting recently with some highly educated people. There were four adults in the room with 4 separate doctorates. We were discussing the plans of the group to establish a Bible College in our city. Part of our conversation took a different turn as the Holy Spirit was directing us and one man, Dr. Randall Worley, told a quick little story that I can use to illustrate this point.

Dr. Worley was in Indiana spending time with one of his mentors at a farm and it was raining profusely. As the two men were watching the rain, his mentor pointed out the rain water gushing through the downspout. "Is that downspout working?" He asked Dr. Worley. "Well, yeah," he replied, "It seems to be working great." "Not really," his mentor answered. "It isn't 'working' at all. It's not doing a thing accept letting the water flow through it, and that's only because it's connect to the gutter."

We can't work up this subject of forgiveness. We can't do it. We just have to remain connected to our heavenly source and allow the Spirit of God to pour His love through us and the forgiveness will flow from Him, not us. We don't work it; we let Him work through us. Romans 13 places an emphasis on the love of God manifesting to others through us.

"Owe no one anything except to love one another,
for he who loves another has fulfilled the law.
For the commandments, 'You shall not commit
adultery,' 'You shall not murder,' 'You shall not
steal,' 'You shall not bear false witness,' 'You
shall not covet, and if there is any other
commandment, are all summed up in this saying,
namely, 'You shall love your neighbor as yourself.'
Love does no harm to a neighbor; therefore love is
the fulfillment of the law."
Romans 13:8-10

All of the laws of God are fulfilled in one word: LOVE. Forgiveness is the greatest expression of love. So it is/was with Jesus so it must be through us.

"Therefore, as the elect of God, holy and beloved,
put on tender mercies, kindness, humility,
meekness, longsuffering; bearing with one
*another, and **FORGIVING** one another, if*
anyone has a complaint against another; even as
*Christ **FORGAVE** you, so you also must do. But*
*above all these things **PUT ON LOVE**, which is*
the bond of perfection. "
Colossians 3:12-14 (emphasis mine)

WHAT DOES THAT LOOK LIKE?

What is real forgiveness? I found this definition given by the Mayo Clinic. I know most don't consider them as Biblical scholars, but I thought their concept was enlightening and could actually pass the test of Scriptural study.

> "Generally, forgiveness is a decision to let go of resentment and thoughts of revenge. The act that hurt or offended you might always remain a part of your life, but forgiveness can lessen its grip on you and help you focus on other, positive parts of your life. Forgiveness can even lead to feelings of understanding, empathy and compassion for the one who hurt you. Forgiveness doesn't mean that you deny the other person's responsibility for hurting you, and it doesn't minimize or justify the wrong. You can forgive the person without excusing the act. Forgiveness brings a kind of peace that helps you go on with life."[2]

Let's look at the major concepts in this definition and apply them with the help of the Holy Spirit and God's Word.

A DECISION

Forgiveness doesn't just happen. It is intentional not accidental. Many things have to be weighed in the balance. It is not just a thoughtless whim of emotion, it is a deliberate judgment that you make whereby you resolve, after consideration, to choose to release the wrong. It is voluntary. That is not easy. I don't think it's supposed to be easy. I believe that it is part of how we are to exhibit the love of God to a godless world. Jesus even told us that offenses would happen and even increase in the latter days. The world knows how hard it is to truly forgive, so when we actually choose to do so, we are showing God's great power. That's right, we choose to forgive. Our volition is part of our soul. It is a soul function. But often the other two faculties of the soul will fight against it. Our feelings will tell us we can't do it. So will our intellect. But with the power of God in our spirit-man flowing through us (like a down-spout) we can overcome those soulish struggles and choose to forgive anyway.

LET IT GO

Let me take a moment to remind you that the command of God is to forgive, not forget. Our mind is one of God's most inspiring creations. It has been said that we never truly, forget anything. Our minds file it away. We speak of letting it go, we are not contradicting ourselves and trying to slip one by you and make you forget by using other words. The decision to let go actually is more related to ownership than memory.

More than letting the "person(s)" go, we are letting go of the ownership of that offense. We actually release ourselves from the grip of the cancerous thoughts and feelings of revenge and resentment. Those can eat not only at our souls, but even at our bodies. That's why the bumper sticker slogan is true:

> "Forgiveness doesn't make the other person
> right, it sets you free"

The overwhelming enslavement of the duo of resentment and revenge has ruined many lives. Too often we can become so preoccupied with the offense (real or imagined) that we have internalized it to the point of it becoming a barrier from receiving from God. Our obsession with the transgression can become even more of a problem than the transgression itself. We become comfortable with it. We begin to identify with it, and even make it part of our identity. We accept a victim mentality and eventually can make the disastrous move from owning the offense to being owned by the offense. It moves from it identifying us to us identifying it. For some people it could be quipped that if you look up un-forgiveness or bitterness in the dictionary you would find their picture. We must let go!

As a boy I loved to climb the dogwood in our back yard. There was a little barbed wire fence near it that would give me a few feet head start. I would jump from the fence, reach the first limb and scurry up the tree. I would get pretty far up and suddenly realize how high I was and begin to freeze. I don't care for heights. I would begin screaming and my father would come out and talk me down, one step at a time. Eventually I had to get to that bottom limb. I would hang from the limb, but never felt like I could drop to the ground, or land on that fence. Usually, panic was the next emotion. My father promised to catch me if I would let go. I might scream or cry. I could say that I couldn't do it. But finally, after asking dad several hundred times if he was sure he could catch me, I would let go. Once I did, he would catch me and place me on good ole' terra firma and I could run and play again. You get the picture, right? Your Heavenly Father is right near you asking you to let go of the offense or trespass that was committed against you. He promises to catch you. You may scream and cry for a while. But, to ever be free to go ahead in your spiritual life you must eventually "let it go." When you do, I promise, God will always catch you.

IT MAY ALWAYS REMAIN A PART OF YOUR LIFE

I know that it is not good news, but I'm afraid it is true. Some hurtful things will never change. You will always hurt from broken marriages, Church splits, stolen items, murderous deeds, and parental neglect or abuse. The list could go on and on, but you get the picture. Some trespasses will always remain a part of your life. We need to apply the love of God to that situation and forgive through His power anyway.

Just because it is a part of the rest of your life doesn't mean it has to always hurt. Once you choose to forgive and allow the power of God's Spirit to pour His love on, in and through you, you can begin to heal the hurt. Your facts or situation may not have totally changed, but you're not focused on it or relying on it for your identity.

As I am writing, it is winter. Believe it or not it can get pretty cold sometimes at the beach. The entire south east suffered a huge winter storm this year and Myrtle Beach was totally shut down by ice. I can feel the cold most in my right leg. Nearly 10 years ago I was carrying my youngest son down some steps and I lost my footing and severely dislocated and broke my leg/foot. I say severely, my foot was turned 180 degrees the wrong way. I looked like the double minded man from James 1. The left leg was pointing forward and the right was pointing backward. I didn't know if I was coming or going. Anyway, I digress. The doctors gave very little hope that I would be able to walk again unassisted. At the very least I would need a cane or walker.

It was a long and hard process to go through the physical therapy. Just as in forgiveness, I had to choose every day, sometimes several times a day, to work on my walking or dexterity. I had many exercises to do and had to slowly develop from being in a wheel chair to a walker, then to crutches, next to a cane and now finally to walk unassisted. Praise God, most people wouldn't even know of the accident by watching me walk.

Let me now appropriate that experience to our topic. In order to fix my "hurt" I had to *choose* to undergo surgery. So it is with the offenses and trespasses that have affected our lives. In order to begin to heal, we must choose to move in that direction. Remember, moving towards healing through forgiveness doesn't mean that what happened to you isn't important or doesn't matter, it just means that you are choosing to "walk" in the Spirit and not let your past dictate your future or your hurt own the rest of your life.

The surgery first of all re-located my foot so that I was now pointing towards the correct location. Then, to actually fix my break they had to place a metal plate in there and fasten it with about 13 screws from both sides. For a long time the wound remained open though covered with bandages. This relates to us in realizing that there was more than just a choice, some difficult and painful decisions had to be made. It didn't feel good right away, and you may not feel all the emotions you hope for as you choose to forgive. It isn't easy. You have to "die to yourself" and be willing to let God surgically remove those things that you have allowed to take root in your spirit. Resentment, hatred, vengeance, etc., all have to be removed and replaced with whatever is necessary for you to begin the process of walking once again in the right direction toward Godliness.

Next, my wife and the doctor's special assistant were the only ones who would change the bandages. This happened several times each day. Once I began to heal enough to begin to put pressure on it, it hurt all over again. I had to choose to look past the hurt if I ever thought I would walk again. Your hurts may continue to be painful, even after your choice. You will have to choose each time to not pick that offense up again, but to release it to God and ask Him to fill you with His Spirit of Love again and again. If you truly want to walk in the Spirit and experience the "life more abundant" that Jesus once spoke about, you will have to continually choose to forgive. Remember, forgiveness doesn't mean what happened to you isn't important or doesn't matter. It does matter, not only to you, but to your loving Heavenly Father. Keep in mind, though, He loves you enough to guide you to freedom through forgiveness and He will help you all the way through your "therapy" as you learn to walk again.

Sometimes, my foot still hurts, especially in the cold. The metal plate and screws get cold and that feels very strange inside of my leg. It is a reminder that will never go away. Just like the long scar on the outside of my leg, and the bumps where you can actually see and feel the screws (I'm pretty sure they are phillip's head). This will always be a part of my life. It will be something I carry to my death. It's just that serious of an accident and repair. That can also be applicable to our hurts and offenses.

As I mentioned earlier, some trespasses are so severe that it will always be a part of your life. You may feel it more on certain days. Even if there is no "feeling" present, they may leave a scar. That's the normal for my foot. It doesn't cause pain every day anymore, but the scar is there. We may have a scar. A scar is nothing more than a reminder that a wound happened and has healed. Sometimes we are stronger because of the scarring. Other times it is a constant reminder of the hurt (like a scar to the face).

The metal I have will finally be separated at my death. As a certified crematory operator, I performed many cremations. In today's world it is common to find metal in the ashes. Hips, rods, plates, you name it, and I've seen it. But the unique aspect is that now, after the death and cremation of the person, the metal is no longer connected. Eventually, the scars and memories will remind us no longer. When we pass into the next dimension of existence and live before Almighty God, those sins, offenses or trespasses will no longer matter. Hallelujah!

FORGIVENESS ISN'T DENIAL

It's been a few pages, so let's revisit this portion of the Mayo Clinic's definition.

"Forgiveness doesn't mean that you deny the other person's responsibility for hurting you, and it doesn't minimize or justify the wrong. You can forgive the person without excusing the act."[3]

Denial. I've hear that is a river in Egypt (De-Nile). In many areas of life we find it easier to cope if we just deny or pretend that it never happened. Hurt can be one of those areas. "Nothing really happened, I'll just keep going on like nothing even happened." we convince ourselves. Once we actually begin the process (and it is a process) of forgiveness, we should not deny the event happened or that the person(s) responsible should be held to account. We do no one any good in the long run by denying the event or its impact on us. We definitely can pardon the person without justifying the deed.

Forgiveness doesn't mean there shouldn't be consequences for the hurt done to you by someone else. There is a Biblical principle: You sow what you reap.

"Do not be deceived, God is not mocked; for whatever a man sows, that he will also reap"
Galatians 6:7

There will often be consequences for people's actions. Wisdom tells us to learn from our mistakes.

Sometimes, after certain difficult circumstances have been forgiven, we need to evaluate our personal lives and relationships. In order to protect yourself or your family it may be necessary to limit your exposure to the other person. It doesn't mean you haven't forgiven them, it just means you have learned much from your experience. Forgiveness doesn't necessarily mean you will always reconcile the relationship with the person who hurt you. It means you have chosen to not hold the issue against them any longer. You no longer fume about it. You no longer tell others about it. You don't even continually tell the other person that you have forgiven them (you know, rubbing it in). You have released them and the love of God has given you the power to let them go. Yet, it doesn't mean that your relationship with that person will automatically resume (if at all) at the same level as before the offense.

FREEDOM

Freedom is a great topic. Movies have been made about it. Sermons have been preached about it. Wars have been fought for it. It is within all of us to long for real freedom. Jesus knew this when He made the radical statements:

"And you shall know the truth, and the truth
shall make you free.
Therefore if the Son makes you free, you shall be
free indeed."
John 8:32 & 36

Carrying un-forgiveness within us binds up our soul. We are enslaved to its every whim. It demands that we think, act, react and even dream within its parameters. When we forgive, however, we are loosened from that slavery and enjoy the freedom that emancipation brings.

I think of freedom in the natural. My roots are in the state of Georgia, a southern state and a member of the Confederacy. Over a century ago the slaves were freed by the Emancipation Proclamation signed by President Lincoln. After a hard fought war and in spite of many prejudiced people, the slaves were given their freedom. The sad thing is that many of them did not know what their free life should look like. They had been held back so much that they were hardly able to forge a living for themselves. Though they desperately desired freedom, they didn't know how to live free. It took time, effort and strength to press on until they began to live in this new age of freedom.

Many times that can also be indicative of us. We have to allow the Holy Spirit of God to show us how to walk in the Spirit with this new freedom. We are suddenly released from the bondages of un-forgiveness and we need assistance in learning how to live in that freedom.

The main object and purpose of forgiveness is not the person who did the wrong, but the wronged. Forgiveness is not about letting the sinner off the hook or saying what they did to us is OK. It is about releasing them so that we are not bound by the hate, resentment or vindictiveness that had us shackled. Basically, forgiveness does not try to decide who was right or wrong, it just means we are not going to let someone else's actions ruin us.

Holding on to the offense is often a major blockage that stops us from receiving from God. How can we clearly pray or discern the will of God if we are "eaten up" by our un-forgiveness?

Refusing to forgive has been likened to drinking poison and expecting the other person to die. Not going to happen.

THE OTHER LORD'S PRAYER

John 17 is the prayer that Jesus prayed while in the Garden of Gethsemane. It is very revealing as Jesus shares His heart with the Father. Jesus makes certain requests of Him concerning both His disciples that are with Him and those who would eventually follow Him (us). There are several statements in this prayer that I think are pertinent to our study. He spends much of this high priestly prayer interceding for there to be unity. Notice the unity sections that I have emphasized in the following four verses from our Lord's prayer.

*"I will remain in the world no longer, but they are still in the world, and I am coming to you. Holy Father, protect them by the power of your name, the name you gave me, so **THAT THEY MAY BE ONE** as we are one.*
***THAT ALL OF THEM MAY BE ONE**, Father, just as you are in me and I am in you. May they also be in us so that the world may believe that you have sent me. I have given*

them the glory that you gave me, ***THAT THEY MAY BE ONE*** *as we are one—I in them and you in me—so that they may be brought to complete unity. Then the world will know that you sent me and have loved them even as you have loved me."*
John 17:11, 21-23 (NIV emphasis mine)

His emphasis on the unity of His disciples is understandable since He was going to be betrayed any moment, tried, scourged and eventually put to death. They could have scattered and never seen one another again. Even after He arose from the dead and was taken into heaven 40 days later, one can understand that the entire message could be lost without a spirit of unity and oneness among them. But why is He concerned about it in our day? We have churches on nearly every corner here in the south. We have Christian TV and radio. We have millions of Bibles in print, and books like this one line the shelves of book stores all across our nation.

I believe that Jesus understood the power of un-forgiveness. He was, and is, very aware that it is a device that satan uses to get an advantage over us and to keep us off purpose. The Apostle Paul called it a "foothold." The picture is that of a person scaling a mountain and looking for some way to ascend the bare faced cliff. The climber finds anything to grasp onto or place his foot on that will give him stability and a way to push forward. Un-forgiveness in our hearts gives satan that type of grip onto our lives. Jesus understood that. He is praying that we all would be one. That nothing would create a chasm between believers, that we would be lovers of one another and not hold grudges against each other. Jesus understood the ancient words of the Psalmist:

"Behold, how good and how pleasant it is
*For brethren to dwell together in **UNITY**!*
It is like the precious oil upon the head,
Running down on the beard,
The beard of Aaron,
Running down on the edge of his garments.
It is like the dew of Hermon,
Descending upon the mountains of Zion;
For there the LORD commanded the blessing—
Life forevermore."
Psalm 133 (emphasis mine)

There is power in unity. There is anointing from God when we are in unity. It even speaks of the Lord commanding a blessing where there is unity. Now, we have to ask the obvious question. How can we be in unity if we won't forgive? Not only that, but could our powerlessness, lack of anointing or blessing be because we are not walking in real forgiveness?

The Apostle Paul understood the heart of Jesus. Concerned that the Church might grieve the Holy Spirit, he writes to the saints in Ephesus that they must forgive one another.

"And do not grieve the Holy Spirit of God, by
whom you were sealed for the day of redemption.
Let all bitterness, wrath, anger, clamor, and evil
speaking be put away from you, with all malice.
And be kind to one another, tenderhearted,
***FORGIVING ONE ANOTHER**, even as God in*
Christ forgave you."
Ephesians 4:30-32 (emphasis mine)

Perhaps we can now see that our tendency to harbor resentment and not forgive is detrimental not only to us, but also to the Body of Christ. No wonder our enemy loves to ensnare us in this trap. We must learn to be quick to forgive. The author of Hebrews understood this as well when he penned:

> *"Pursue peace with all people, and holiness,*
> *without which no one will see the Lord: looking*
> *carefully lest anyone fall short of the grace of*
> *God; lest any root of bitterness springing up cause*
> *trouble, and by this many become defiled;"*
> Hebrews 12:14-15

Many could become defiled because we let a root of bitterness spring up within us. Only an attitude of love and forgiveness can stop that from happening and open the channel for power, anointing and blessing the Psalmist spoke of earlier.

THE NEW COVENANT

Now, I don't want to shake you up, but if you've read this far, you know I probably will. I believe this book will confirm things that you already knew were true as well as challenge some of the preconceived notions that the Church has just accepted over the years. One of the areas of challenge is to understand when the New Covenant took place. Let's allow Jesus' own words to answer that question.

*"For this is My blood of the new covenant, which
is shed for many for the remission of sins."*
Matthew 26:28

*"And He said to them, 'This is My blood of the
new covenant, which is shed for many.'"*
Mark 14:24

*"Likewise He also took the cup after supper,
saying, 'This cup is the new covenant in My
blood, which is shed for you.'"*
Luke 22:20

The Apostle Paul also quoted the Lord in reference
to what instituted the New Covenant.

*"In the same manner He also took the cup after
supper, saying, 'This cup is the new covenant in
My blood. This do, as often as you drink it, in
remembrance of Me.'"*
1 Corinthians 11:25

Anyone can easily tell from these words what should
be considered as the initiation of this New Covenant. The
shedding of His blood for us!

Why is that important? The crucifixion, of course,
happened at the end of Jesus' ministry. That means that
anything that happened prior to His death, even though
He was alive, was still under the Old Covenant. Yes, the
Old Covenant is still taking place in the New Testament!
Actually, according to His own definition, all of Jesus' life
took place under the Old Covenant. The New Covenant
did not begin until His death. That being said, we have
to understand that 27 out of the 28 chapters of Matthew

take place in the Old Covenant. The same can be said of 15 of the 16 in Mark, 23 of the 24 in Luke and 19 out of the 21 in John. Nearly all of the Gospel writing is about what took place *before* the New Covenant.

This is critical because everything changed with the New Covenant.   Listen to how the Hebrew writer explained it:

"For if that first covenant had been faultless, then no place would have been sought for a second. Because finding fault with them, He says: 'Behold, the days are coming, says the LORD, when I will make a **NEW COVENANT** *with the house of Israel and with the house of Judah— not according to the covenant that I made with their fathers in the day when I took them by the hand to lead them out of the land of Egypt; because they did not continue in My covenant, and I disregarded them, says the LORD. For this is the covenant that I will make with the house of Israel after those days, says the LORD: I will put My laws in their mind and write them on their hearts; and I will be their God, and they shall be My people. None of them shall teach his neighbor, and none his brother, saying, 'Know the LORD,' for all shall know Me, from the least of them to the greatest of them. For I will be merciful to their unrighteousness, and their sins and their lawless deeds I will remember no more.' In that He says, 'A new covenant,'* **HE HAS MADE THE FIRST OBSOLETE.** *Now what is becoming obsolete and growing old is ready to vanish away."*
Hebrews 8:7-13 (emphasis mine)

Why is this so crucial? Even this prayer, taking place during one of Jesus' sermons, took place before the New Covenant. It is filled with Old Covenant concepts and working. I think of the relationship of being forgiven **AS** we forgive others. It is developed out of works mentality based on the Old Testament law. We are no longer under that law.   We operate under new guidelines and expectations in the New Covenant.

The Scriptures now tell us that we "can do all things through Christ who strengthens us". We are now crucified with Him. Even that the life we now live in the flesh is because of, and empowered by, Him. Old things have passed away, all have become new. In this New Covenant, we forgive out of being forgiven.   The completed work of Jesus Christ, the Messiah, changes the nature of those who believe.   We are not under condemnation, but rather we exude the powerful, life-giving grace of God that brought about our forgiveness. Again, Paul detailed this in a couple of sections of Scripture as he was informing the churches of his day.

"And do not grieve the Holy Spirit of God, by
whom you were sealed for the day of redemption.
Let all bitterness, wrath, anger, clamor, and evil
speaking be put away from you, with all malice.
And be kind to one another, tenderhearted,
FORGIVING ONE ANOTHER, EVEN AS
GOD IN CHRIST FORGAVE YOU."
Ephesians 4:30-32 (emphasis mine)

"Therefore, as the elect of God, holy and beloved,
put on tender mercies, kindness, humility,
meekness, longsuffering; bearing with one
*another, and **FORGIVING ONE ANOTHER**, if*

*anyone has a complaint against another; even **AS
CHRIST FORGAVE YOU, SO YOU ALSO
MUST DO.** But above all these things **PUT ON
LOVE**, which is the bond of perfection."*
Colossians 3:12-14 (emphasis mine)

The basis of our being forgiven is no longer related
to how we forgive. According to these New Covenant
verses, we forgive because we have **ALREADY BEEN
FORGIVEN**.

Now the nature and Spirit of Jesus lives within us
and it is in His nature to forgive. It is the Spirit of the
New Covenant to be forgiving. Our sins have already
been forgiven and our name written in the Lamb's Book
of Life. Our sins are not in danger of being "un-forgiven."
Remember what the New Covenant says about that?

*"If we are faithless,
He remains faithful;
He cannot deny Himself."*
2 Timothy 2:13

Thank God for our forgiveness! And, thank God for
filling us with His great love and mercy so that we are
willing to allow Christ Jesus to forgive through us, and
keep us from limiting what God can do in our lives.

As we end this chapter focused on forgiveness, I want
to share a collection of quotes on forgiving. I hope they
encourage, enlighten and entertain.

"Always forgive your enemies - nothing annoys
them so much."
—Oscar Wilde

"Forgiveness is God's command."
—Martin Luther

"Without forgiveness, there's no future."
—Desmond Tutu

"Forgiveness is an act of the will, and the will can function regardless of the temperature of the heart."
—Corrie Ten Boom

"The Glory of Christianity is to conquer by forgiveness."
—William Blake

"We win by tenderness. We conquer by forgiveness."
—Frederick William Robertson

"Forgiveness is the fragrance that the violet sheds on the heel that has crushed it."
—Mark Twain

"For 'tis sweet to stammer one letter of the Eternal's language; — on earth it is called Forgiveness!"
—Henry Wadsworth Longfellow

SECTION THREE

THIRD
"G"

GUARD

"In this manner, therefore, pray:
Our Father in heaven, Hallowed be Your name.
Your kingdom come.
Your will be done on earth as it is in heaven.
Give us this day our daily bread.
And forgive us our debts, as we forgive our debtors.
And do not lead us into temptation,
but deliver us from the evil one.
For Yours is the kingdom and the power and the
glory forever. Amen"
Matthew 6:9-13

CHAPTER NINE

WE WILL BE GUARDED BY HIS

LEADERSHIP:

"And Lead Us"

Gaining insight and *growing* in our walk with God have been the focus of the previous two sections. They are both vital and foundational in our progress as believers. We will spend the next three chapters discussing the ways that this prayer shows us that our Heavenly Father *Guards* us (the 3rd G). We will understand how He is our Protector. He will always defend us. God looks after His children and safeguards them. We can always count on

His presence.   He affirms His intentions clearly in His word:

> *"No man shall be able to stand before you all the*
> *days of your life; as I was with Moses, so I*
> *will be with you. I will not leave you nor forsake*
> *you."*
> Joshua 1:5

The first part of this request speaks of God leading us. It is in the negative sense in that; we do not want Father God to lead us into temptation. This requires trust on our part that as He leads us, and we subsequently follow, He will not take us down that path towards enticement to sin. The entire premise is extremely intriguing, don't you think? We will spend some time studying in-depth the implications of God actually leading us into the possibility to sin in the next chapter.   This chapter focuses on strengthening our understanding of, and reliance upon, our Heavenly Father's leadership.

God is an experienced Guide.   There are many Biblical references and passages that reveal the guiding prowess of our Heavenly Father.   We must learn to submit our own selfish desire to lead, and embrace His will and direction for our lives. God has a plan for the world and our place in it.

He has delivered you from the power of sin, not just to take you to a place called heaven, but to allow you to be an integral part of building His kingdom on earth. Everything that we have studied in this prayer so far should be increasing our awareness that we can unreservedly trust Him. That is how we please God, not with a list of do's and don'ts, but through trust (faith Hebrews 11:6).

ROW, ROW, ROW YOUR BOAT

I have often had the privilege of going whitewater rafting in the mountains of North Carolina. As each of my sons became a teenager, I took them on a father and son trip to the mountains. We spent several days together discussing their transition into manhood and my expectations of them as a young man in our household. With each son, we ended the trip by going rafting down the Nantahala River.

The Nantahala is not a real difficult river to run. I would describe it as a smooth rapid river ride with bursts of whitewater excitement. I have gone down it in both a guided boat and in my own rented one man "duckie." As far as I am concerned, that's the best experience for a teenager or adult.

It really made an impact on my son, Joshua, who has gone down the rougher waters, and even taught rafting and kayaking at the summer camp he managed. He actually now owns 2 kayaks. I've seen videos of him going over waterfalls and he has taken his kayak into the ocean when he comes to visit us at the beach.

My first time down the river I had a guide. My oldest son, Jason, and I were in a large boat with an experienced river guide directing us through the entire trip. I didn't know anything about the river. We received a quick, 10 minute training by the river boat company just prior to jumping on an old, dilapidated bus and barging down the crooked, one lane road through the gorge to the launch site. I promise you, the bus ride was just as scary as the river run. Seriously, if you made it through the bus trip, the river was a breeze, no problem.

In this brief class, we all learned about the different classes of whitewater. We heard that most of the trip we would experience class 1 and 2 rapids, and that at the end of the trip we would traverse a class 3. It was exhilarating at first. They showed us how to hold the paddle and to look out for fishing hooks that might be hanging from trees near the riverbank.

Then the topic shifted dramatically. Now we are learning how to survive if you are thrown out of the boat. WHAT!? Assume this position, help this person, hold on to the paddle or you'll get charged for it. THEN the big one, if you don't get the boat out of the river at the proper point, you will go down the next section which is for experienced, licensed rafters only. Class 5 and 6 rapids. People have died there! People who "knew what they were doing" have died there!! My son looks up at me and I feel myself swallow hard and I tell him, "I think that is important." DUH!

The main point to understand for me was that I needed someone to guide me that first time. I needed to hear the calm, assuring voice of someone who knew the river and how to successfully go down it. I wanted someone in control if I were to be thrown out of the boat. Everyone in the boat wanted to feel the security of having a guide who knew where the difficult parts were and how to get through them. And of course, everyone wanted to get out of the river at the right point. I mean, we came to have fun, NOT DIE!! As we were piling into the boat, we were introduced to the guide for our raft. I wanted to know everything I could about him. I asked where he was from (I don't know why that mattered), how long he had been working for the rafting company and even if he had ever "lost" someone to the river. I didn't want a newbie to help us paddle. I wanted an experienced guide who knew what he was doing and had "been there and done that" before. Think about those characteristics as we "paddle" our way down the fast moving topic of God's leadership in our life.

ABRAHAM

When the topic of leadership is brought up, I often think of the Patriarch of the Jewish faith, Abraham. He didn't start out that way of course. No, he was a married, fatherless man living in the area of the Persian Gulf in a city named, Ur. According to Genesis 12:1-3, this was when he began to learn how to follow the leadership of God.

"Now the LORD had said to Abram:
'Get out of your country,
From your family
And from your father's house,
To a land that I will show you.
I will make you a great nation;
I will bless you
And make your name great;
And you shall be a blessing.
I will bless those who bless you,
And I will curse him who curses you;

And in you all the families of the earth shall be blessed.'"

Abraham obeyed and, through trial and error, learned how to follow the leadership of God. It was not always easy or evident. Through these verses we see several important aspects of following the leadership of God.

First, Abram was to leave without knowing where he would stop. He was basically traveling blind without even a map (and certainly no GPS or Smart Phone). He was just waiting on God to say, "Turn right here," or "Take a left at the tall cactus."

Second, he was given a great promise if he would follow God's leadership. If he would just trust God (have faith), God was going to make a great nation out of him and his descendants. The hand of blessing would be so strong upon him, that it would even transfer to those who blessed him. God was going to lead him in such a way that all the families of the entire world would be blessed because of Abram. It's a big deal. God is making some awesome promises in response to Abram's loyalty and devotion. I know that He was thrilled. He had to be excited at the prospect of this new land and the new life God was promising him. Each step probably built an attitude of expectation. "We will be blessed!" Abram kept thinking. "No more lack, no more want. We will be taken care of by God Almighty. This is going to be great!"

A careful study of the story that follows reveals that once Abram is in the land God was giving him, there was a famine. No food. It doesn't look like a blessing. Looks can be deceiving. It looked better in Egypt so Abram decides to run there for food (not directed by God). There, he also lies about his wife, Sarai (says she is his sister). He eventually becomes wealthy (blessed). In the process Sarai is given a handmaid, Hagar, who ultimately bears Abram's child, Ishmael. He is the father of the Arabian people that have fought against Israel for millennium. God does make good on His promises to Abram, but we can see that many problems can surface when you abandon God's guidance.

Think of the heartache Abram (and the rest of the world) would not have experienced if he had just followed God's leadership and trusted God, even in the middle of a famine. But, just like Abram learned and eventually became known by the intimate phrase, "Friend of God," so we can learn. Our times of chasing our own path and following our own limited leadership do not have to define us. I have personally stepped outside of the leadership of God on many occasions. I have a choice to make. I can either bury myself in guilt and shame, blaming everything on my past sins and arrogance, or I can learn from those things, move on under the leadership of my Heavenly Father and enjoy every day as He guides me and helps me make less and less of those selfish mistakes. Most days I choose the latter.

JOSEPH

God's guidance and leadership can create a chain of events that are marvelous. Jacob (renamed Israel) had a son, Joseph, whom he loved very much. Evidently, God's hand was upon the boy from a very early age. He is recorded as experiencing prophetic dreams regarding his eventual elevated status in life and the fact that his people and family would bow before him.

These dreams angered his jealous, older brothers. They abducted him, sold him to slave traders and faked his death. These traders were Ishmaelites, descendants of Abraham's son, Ishmael, we spoke of earlier when he abandoned God's guidance for a season. Jacob was devastated and the brothers would carry the guilt from that decision for years to come.

The slave traders took Joseph to Egypt where he was purchased by Potipher, the head of Pharaoh's guard. He quickly became the loyal and trusted steward of the house. He caught the eye of Potipher's wife and she tried many times to seduce him. In spite of her attempts, he remained chaste and faithful to God and his upbringing. Once, she had him alone and grabbed his garment and tried to force him to have sex with her. He refused, shook off his garment and ran. Aware of her fate should this incident reach her husband, she screamed and told Potipher that Joseph had tried to rape her. He believed her and Joseph was sent to prison.

His work ethic and the favor of God found Joseph quickly in a place of responsibility again, even in the jail. Some of the other inmates were disheartened by confusing dreams and they spoke to Joseph about them. Through God's gifting, he gave them interpretations of their dreams. His interpretations were true.

Pharaoh, Supreme ruler of Egypt, had a disturbing set of dreams about two years later. None of his advisors or counselors, not even the priests from the great Egyptian temples, could assist the Pharaoh with an interpretation of his dreams. Then, his chief butler (who had been in prison and had his own dream interpreted by Joseph) told the king of his experience with the prisoner. Because the dreams troubled Pharaoh so deeply, Joseph is called and was given the chance to hear the dreams.

Upon hearing the dreams, Joseph gave an interpretation that calmed the king. He also gave the king counsel as to how to prepare for the famine the dream had prophesied. It was then that Pharaoh made Joseph Prime Minister over all of Egypt.

Now why did I tell you all this? I could have directed you to the verses in Genesis and let you read them from there. I had you read this so that I could highlight the areas of the story I want you to consider. All of the parts of this storyline are important parts of the leadership of God in order to get Joseph in the position to save many people, even his own.

Being sold to slave traders was not a hallelujah moment. But if it didn't happen, he would not have been taken to Egypt and never become Prime Minister! The same logic can be used about his years in prison. Even later, Joseph would face his brothers and tell them that though they did it for evil, God had a bigger, better plan for the good of many people.

It all reminds us of the words of the Apostle Paul in his letter to the church at Rome:

> *"And we know that all things work together for good to those who love God, to those who are the called according to His purpose."*
> Romans 8:28

Sometimes, like I'm sure Joseph did, we are able to look back over the days of our lives and see the invisible, yet purposeful, leadership of God. Perhaps we may see that we are blessed to still be alive. Maybe we can understand the hurt or loss better as we see how God's plan unfolded in other ways. The main point here is that God's leadership will always bring us to a better place, spiritually, and give us the opportunity to minister to the world around us. Even though, as with Joseph, not every event of our lives feels good, the verse doesn't promise that *everything* will be good or feel good, does it? No, it promises that all things will work *together* for good!

MOSES

Just a few years ago, Priceline.com, the online travel company, depicted their number one representative, William Shatner, as "The Negotiator." Now I like Mr. Shatner and actually, I am somewhat of a "treckie." But, I don't think he holds a candle to one of the best negotiators in the Bible, Moses.

I am sure some of you are questioning why I call the great prophet, deliverer, messiah, and intimate friend of God (He did see part of God) a negotiator. Well, because it's true. When God first called Moses from the burning bush, Moses tried to negotiate out of the calling. He offered one excuse after another. God used that negotiating ability as Moses stood before Pharaoh asking for the Jewish people to be set free. Moses even negotiated again with God over the fate of the Israelites. At one time, God spoke of destroying them all and starting over with Moses. Moses interceded (negotiated) with God for their lives.

Yet even when we see this gift of negotiation at work, it never changes the actual leadership of God in respect to both Moses and the Hebrew nation. In fact, Moses actually made the leadership of God a part of his successful negotiations:

"Then Moses said to the LORD, 'See, You say to
me, 'Bring up this people.' But You have not let
me know whom You will send with me. Yet You
have said, 'I know you by name, and you have
also found grace in My sight.' Now therefore, I
pray, if I have found grace in Your sight, show me
now Your way, that I may know You and that I
may find grace in Your sight. And consider that
this nation is Your people.'
And He said, 'My Presence will go with you, and I
will give you rest.'
Then he said to Him, 'If Your Presence does not
go with us, do not bring us up from here. For
how then will it be known that Your people and I
have found grace in Your sight, except You go
with us? So we shall be separate, Your people and
I, from all the people who are upon the face of the
earth.'
So the LORD said to Moses, 'I will also do this
thing that you have spoken; for you have found
grace in My sight, and I know you by name.'"
Exodus 33:12-17

Though Moses may not have realized it as a child,
God had a path that He was leading Moses down. God
was guiding him and preparing him for an incredible
task. He was taught in the greatest schools of the time
and was introduced to the culture that he would one day
have to re-enter as the messenger of God. He knew the
language of the privileged, the protocol of the palace and
the way around the buildings. Next, Moses learned the
skills of a shepherd. While in the desert (hiding from
Pharaoh), he lived with, worked for and became a part of
the family of Jethro, priest of Midian. Moses became a

shepherd by trade and learned important lessons that would, in due course, be used by God as He led Moses to deliver His people and guide them across the Sinai Desert towards the Promised Land. He knew how to survive in the desert. He understood a herd or flock mentality. God prepared Moses for nearly 80 years to accomplish the task of delivering Israel from the bondage of the Egyptians.

One very eventful and memorable example of God's leadership is found in the deliverance of Israel. Moses was given very distinct guidelines to share with the people in order to survive the 10th plague. They were to prepare a spotless lamb, kill it and place the blood over the doorposts of their home that evening.

If the angel of death saw the blood, he would pass over their home. If he didn't, then the first born was to be killed. Following His leadership to the smallest detail was essential for life.

Once they were released from bondage, God was very specific in where Moses was to take them. God had a plan and it included their complete obedience to His guidance in order to work.

"Now the LORD spoke to Moses, saying: 'Speak to the children of Israel, that they turn and camp before Pi Hahiroth, between Migdol and the sea, opposite Baal Zephon; you shall camp before it by the sea. For Pharaoh will say of the children of Israel, 'They are bewildered by the land; the wilderness has closed them in.' Then I will harden Pharaoh's heart, so that he will pursue them; and I will gain honor over

> *Pharaoh and over all his army, that the*
> *Egyptians may know that I am the LORD.' And*
> *they did so".*
> Exodus:14:1-4

By following the LORD's leadership, they were placed in an inescapable and indefensible position. Once Pharaoh and his army followed them there, the children of Israel were trapped between the army and the Red Sea. Because of their position (based on their obedience) God was able to perform one of the great miracles of the exodus from slavery, the dividing of the Red Sea.

God also uses Moses to direct the new nation with a set of laws, commandments and worship rites. Down to the minutest detail, God gives the plan for the tabernacle, the feasts, as well as blessings and curses for breaking the law.

Even in the end, after Moses successfully maneuvers these hard headed people around the desert for 40 years and brings them to the brink of the Promised Land again, he is not allowed to cross over with them. He is refused entry because of an incident where he didn't exactly follow the leadership of God. It was one of the times in the desert when there seemed to be no water, and the people began to complain and regret that they ever left Egypt (a common theme with them). This is what happened.

> *"So Moses and Aaron went from the presence of*
> *the assembly to the door of the tabernacle of*
> *meeting, and they fell on their faces. And the*
> *glory of the LORD appeared to them.*
> *Then the LORD spoke to Moses, saying, 'Take the*
> *rod; you and your brother Aaron gather the*

congregation together. **SPEAK TO THE ROCK** *before
their eyes, and it will yield its water; thus you shall bring
water for them out of the rock, and give drink to the
congregation and their animals.' So Moses took the rod
from before the LORD as He commanded him.
And Moses and Aaron gathered the assembly
together before the rock; and he said to them,
'Hear now, you rebels! Must we bring water for
you out of this rock?' Then Moses lifted his hand
and* **STRUCK THE ROCK TWICE** *with his rod;
and water came out abundantly, and the
congregation and their animals drank.
Then the LORD spoke to Moses and Aaron,
'Because you did not believe Me, to hallow Me in
the eyes of the children of Israel, therefore you
shall not bring this assembly into the land which
I have given them.'"*
Numbers 20:6-12 (emphasis mine)

DAVID

As much as Joseph, David had a reason to wonder about the leadership of God in his younger years. David's father, Jesse (the grandson of Ruth), was a shepherd and raised his boys in that lifestyle. David, though young, was already in the training stages of that rough life. He would spend hours, sometimes days, out with the flock. He guarded them and led them to good food and clear water. He also searched for the ones who had wandered away from the group, often putting himself in harm's way for their welfare.

One day, while David was out watching over his flock, he hears a faint cry. He turns and sees one of his father's servants running toward him. He can't make out what the servant is screaming. He wants to run to him, but he can't leave the sheep. Finally, the out-of-breath servant reaches the boy. "You must go now to your father's house. There is a prophet there and your dad sent me to take your place with the sheep. Hurry! They are all waiting on you."

Surprised, and no doubt troubled over this news, David begins to sprint to the house. "What have I done?" may have been one of his thoughts. He was used to being the least of the brothers and they blamed him for everything that happened. As he approached the house, he slowed the pace so as to not be totally out of breath (he might have to speak to his own defense). He smells food. Good food!! He is hungry from spending the past few days out with the sheep. He runs through the door and immediately stops in his tracks.

"This is strange." he thought as he surveyed the room with a quick glance. Everyone was staring at him. His dad was standing near all of his brothers.

The brothers were all standing in a line from oldest to youngest. The table was set with a meal that would make last Thanksgiving look like a pitiful snack. And, there was Samuel. He had heard of him before. Samuel was God's man. God performed a miracle so that Samuel could be born and raised in the priesthood. Samuel was the man who had anointed King Saul and was a counselor to the great King. What was this strange setting?

Suddenly, and with no explanation, the prophet Samuel takes hold of the young teenager. He pronounces a blessing, pours oil over David's head, proclaims that

David will be the next King of Israel. Immediately, the Spirit of the Lord came upon him from that day forward.

Then Samuel left. David is left staring at his father through the oil that is running down his face, and feeling the jealous piercing gaze of his brothers. "Me, King?" David thought, "What?' "How?"

Let me shorten the story some. After his anointing to be the next King of Israel, David does not move to Jerusalem and hand King Saul a change of address form from the post office. No, he goes back to tending sheep. God has a specific plan in place for David. David trusts God. He learns from being a shepherd (much like Moses). He worships God on the mountains and in the valleys of Bethlehem's region.

It is nearly 20 years before God finally elevates the boy to the throne. During those years David will become a giant slayer, a general in the King's army, a son-in-law to the king, a best friend to the prince, and a fugitive being chased by the king into the caves. All of this to prepare him to become the most loved and renowned King in Israel's history. Even today the Israeli flag features the "Star of David."

David experienced great favor in his relationship with God. Though the average Hebrew may have prayed and made sacrifice, David enjoyed a unique intimacy with the LORD. He was even allowed by God on several occasions to use the Urim and the Thummim to seek God's guidance over whether to attack certain enemies.

THE LORD IS MY SHEPHERD

In what is possible David's most famous and beloved Psalm, it is distinctly obvious that he realized the priority of relying on God for guidance. David understood the mind of a shepherd. He could relate to the responsibilities of a shepherd as well as the tender nature that a shepherd must cultivate in order for his sheep to feel secure. He also appreciated the protective nature of a shepherd, having honed his courage and sling skills keeping bears and lions from attacking his flock. Think of the term *guidance* as you read this emphasized quote of the 23rd Psalm.

"The LORD is my shepherd;
I shall not want.
He makes me to lie down in green pastures;
HE LEADS ME *beside the still waters.*
He restores my soul;
HE LEADS ME *in the paths of righteousness*
For His name's sake.
Yea, though I walk through the valley of the
shadow of death,
I will fear no evil;
For You are with me;
Your rod and Your staff, they comfort me.
You prepare a table before me in the presence of
my enemies;
You anoint my head with oil;
My cup runs over.
Surely goodness and mercy shall follow me

> *All the days of my life;*
> *And I will dwell in the house of the LORD*
> *Forever."*
> Psalm 23 (emphasis mine)

David knew the purpose of a shepherd was more than just to be a babysitter for the "critters." He had responsibility. He knew the best place for the sheep to eat and drink. He knew the safest places for them to graze. He could also defend them if there was a surprise attack. He had a rod and a staff for gentle guidance and protection. The best sheep were an indication of a great shepherd who was alert and responsible, yet not in a way that would cause stress or alarm among the animals.

David understood those principles and recognized that God was the Good Shepherd that he needed. In true Davidic fashion, the focus of the Psalm moves into a more intimate discourse. He begins by talking about God is his Shepherd as though he is explaining it or witnessing to it to another person or group. Yet by the middle of the chapter he has started talking directly to God, "For You are with me." Guidance or leadership is all through this Psalm.

God's guidance is all through the Bible. Sometimes it makes complete sense to our minds and at other times it seems to go contrary to our logic, but God is always leading. So that you may be thankful for what simple things God has led you to do, consider these strange, yet effective directions from God to His prophets.

Isaiah was instructed to walk around naked and barefoot for 3 years, *Isaiah 20:2-3*. Ezekiel was told to eat a scroll and then go prophesy to Israel, *Ezekiel 3:1*. He was also told to construct a model of Jerusalem out of clay and then lay siege to it. Next, Ezekiel was to lie on one side for 390 days eating only bread made from several types of grain (a thing forbidden in the Law) and baked with human excrement. When he objected to cooking with human excrement, God relented and let him use cow manure, *Ezekiel 4*. Ezekiel also had to shave his head and beard with a sharp sword. He had to burn one-third of it, strike another third with a sword and the last third scatter to the wind, *Ezekiel 5*. Hosea had to marry a prostitute and then name two of his children "I have no pity" and "Not my people," *Hosea 1*. Jeremiah had to make a yoke and wear it every day, *Jeremiah 27*. These are just some of the weird things God has asked people to do. Yet even in these cases, God's plan and message are clear and proclaimed as such.

God is still guiding His people. It may not always make sense to our natural minds, but He works all things together for our good. Again, this is not saying that all things are good, but together, they can make something good. Think of a recipe for baking cake from scratch. Here are some of the items you may need: egg whites, all-purpose flour, baking powder, baking soda, salt, butter or shortening, sugar, vanilla and buttermilk. These ingredients are not intended to be eaten one at a time. Who wants some raw egg whites? Maybe a big spoonful of shortening! Gross! Maybe some sugar, but not cups of it. If you follow me, you will understand that some ingredients are bitter, some are sweet. Some are fluid and some are solid. Just like the experiences in our lives. Some are sweet while others are very bitter to swallow. Individually they are not as tasty. But once they are combined in the proper order and amount, mixed together, heated at the correct temperature, something lovely, tasty and GOOD come out. All those ingredients work together to form something good.

As we close this first chapter on guidance and the leadership of God in our life, I am creating a list of wonderful Scriptures that will encourage you. Scan these verses over the next few pages. Allow their messages to give you confidence that God is actually actively leading **YOU**.

*"And the Lord went before them by day in a pillar of cloud **TO LEAD THE WAY**, and by night in a pillar of fire to give them light, so as to go by day and night."*
Exodus 13:21 (emphasis mine)

*"You in Your mercy have led forth The people whom You have redeemed; **YOU HAVE GUIDED THEM** in Your strength To Your holy habitation."*
Exodus 15:13 (emphasis mine)

*"**LEAD ME, O LORD**, in Your righteousness because of my enemies; Make Your way straight before my face."*
Psalm 5:8 (emphasis mine)

*"**LEAD ME** in Your truth and teach me, For You are the God of my salvation; On You I wait all the day."*
Psalm 25:5 (emphasis mine)

*"Teach me Your way, O Lord, And **LEAD ME** in a smooth path, because of my enemies."*
Psalm 27:11 (emphasis mine)

*"For You are my rock and my fortress; Therefore, for Your name's sake, **LEAD ME AND GUIDE ME**."*
Psalm 31:3 (emphasis mine)

*"I will instruct you and teach you in the way you should go; **I WILL GUIDE YOU** with My eye."*
Psalm 32:8 (emphasis mine)

*"For this is God, Our God forever and ever; **HE WILL BE OUR GUIDE** Even to death."*
Psalm 48:14 (emphasis mine)

*"From the end of the earth I will cry to You, When my heart is overwhelmed; **LEAD ME** to the rock that is higher than I."*
Psalm 61:2

*"**DIRECT MY STEPS** by Your word, And let no iniquity have dominion over me."*
Psalm 119:133 (emphasis mine)

*"Even there **YOUR HAND SHALL LEAD ME**, And Your right hand shall hold me."*
Psalm 139:10 (emphasis mine)

*"And see if there is any wicked way in me, And **LEAD ME** in the way everlasting."*
Psalm 139:24 (emphasis mine)

*"Teach me to do Your will, For You are my God; Your Spirit is good. **LEAD ME** in the land of uprightness."*
Psalm 143:10 (emphasis mine)

"Trust in the LORD with all your heart,
And lean not on your own understanding;
In all your ways acknowledge Him,
And *HE SHALL DIRECT YOUR PATHS*."
Proverbs 3:5-6 (emphasis mine)

*"A man's heart plans his way, But **THE LORD
DIRECTS HIS STEPS.**"*
Proverbs 16:9 (emphasis mine)

*"He will feed His flock like a shepherd; He will
gather the lambs with His arm, And carry them
in His bosom, And **GENTLY LEAD** those who
are with young."*
Isaiah 40:11 (emphasis mine)

*"They shall neither hunger nor thirst, Neither
heat nor sun shall strike them; For He who has
mercy on them **WILL LEAD THEM**, Even by the
springs of water **HE WILL GUIDE THEM.**"*
Isaiah 49:10 (emphasis mine)

*"I have seen his ways, and will heal him; **I WILL
ALSO LEAD HIM**, And restore comforts to him
And to his mourners."*
Isaiah 57:18 (emphasis mine)

*"The Lord will **GUIDE YOU CONTINUALLY**,
And satisfy your soul in
drought, And strengthen your bones; You shall be
like a watered garden, And like a spring of water,
whose waters do not fail."*
Isaiah 58:11 (emphasis mine)

*"As a beast goes down into the valley, And the Spirit of the Lord causes him to rest, So **YOU LEAD YOUR PEOPLE**, To make Yourself a glorious name."*
Isaiah 63:14 (emphasis mine)

God's guidance and leadership can create a chain of events that are marvelous.

-Dr. Lonnie E. Riley-

CHAPTER TEN

WE WILL BE GUARDED FROM

TEMPTATION:

"Not Into Temptation"

I *can resist anything but temptation.* – Oscar Wilde. Sometimes I guess we all feel that way. Certain things are considered temptations that I'm sure are not the intent of this prayer. If you are on a diet and while walking through the grocery store there is a lady handing out warm, gooey, chocolate chip cookie samples, I'm sure that is "temptation." You may even begin to rationalize this with self-leading questions like, "I've done very well on this diet, I deserve a little indulgence," or maybe "Nobody around here knows that I'm dieting. No one will ever know if I cheat a little." That is not the actual topic of the prayer, but the mindset is basically the same.

Temptation is common. Even Jesus was tempted. What is temptation? It is the enticement to sin - to do what is clearly wrong. It is the allure to even do what is right, but with selfish or other wrong motives. It is also the rationalization that will cause you to impotently do nothing when there is a clear message from God to either do or not do. Sins may be considered those of either commission (you committed the act) or omission (you omitted obeying a command).

Though there are many instances of people being tempted and being caught in the act of commission of sin (falling), there is a difference, you know. It is not a sin to be tempted. Jesus was tempted, yet the Scriptures are clear that He was without any sin. The actual "sinning" takes place when you give into the temptation. To help us through this first part of the chapter, I have selected 3 Old Testament characters to study: Eve, Achan and King David.

EVE

Nearly everyone in the modern world is at least somewhat familiar with the character of Eve. She is the first female. She is the wife of Adam, the first man. She was his helpmate as they were to fulfill the commission of

God to tend the Garden of Eden, take dominion over the earth, and to multiply and replenish the earth.

Eve was perfect. She had the same nature that Adam had which gave them the distinct designation of being created in the image of God. There was nothing separating her from both of her relationships, God and Adam. She was under the same commands as Adam as well as the same blessings. For both of them, there was nothing withheld save the fruit from the tree of the knowledge of good and evil.

That's it. Everything else was not only permissible, but also enjoyable. Eve had the exact force of physical, emotional, intellectual, volitional and spiritual power that Adam had. Yet, all of us know that she was tempted and persuaded to eat of the forbidden fruit. Here is the Biblical account:

> *"Now the serpent was more cunning than any*
> *beast of the field which the LORD God had made.*
> *And he said to the woman, 'Has God indeed said,*
> *'You shall not eat of every tree of the garden?'*
> *And the woman said to the serpent, 'We may eat*
> *the fruit of the trees of the garden; but of the fruit*
> *of the tree which is in the midst of the garden,*
> *God has said, 'You shall not eat it, nor shall you*
> *touch it, lest you die.'*
> *Then the serpent said to the woman, 'You will not*
> *surely die. For God knows that in the day you eat*
> *of it your eyes will be opened, and you*
> *will be like God, knowing good and evil.'*
> *So when the woman saw that the tree was good*
> *for food, that it was pleasant to the eyes, and a*
> *tree desirable to make one wise, she took of its*
> *fruit and ate.*

> *She also gave to her husband with her, and he ate."*
> Genesis 3:1-6

That one decision, which Eve made of her own free will and subsequently Adam did as well, changed the course of human events forever. There are several characteristics of the temptation that she faced that I think will help us in regard to dealing with temptation in our own lives.

First, Eve *listened*. Temptation usually has a voice. It can be that of your friends trying to coax you into stealing a candy bar as a child. Perhaps it comes in the form of a boss or co-worker who is trying to hide some type of irregularities at work. Maybe it comes from someone you find attractive, but you are not married to them. Yet, I would venture to surmise that the voice you hear most often in regards to temptation is your own.

You are fighting a battle inside of your head. Our minds are a battlefield. The Scriptures are clear in declaring the power of our own minds. Because of this truth we are told to *renew* our minds, *guard* our minds, and even given a list of things in Philippians 4 to think about, and with which to fill our minds. We are told to *cast* down thoughts and to bring them under submission to Jesus. Thoughts are powerful and they are the breeding ground for temptations.

Second, Eve *looked*. I am not referring to a quick glance to identify the color of the fruit. She looked with intensity and concentration. Looking at the temptation only begins to solidify it in our minds. The Scripture says that she "saw" that it looked pleasant, edible and appetizing.

I remember as a very young boy that my mother, Ann Wiggins, was one of my Sunday school teachers in the beginners' class. I learned so much from their excellent storing telling skills, visual aids as well as the simple music that we sang that implanted Biblical truth into our little hearts and minds. In particular, there was a simple little song that embedded this point into me.

"Oh, be careful little eyes what you see.
Be careful little eyes what you see.
For the Father up above is looking down in love.
Be careful little eyes what you see."

The next verses just changed out the "eyes what you see" with "ears what you hear," "hands what you do," "feet where you go," "mouth what you say." All of these are extremely significant instructions for us to follow in order to avoid temptation.

Scriptural admonitions regarding keeping our eyes focused away from temptation abound throughout the Bible. Most importantly, though, we are admonished to "look" to Jesus as the Author and Finisher of our faith, Hebrews 12:2. Keeping our eyes focused on Him (not literally, but on the Christ-like example of His self-sacrificing life).

Third, Eve *longed for*. The word, desirable is used here. The Hebrew, *Khaw-mad'*: meaning to delight in, covet, desire, pleasant, precious or lust.[1] The same word is used in the last of the ten commandments to "not covet." After listening to satan, looking at the temptation she began to covet it, lust after it or long for it. She wanted it. She had to have it! Eve convinced herself, with satan's assistance, that God didn't really mean it and that she deserved it. So, as James says, *"when desire* *has conceived, it gives birth to sin."²* So it was with Eve. So it is with us.

ACHAN

This is also a very tragic story. After the death of Moses, Joshua was chosen to lead the children of Israel from the desert plains into the Promised Land. They rededicated themselves to God and His covenant with them, and miraculously crossed a flooded Jordan River on dry ground.

Once across, they faced their first foe, Jericho. God gave them a surprising battle plan and Joshua followed it exactly. Victory! The entire city fell and Israel won.

Now, part of the distinct plan that God gave them included that all of the spoils of the victory over Jericho would belong to God. They were not to take anything for themselves. It was a "First Fruits" offering to God in order to build up the treasury of the Tabernacle of God.

"And you, by all means abstain from the accursed things, lest you become accursed when you take of the accursed things, and make the camp of Israel a curse, and trouble it. But all the silver and gold, and vessels of bronze and iron, are consecrated to the LORD; they shall come into the treasury of the LORD."
Joshua 6:18-19

That seems very clear. The command is precise, as well as the result of breaking the command. The next battle that Israel fought was with AI. They were small and seemingly insignificant to them. Israel's arrogance caused them to send less people into battle and assume that God was going to give them a great victory again. WRONG! They were defeated and "run out of town," as they used to say in the old west. Thirty-six men lost their lives in the skirmish. They scurried back home like a dog with its tail tucked between its legs. It caused the entire nation to stand in wonderment, to doubt. The Scripture describes it as their hearts melted and became like water. God had promised to be with them, what happened?

Joshua hit his knees in prayer and inquired of the LORD what had happened. God lets him know that there is sin in the camp because someone took of the spoils of Jericho. Through a Spirit led process, Achan is found to be the guilty one. He was a member of the blessed tribe of Judah. The Messiah was prophesied to be a decent of Judah. This descendant was taken out of the camp, along with his family and all of his possessions. First, they stoned them to death and then they burned what remained. What would cause him to do such a thing to the God Who had just handed Jericho to them? Here is Achan's confession:

"And Achan answered Joshua and said, 'Indeed
I have sinned against the LORD God of
Israel, and this is what I have done: When I
__SAW__ among the spoils a beautiful Babylonian
garment, two hundred shekels of silver, and a
wedge of gold weighing fifty shekels, I
__COVETED__ them and took them. And there they
are, hidden in the earth in the midst of my tent,
with the silver under it.'"
Joshua 7:20-21 (emphasis mine)

I believe that all three of the characteristics from Eve's temptation (listening, looking and longing) where present with Achan's temptation as well. He must have been *listening* to his own inner voice. I don't know what it said, but it was very convincing. Perhaps it was, "Hey, I deserve it. I've been in the desert for years and I haven't had any new clothes or any money." Maybe he thought, "No one is around. They'll never know about it, especially if I hide it under my tent." He was listening to his own voice.

The verses above say that Achan saw the items. He *looked* at them, thereby allowing them access into his continuing thought process through the eye gate. The more he looked at them, the better they looked.

Then Achan admits that he took them because he coveted them. The same Hebrew word is used here that we saw in Eve's case. His listening to himself and looking at the temptation created a *longing* within him that caused him to sin. Romans reminds us that, "The wages of sin is death." That was true in this case. Achan lost his life, his family's, his livestock and inadvertently caused the death of the soldiers during the failed attempt on AI.

KING DAVID

Our next example of temptation is reflected in the life of Israel's most beloved king. David had risen to the throne of Judah first, and eventually over the combined house of all Israel. David was known as a warrior. God knew that he had a warrior's spirit and that was the reason God gave for not allowing David to build the temple. Not only is he known for being a strong soldier, but also for being an intimate worshipper. Many of the Psalms are written by him at all the differing stages of life. Prior to the creation of the temple, David brought the Ark of the Covenant to Jerusalem and placed it in a tent. It became known as the "Tabernacle of David", because the tabernacle of Moses was still being used in Gideon. Yes, Israel had two tabernacles at the same time. One was offering animals and the other was offering praise 24/7. This tabernacle of David's so pleased Almighty God that the recreation of that type of worship is prophesied as a sign of the end times, *Amos 9:11, Acts 15:13-18*. King David is most known as a man after God's own heart.

Sad to say, ranking among those lofty accolades, David is also widely known as both an adulterer and a murderer.

David refused to accompany his army as it went to war. Instead he stayed in the palace. One night he was walking on the flat roof of his home and noticed a woman, Bathsheba, bathing. He had her brought to him and they slept together. She became pregnant. David tried to hide the fact that he was the father by bringing Bathsheba's husband home from war. He thought they would sleep together and everyone would believe her husband, Uriah, was the father of the child. The plan didn't work. Uriah was such an honorable man that he wouldn't go home and enjoy his wife while all his fellow soldiers were at war. Ultimately, King David sends Uriah back to the battle with a note to the general saying to place him at the front lines and then back away so that he would be killed. That plan worked. Now David is guilty of adultery and murder. As a result, the child Bathsheba is carrying dies and David's children/family becomes a wreck with several of them dying prematurely. Again, what does Paul tell us are the wages of our sin? Let's look at the description of the temptation and sin quickly.

> *"Then it happened one evening that David arose from his bed and walked on the roof of the king's house. And from the roof he **SAW** a woman bathing, and the woman was very beautiful to behold. So David sent and inquired about the woman. And someone said, 'Is this not Bathsheba, the daughter of Eliam, the wife of Uriah the Hittite?' Then David sent messengers, and **TOOK HER**; and she came to him, and he lay with her, for she was cleansed from her impurity; and she returned to her house. And the woman conceived; so she sent and told David, and said, 'I am with child.'"*
>
> 2 Samuel 11:2-5 (emphasis mine)

Do you think we will find the same characteristics evident in this temptation? I do. He undoubtedly had much the same type of inner conversation that Achan did and he *listened* intently to that voice. David didn't take those thoughts captive and pull them down, instead he fed them. Of course the verses indicate that he *saw* her bathing and that she was very beautiful. He was *looking* in the wrong direction and continued to *look* in that direction intense looking and listening gave way to lust. David actually "coveted" her and had her brought to the palace where they committed adultery.

These illustrations from the Bible should make each of us aware that we are susceptible to be tempted and to fall. We need to continually pray for God to give us strength, wisdom, and courage to deny ourselves and our desires in preference to His will. Having explained some of the characteristics and distinctiveness of temptation, we must now tackle more of the meaning of this phrase in the prayer. Jesus is instructing His disciples (ergo us) to ask their/our Heavenly Father to please not lead them/us into temptation.

PLEASE DON'T LEAD US THERE GOD

The very concept that God even *might* decide to lead us into temptation is extremely troubling to me. Concepts like that run foreign to my view of God and His leadership for my life. So, how or where do the two thoughts merge? What is Jesus telling us about the Father when we are told to pray this way?

Sometimes we lose the understanding that Greek (the original language the Gospels were written in) is a very unique language. If you ever utilize a Strong's Exhaustive Concordance, you will understand the point I am about to make. I am going to look up the word "temptation" finding that the Strong's Greek reference number is 3986. This reveals the Greek word "peirasmos" (πειρασμός). The definition given by the concordance for this word is:

> "from <G3985> (peirazo); a putting to *proof* (by experiment [of good], *experience* [of evil], solicitation, discipline or provocation); by implication *adversity* :- temptation, × try."[3]

From this definition we can see several things that may enlighten us. One is that there are several words, phrases or thoughts that can be translated from this one word. A putting to the proof has a different connotation than that of temptation, especially when you consider that it can be done by utilizing good or evil. We always consider temptation as evil, right? Other options that this Greek word can be translated as are: solicitation (an effort to get a response), discipline (using thinking of punishment) or provocation (intimating that which stirs up or incites, usually to anger). It may imply adversity (difficulty or hardship), as in temptation or trial.

The most interesting thing in this definition is that that there is a relation to another word from which this one is derived, "peirazo" (πειράζω). So we truly need to see what this root word's definition reveals to us in 3985.

> "from <u><G3984></u> (peira); to *test* (object), i.e.
> *endeavor, scrutinize, entice, discipline* :- assay,
> examine, go about, prove, tempt (-er), try."[4]

This helps us focus a little better. The root word here implies to test. As in to scrutinize, entice or discipline. To assay is to analyze, or examine; to prove or tempt. We are beginning to see a clearer focus more on the examination, testing or trial of our faith rather than just in reference to temptation.

But wait, even this word came from another root, "peira" (πεῖρα). If we are going to be true to the meaning of Scripture we have to do our due diligence by looking up reference number 3984. We must dig out exactly what God is trying to teach us here, not just take the translation as the authority. I am beginning to see why the Good News Translation renders it, *"Do not bring us to hard testing."*

> "from the base of <u>\<G4008\></u> (peran) (through the idea of *piercing*); a *test*, i.e. *attempt, experience* :- assaying, trial."[5]

We are seeing an even deeper association with analyzing or testing. The word is mainly translated as "trial." But, the real work of someone who is seeking the root of Biblical words is still not done. Even this word is derived from another: "peran" (πέραν) 4008. Grab your shovel; let's dig in one more time.

> "apparently accusative of an obsolete derivative of peiro (to *"pierce"*); *through* (as adverb or prep.), i.e. *across* :- beyond, farther (other) side, over."[6]

Finally, we find the base word which is basically an obsolete spin-off of the verb "to pierce." We have translated it as across, beyond, farther, other side or over. Now, having taken the time to study the original word that was translated "temptation," I see a huge point of difference. The root of this word seems to focus more on a trial or test rather than a temptation. What is the difference? Let's examine that next.

We see that the Scripture declares in James that we should look at trials or tests differently.

> *"My brethren, count it all joy when you fall into various trials, knowing that the testing of your faith produces patience."*
> James 1:2-3

We should have an attitude of joy when we face these trials or tests because they produce the good in us. However, we are admonished to escape or flee from temptation.

> "No temptation has overtaken you except such as is common to man; but God is faithful, who will not allow you to be tempted beyond what you are able, but with the temptation will also make the way of escape, that you may be able to bear it."
> 1 Corinthian 10:13

God uses testing or trials to build our character. He wants us to trust that He will give us a way of escape from the temptations. Hmmm. Escape from temptations, be joyous when tested, big difference! Now, regarding this prayer, "lead us not into temptation," let's also remember what we are told about God and the origin of temptation.

> "Blessed is the man who endures temptation; for when he has been approved, he will receive the crown of life which the Lord has promised to those who love Him. Let no one say when he is tempted, 'I am tempted by God'; for **GOD CANNOT BE TEMPTED BY EVIL, NOR DOES HE HIMSELF TEMPT ANYONE.** But each one is tempted when he is drawn away by his own desires and enticed. Then, when desire has conceived, it gives birth to sin; and sin, when it is full-grown, brings forth death."
> James 1:12-15 (emphasis mine)

The Holy Spirit directed James to explain some things in regard to God and temptation. He clearly states that we are blessed when we endure temptation. He also unequivocally states that none of us should accuse God of tempting them (or leading them into temptation) because that is not part of His nature. He can't be tempted neither does He tempt anyone.

Now this is beginning to make some real sense. If God doesn't tempt anyone, I don't see that He would lead us into that situation. If that is so, then we really wouldn't need to pray that way.

Next, in order to make sure we understand, James lays out the origin and process of temptation. It begins with a drawing away by our own desires. Drawn away from what or perhaps better stated, who? Could it be that we are drawn away from our Heavenly Father and His will by asserting ourselves, taking the lordship of our own lives and focusing on our will? I think so.

That is how temptation is initiated, a drawing away. Drawing away is to move an object by exerting force on it. Our desires put us in opposition to His desires and we are drawn to our own will. I can certainly see the importance of praying, "Your will be done." The enticement creates the pressure. Once that desire is birthed, it grows in the enticement stage and in due course gives birth to the act of sin. And as Romans tell us, the wages of sin is what? DEATH.

Basically, temptation first comes as a thought (desire). We meditate on it (listen). We visualize it (look). We visualize our preferred outcome (long for). And then, when acted upon, it becomes sin. You can see these evident in the temptations of Eve, Achan and David as well.

Hopefully, I have clearly shown the difference between temptation and test or trial. The real root of this word leans more toward meaning, "Lead us not into a test." Though testing may be profitable for us, we really don't want to go through them, do we? I don't wake up in the morning and say first thing, "I sure hope I have a test or trial today." No, I will pray as Jesus taught His disciples nearly 2,000 years ago for God to NOT lead me into a test or trial today. Yet, in all things I must continue to have the submissive attitude of desiring His will over my own.

How can a testing or trial actually be beneficial to us? Let me illustrate from my personal life. When my oldest son, Jason, was very little, I began to teach him what to do if he were ever separated from me in a store. I showed him the customer service counter in front of the store. We discussed that if he were ever separated from me to NOT talk to anyone else or draw attention to himself, but to go straight to that counter and ask them to page his daddy. I did this nearly every time we shopped at the department store. I would quiz him on it to make sure he had the procedure correct in his mind. Sometimes he would initiate the conversation as we passed by the service desk.

Wanting to make sure that Jason had been listening and could actually do what he needed to in the event of an emergency, one day I "tested" him. He became enthralled with the toy section, so I carefully backed up and hid in the next aisle. It took a few minutes, but in time he looked around and realized he was all alone. He had a panicked look at first. (Yes, it was very hard to remain hidden at that point.) He called for me. I bit my lip and didn't answer. He called several more times. I remained quiet. He looked around some, and his eyes began to water. I was about to jump out and scoop him up.

Then suddenly it clicked. Jason spoke to no one and made a beeline to the customer service counter; spoke to the lady there, and the next thing I knew, I was being paged over the loud speaker. I came out from my hiding place in full view of the front desk. He saw me. His eyes grew wide and he sprinted right toward me, jumped into my arms and squeezed me like he would never let me go. I loved on him for a minute and told him how proud I was that he had done exactly what I had trained him to do.

Jason passed the test.

Now I truly knew that he was ready in case we were ever really separated. The training had paid off. Not only was I confident, but he was a well. Jason knew I was proud of him and he knew that the system I taught him worked and that we would be reunited if he followed the plan.

God actually did a similar test with Abraham. He had him do something in order to test his obedience. God told him to take Isaac, his son of the promise, to the land of Moriah and offer him as a sacrifice. I don't know exactly how Abraham reacted, but I would not have been able to sleep. I would have had one of those all night prayer meetings interceding for my son. The story goes that the next morning he rose up with Isaac and a couple of his servants, cut some wood for the burnt offering and headed out of town. Three days later, Abraham sees the mountain where the sacrifice is to take place. He then tells the servants to stay there because only he and Isaac will go up and make the sacrifice. Then he makes a wonderful FAITH FILLED statement, he actually says:

> *"And Abraham said to his young men, 'Stay here with the donkey; the lad and I will go yonder and worship, **<u>AND WE WILL COME BACK TO YOU.</u>**'"*
> Genesis 22:5 (emphasis mine)

Abraham actually tells them, in faith, that both of them will come down from the mountain. He knows that the command from God was to sacrifice his son, but he also knows the promise of God. Isaac was the promised child and that the LORD had named him Abraham's successor.

The father and son begin their ascent up the mountain. Abraham puts the wood on Isaac's back and carries the fire himself. As they are climbing, Isaac asks his father about the sacrifice. He notes that they have the wood and fire, but no sacrifice. Abraham throws his faith out there even further and says to the boy:

> *"And Abraham said, 'My son, God will provide for Himself the lamb for a burnt offering.' So the two of them went together."*
> Genesis 22:8

Once they get to the right place, Abraham takes some rocks and builds an altar. He lays the wood out on top, then grabs his son and binds him. He picks Isaac up and places him on top of the wood. Next is the horrifying scene. Abraham pulls his knife out of its sheath, raises it with both hands as he prepares to plunge the blade into his promised son, killing him along with the vision of a great nation.

At that crucial point, the Angel of the LORD calls out and tells Abraham to stop. He turns around and finds a ram caught in some thorny bushes. He grabs the ram and sacrifices it unto God instead of Isaac.

After the sacrifice is made, Abraham hears from God once again,

> *"Then the Angel of the LORD called to Abraham a second time out of heaven, and said: 'By Myself I have sworn, says the LORD, because you have done this thing, and have not withheld your son, your only son—blessing I will bless you, and multiplying I will multiply your descendants as the stars of the heaven and as the sand which is on the seashore; and your descendants shall possess the gate of their enemies. In your seed all the nations of the earth shall be blessed, because you have obeyed My voice.'"*
>
> Genesis 22:15-18

Essentially, God is saying to Abraham, "I'm proud of you, son. You did exactly what I wanted you to do. I know that you love Me more than the promise. I know that your faith in Me is stronger than your love for your son or your hope for a great nation. Because of that, I'm giving you both."

He passed the test.

How in the world was Abraham able to take such extreme action regarding his son? How could he make

such radical statements as those? He had never been in
that exact position before. Neither did he have a Bible to
read about someone else passing this kind of test.
However, Abraham had left all to follow God. He had
seen his God provide in miraculous ways and trusted
God's promises. The book of Hebrews sheds a little light
on Abraham's thought process in this time of testing.

> *"By faith Abraham,* ***WHEN HE WAS TESTED,***
> *offered up Isaac, and he who had received the*
> *promises offered up his only begotten son, of*
> *whom it was said, 'In Isaac*
> *your seed shall be called,'* ***CONCLUDING***
> ***THAT GOD WAS ABLE TO RAISE HIM UP,***
> ***EVEN FROM THE DEAD,*** *from which he also*
> *received him in a figurative sense."*
> Hebrews 11:17-19 (emphasis mine)

That is faith, my dear friend. God is true. The
promise is fulfilled. And, Abraham passed this great test
with flying colors.

None of us likes to go through testing and trials. I
never really liked having tests in school either. I was
always worried about them. But without these tests,
students couldn't prove that they knew and understood
the concepts required to pass the grade. In much the
same way we prove our faith and God's faithfulness when
we successfully encounter these tests.

Jesus instructs us to pray that we not have to go
through these trials, that God would not lead us there.
Yet at the same time, Peter tells us to not be surprised
when we face them. He should know, though he
undoubtedly prayed this prayer that Jesus taught them

often, he also had to prove himself. He was even warned about it by Jesus.

> *"And the Lord said, 'Simon, Simon! Indeed,*
> *Satan has asked for you, that he may sift you as*
> *wheat. But I have prayed for you, that your faith*
> *should not fail; and when you have returned to*
> *Me, strengthen your brethren.'"*
> Luke 22:31-32

Peter was tested to the very core of his being as well. His pride was slaughtered as he ran away when Jesus was arrested. His leadership was diminished to nothing. His self-confidence was obliterated. He ran and cried "bitterly" once he heard the rooster crow. He was so low and in such a place of shame that Jesus actually mentioned Peter's name when He told Mary to share the news with the disciples. He did overcome. He was forgiven and filled with the Holy Spirit. He preached the sermon on that first Pentecost where thousands were converted. The trial revealed things that he had to come to grips with, but it was necessary for him to be the leader Jesus wanted him to be.

As we close this chapter, let me leave you with the Apostle Peter's words on the subject.

> *"If anyone speaks, let him speak as the oracles of*
> *God. If anyone ministers, let him do it as with the*
> *ability which God supplies, that in all things God*
> *may be glorified through Jesus Christ, to whom*
> *belong the glory and the dominion forever and*
> *ever. Amen. Beloved, do not think it strange*
> *concerning the fiery trial which is to try you, as*
> *though some strange thing happened to you; but*

rejoice to the extent that you partake of Christ's sufferings, that when His glory is revealed, you may also be glad with exceeding joy."
1 Peter 4:11-13

CHAPTER ELEVEN

WE WILL BE GUARDED BY HIS

DELIVERANCE:

"But Deliver Us From Evil"

"Thou foul spirit, COME OUT!!" Sorry, but I had to get that out of my system before we could intelligently deal with this portion of the prayer. I remember watching some guy on television who would put his fingers in people's ears and shout that phrase (with full Shakespearean dramatic flair). What comes to your mind when you hear the word, "deliverance?"

As we move into this last phrase, "But deliver us from evil," we are going to have to deal with some definitions so that we can have clarity about what Jesus is trying to get across to His disciples, and ultimately us.

This is actually a continuation of the previous chapter. The two phrases are connected with "but." We are tying the thoughts together. Lead us not, *but* deliver us. Don't do one, *but* do the other. Please don't put me to the test, *but* please deliver me from evil (or the evil one).

As we saw in the previous chapter, you don't have to give in when tempted and trials may come to make us stronger. Actually, part of the goal of the Christian life is to be strong enough in the Lord and the power of His might that when temptations come (and they will come) we do not fall for them. This correlation of the phrases puts everything into perspective.

Let's focus on "deliverance" first. A lot of things come to our minds when we speak of deliverance, or being delivered. The word is "ponēros" (πονηρός) in the Greek. It can mean deliver, rescue, set free, save, liberate or release.[1]

If we are to be delivered, the implication is that we are bound, enslaved, captured, or oppressed. In other words, something or someone has to have a grip on you in order to be delivered from it. Just like "give us this day our daily bread" presupposes we are going to be hungry and need some food.

GOD IS AN EXPERT AT DELIVERANCE

If we are to pray for our Heavenly Father to deliver us, we need to have faith in His delivering power. Let the following stories from the Scriptures build that faith as we see that God is an expert at deliverance.

After the fall of Adam and Eve in the Garden of Eden, mankind was born in the image of sinful man. Sin had a grip on their souls and bodies, and they gravitated towards evil. In time, all of the people's thoughts were continually evil and God decided to deal with them. His plan was to bring a massive flood to the earth and cleanse it from these evil people. His judgment was decided. It would be so. Then we hear that Noah found grace in God's eyes. God gave Noah a chance to be *delivered* from the judgment. If Noah built a boat, God would *save* him, his family and a representation of the animals of the earth. God gave him the boat plans and brought the animals to the Ark. God *delivered* Noah and his wife, his three sons, Shem, Ham and Japheth, and their wives from the most horrific judgment mankind has ever known.

Abraham took his nephew, Lot, with him when he left the Ur of the Chaldeans for the land of Canaan. After God blessed Abraham with riches, it became difficult for everyone to share the same land in order to feed their flocks. Abraham and Lot decided to split up and form two tribes. Lot eventually moved into Sodom. The sin of this town was so great that God sent angels to destroy it with fire. Abraham interceded for the city, but there were not 10 righteous there. Nevertheless, the angels found Lot and escorted him, his wife and his two daughters out of the city before it was destroyed. The fired engulfed the city and all of its inhabitants, but Lot and his family were *delivered.*

One of the most profound and memorable acts of God's mighty deliverance can be found in the story of the Exodus. All of Jacob's family was moved to Egypt by his son, Joseph, who had been elevated to the position of Prime Minister. There was a great famine in the land and Joseph was responsible for preparing during the abundant years to save grain for the people during the lean years. He brought his family there and they were treated like royalty. Over the years, after Joseph's death, the clan had grown to a multitude and the Pharaoh had enslaved Jacob's descendents. God prepared a series of events that brought a Prophet, Moses, to Egypt. Through God's mighty power, the *release* of the slaves was granted and a *free* nation was formed. This is the story which surrounds the Hebrew festival of Passover.

As a young man, David, the future of king of Israel, was sent by his father to deliver some food to his brothers who were fighting in King Saul's army. When he arrived, he was shocked to observe a Philistine giant named, Goliath, mocking Israel and challenging someone from the army to fight him in a winner-take-all contest. No one responded. They were all fearful of this giant. David, now filled with the Holy Spirit since his anointing, speaks up and ultimately fights this monster. A young teenager pitted against a seasoned champion is warfare where the stakes are enormous. The losing warrior's country would surrender to the winner's. David put a stone in his sling and sent the projectile toward the giant. God directed this rock to the most vulnerable part of

Goliath's armor and the giant was killed. God *delivered* the nation of Israel from this evil and wicked nation.

As prophesied, David eventually became King over Israel. The kingdom of Israel grew under his reign and prospered beyond imagination under his son, Solomon. After King Solomon, the country divided and had different kings. Over the years, the nation moved away from worshipping God and developed an interest in, and a devotion to, idols. A result of not honoring God was that they lost His protection. They were ultimately defeated by the Babylonians and taken captive. Jerusalem was destroyed and the prisoners were moved to Babylon. Some of those taken were the children of the royal houses of Israel. One young man stands out among all others, Daniel. He is wise and gifted. He is also very devout toward God and leaned upon Him for everything. Over time, Daniel is promoted among the Babylonians and has the trust of the king.

Others seek to displace him and take over his influential position. By caressing the king's ego, they persuade him to sign a law that prayers can only be made to him, no other deity, under punishment of death. Daniel is faithful to God and continues to make is daily prayers. He is caught and sentenced to be thrown into a den of hungry lions. The next day, the king (realizing he had been played) runs to the cave and calls for Daniel. Daniel answers, because God has *saved* him from the mouth of the lions.

Three of Daniel's closest Jewish friends also experienced the miraculous deliverance of God. The king erected a huge statue of himself and demanded that everyone in the kingdom bow down and worship it. Shadrach, Meshach, and Abed-Nego refused. They were tossed into a furnace of fire when they continued to refuse. The soldiers who threw them in died immediately from the intense heat. After a while, the king looked in and saw them alive, walking in the fire and accompanied by the Son of God. They were brought out alive and unharmed. God was their *deliverer* (JHVH Mephalti).

The Babylonians were defeated by the Medes and Persians. In time, a ruler of the Persians was in charge. His wife publicly dishonored him and was supposedly killed. He looked for another queen and chose Esther, a Hebrew originally named Hadassah. It was revealed to her from her uncle, Mordecai, that the king's Prime Minister, Haman, had influenced the king to kill all Israelites.

At that time, the king didn't know that Esther was Jewish. She prayed and fasted. She had her countrymen do the same. Next, she walked into the throne room, unannounced and stood before the king. This could also be seen as public dishonor, but he was gracious and welcomed her. After a series of banquets, Esther reveals Haman's sinister plot. The king has him hanged and the entire Hebrew nation is *delivered* from extinction. This is the story behind the Jewish festival named Purim.

The New Testament has great, faith building accounts of God *deliverance*. In the 3 ½ years of public ministry of Jesus, He was regularly used by the Father to bring deliverance to people. He even concentrated on deliverance when He explained His purpose for coming:

> *"And He was handed the book of the prophet*
> *Isaiah. And when He had opened the book, He*
> *found the place where it was written:*
> *'The Spirit of the LORD is upon Me,*
> *Because He has anointed Me*
> *To preach the gospel to the poor;*

He has sent Me to heal the brokenhearted,
TO PROCLAIM LIBERTY *to the captives*
And recovery of sight to the blind,
TO SET AT LIBERTY *those who are oppressed;*
To proclaim the acceptable year of the LORD.'"
Luke 4:17-19 (emphasis mine)

Even a close review of Jesus' life reveals His frequent ministry of *deliverance*. He *delivered* from sickness, demonization and strife. He *delivered* from the bondage of sin. His ultimate purpose was to *deliver* all of humanity from sin, self, and satan, if they would only believe.

Peter was cast into prison and awaiting certain execution. James had already paid that ultimate price for his faith. The church held a special prayer meeting on behalf of Peter and he was dramatically *rescued* by God.

Paul and Silas were jailed for their faith in Philippi. The Scriptures reveal that they began to sing around midnight. Suddenly, the building was shaken and they were *released*.

Deliverance seems to be one of the greatest themes that flows through the entirety of God's word. Even as the consummation of all things comes to pass, He is still recognized as the ultimate Deliverer. As His church and children, we are called into the ministry of *deliverance*, more on that later in the chapter.

WHAT IS EVIL?

We now move to the other part of this phrase, "From evil." We are asking something very specific from our Heavenly Father that He would exercise His influence and power to deliver us from evil.

This is a matter of some contention in theological circles. Most of us are accustomed to the King James Version of the prayer. However, there have been many discoveries and a better understanding of the Greek language that has helped us comprehend the original purpose of the writers. The contention is whether the language supports the phrase "from evil", or the understanding of "from the evil one." That is a significant difference.

Either way we must come to an understanding that there is evil in the world. We contend that God is good and philosophically there cannot be a definable good without a definable opposite, evil. Both must have a reference point that supports whether they are good or evil. There must be a standard by which they are measured and defined. The standard used by the Church should be the Word of God.

What this prayer shows us is that we need to take evil seriously. We can't just pretend that deep wickedness doesn't exist or doesn't really matter. Our mindset can't be "if we'd only educate people or raise them better, everybody would be fine". Reality is not that way. Tangible, world-embracing evil (spiritual evil) exists. When we don't pray about evil, we're making a huge mistake.

The church must be aware of evil and the evil tendencies of this age. If we are to minister effectively to this world, we must realize the conflict that exists between our message and the overall view of its inhabitants under the influence of evil.

EVIL ONE

Let's take a look at the original language and see what is being said or implied in the Greek text about this term we have had translated as "from evil". I appreciate the understanding I receive from Adam Clarke's Commentary:

> "But deliver us from evil—*Απο του πονηρου*, from the wicked one. Satan is expressly called o *πονηρος*, the wicked one. Matthew 13:19, 38, compare with Mark 4:15; Luke 8:12. This epithet of Satan comes from *πονος*, labor, sorrow, misery, because of the drudgery which is found in the way of sin, the sorrow that accompanies the commission of it, and the misery which is entailed upon it, and in which it ends."[2]

As Clarke suggests, when this exact Greek verb is used with this particular preposition, it almost always means to rescue from a specific person, not from an abstract idea or concept. Clark is not alone in this matter. Many scholars agree that the most literal translation of the phrase "deliver us from evil" actually reads "deliver us from the evil one." Barne's states it this way:

> "*Deliver us from evil.* The original, in this place, has the article—deliver us from *THE evil*-that is, as has been supposed, the evil one, or Satan. He is elsewhere called, by way of eminence, *the evil one*, Matthew 13:19, 1 John 2:13, 14, 3:12. Deliver us from his power, his snares, his arts,

his temptations. He is supposed to be the great parent of evil, and to be delivered from him is to be safe. Or it may mean, deliver us from the various evils and trials which beset us, the heavy and oppressive calamities into which we are continually liable to fall."[3]

From a translation standpoint, I agree with both of these great scholars in seeing the focus being on the evil one, as opposed to evil. Interesting stuff I know, but what does that mean? What is the big deal? Is there a real difference in the two (evil or evil one)?

Evil, according to a Christian or Godly view of the universe, is any action, thought or attitude that is contrary to the character or will of God. To be sinful then is to be evil. This is shown throughout both the Old and New Testament. There is no moral action commanded in the Bible that is contrary to God's character or God's will.

Evil, therefore, in a Christian world view, is contrasted by and in conflict with God's character or God's will. Evil, then, shows itself through deviation from the character or will of God. Evil is a broad concept and encompasses the wrong actions of all beings in the universe, not just human beings.

A century ago, sections of the Christian church were starting to act as if the Western mindset was correct in pretending that if we only educated people better, if we only made sure their family situation was right, all the things that we call evil would disappear. Two world wars, countless smaller wars, police actions, genocide, the Holocaust, pollution and much more has removed that fantasy. Yet, in light of all that evidence, there are still times that we act as if evil isn't that serious.

Even in our age, evil is rampant. I rarely spend much time watching the national news because of the barrage of evil that takes center stage. Good is hardly ever rewarded and evil is "juicy" news. Ours is a wicked age, but that is nothing new. Since the fall of man there has always been an evil element in society. The Apostle Paul recognized it even in his day:

> *"Grace to you and peace from God the Father and our Lord Jesus Christ, who gave Himself for our sins, that He might **DELIVER US FROM THIS PRESENT EVIL AGE**, according to the will of our God and Father, to whom be glory forever and ever. Amen."*
> Galatians 1:3-5 (emphasis mine)

If this prayer were only meant to deliver us from the concept of evil or the philosophical tenant that is opposed to what we believe is good or even the actual wrong and sinful things around us, it would be limited in its scope. How can it be limited if it is universal, cultural, and a part of this age? It is limited because it does not recognize its inception or its conclusion. In order to more accurately comprehend the broad scope of evil, we must include the more narrow interpretation of this phrase which deals with the evil one.

Deliver us from the evil one, places a face on the term evil. It brings the connotation of, "Deliver us from the devil." There is spiritual evil in the world and it is personified in this being called the devil or satan. He is not just an influence, an idea or an abstract design. He is a person. He is our chief enemy, and he is the one who sets out to see that we do not keep God's name holy, or that God's will be done and His kingdom come among us.

The devil does not want us to get our daily bread and be thankful for it. He does not want us to have the clear conscience that comes with the forgiveness of sins. He is the one who wages war against us, and it is against the devil and all this evil that we pray to be rescued.

Ethical or moral evil has its source in the being that rebelled against God by his own free will. This was the Archangel Lucifer. By his revolt against the Creator, he became the devil. From then on, the devil has had one purpose, to block the fulfillment of the will of God. He does everything he can to obstruct the work of God.

A very important distinction for us to understand is that the origin of evil is not Adam and Eve. Our ancestors were not bad people who created evil. Rather, Adam and Eve listened to the devil who was already evil—that was their sin. In obeying the devil, they disobeyed God. Adam and Eve gave themselves over to the power of the devil and the corruption of evil. And so, by their disobedience, the devil was successful for a time in thwarting the will of God. We need to understand that this evil one, satan, is the embodiment of evil. He is the symbol of all evil, even those evils over which he is not directly responsible but for which we are so willing to give him the credit.

GOD ISN'T SCARED

Somehow, in his devious book of tricks, satan has implanted the concept in the church's mind that satan roughly equals God in being and power. That couldn't be less true. There is no similarity between the two. In no way, shape or form is satan even a minute resemblance of

Almighty God. In fact, if satan were to think about it, he would realize that he can only do as much or live as long as God permits. Satan is a creature defined by fear, because he knows he is no match for God. He knows his time is running out. He knows that a day is coming when he will be swept away. In fact, the root of the word "deliver" has to do with a rushing current. That rushing current overwhelms satan.

God has no reason whatsoever to fear satan. Sometimes we may doubt God's being and power. We may even underestimate God's being, power, wisdom, holiness, justice, goodness, and truth. Furthermore, we might also overestimate satan's being, power, wisdom, badness, and lies. But don't expect God to make that same mistake. There is no passage in the Bible where God expresses fear of satan, or any evil for that matter.

God does take evil seriously. He also takes the devil seriously. However, let me be perfectly clear on this next point, God does not fear evil. God does not fear satan. He has no reason to fear. At present, God permits satan to bark, growl, and even bite. Through deception, the devil won the authority God had given to Adam and Eve. Through agape love like the world had never seen, Jesus won that authority back. The day is coming when God will take satan in hand and fling him into hell in final and lasting defeat.

God fears nothing. God fears no evil. Therefore, every time we pray "Deliver us from evil" we confess and celebrate that God is unafraid of evil. God is fearless in the face of evil and the evil one. And as such, we become like the Psalmist who expresses, "I fear no evil, for You are with me" and "You prepare a table before me in the presence of my enemies." God is always on our side. I love the hymn penned by Martin Luther, "A Mighty Fortress Is Our God." Here is the third stanza.

> "And though this world, with devils filled, should
> threaten to undo us,
> We will not fear, for God hath willed His truth
> to triumph through us:
> The Prince of Darkness grim, we tremble not for
> him;
> His rage we can endure, for lo, his doom is sure,
> One little word shall fell him."[4]

AN ORGANIZED ENEMY

Satan has developed an army of evil spirits (demons) that work his bidding. The word of God announces that one-third of heaven's angels joined him on his doomed plot to replace God. He has to have these evil (unclean) spirits because he is not omniscient, omnipresent or omnipotent. He is a created being with imperfect intellect, restricted presence, and limited power. You can see how his quest against God was, is, and will be doomed.

The Scriptures give us several classifications of evil spiritual beings. There are categories of some semblance of order among the evil ranks. Satan is not disorganized and we should not allow ourselves to be lulled into a false security by thinking otherwise. Consider these verses:

> *"Who shall separate us from the love of Christ?*
> *Shall tribulation, or distress, or persecution, or*

famine, or nakedness, or peril, or sword?   As it is
written:
'For Your sake we are killed all day long;
We are accounted as sheep for the slaughter.'

For I am persuaded that neither death nor life,
nor angels nor principalities nor powers, nor
things present nor things to come, nor height nor
depth, nor any other created thing, shall be able
to separate us from the love of God which is in
Christ Jesus our Lord."
Romans 8:35-39

"For we do not wrestle against flesh and blood,
but against principalities, against powers,
against the rulers of the darkness of this age,
against spiritual hosts of wickedness in the
heavenly places."
Ephesians 6:12

"For by Him all things were created that are in
heaven and that are on earth, visible and
invisible, whether thrones or dominions or
principalities or powers. All things were created
through Him and for Him."
Colossians 1:16

"Having disarmed principalities and powers, He
made a public spectacle of them, triumphing over
them in it."
Colossians 2:15

We see differing titles for these demonic spirits;
principalities, powers, rulers, thrones and dominions.   It

is clearly evident from Scripture that satan has a hierarchy that he has put into place for control of his minions. The Gospels most frequently refer to them under the overarching categories of evil or unclean spirits. We can understand it better by relating his organization to our military. He is the general of his forces and has a ranking system that places all other spirits in their position.

JESUS DELIVERED

We now recognize that one of the great marks of the ministry of Jesus was that of delivering those who were demonized. There are several stories in the Gospels where Jesus confronts evil spirits and casts them out. The most memorable is probably the confrontation with the Gadarene demoniac.

"Then they sailed to the country of the Gadarenes, which is opposite Galilee. And when He stepped out on the land, there met Him a certain man from the city who had demons for a long time. And he wore no clothes, nor did he live in a house but in the tombs. When he saw Jesus, he cried out, fell down before Him, and with a loud voice said, 'What have I to do with You, Jesus, Son of the Most High God? I beg You, do not torment me!' For He had commanded the unclean spirit to come out of the man. For it had often seized him, and he was kept under guard, bound with chains and shackles; and he broke the bonds and was driven by the demon into the wilderness.

*Jesus asked him, saying, 'What is your name?'
And he said, 'Legion,' because many demons had
entered him. And they begged Him that He
would not command them to go out into the
abyss. Now a herd of many swine was feeding
there on the mountain. So they begged Him that
He would permit them to enter them. And He
permitted them. Then the demons went out of the
man and entered the swine, and the herd ran
violently down the steep place into the lake
and drowned. When those who fed them saw
what had happened, they fled and told it in the
city and in the country. Then they went out to see
what had happened, and came to Jesus, and
found the man from whom the demons had
departed, sitting at the feet of Jesus, clothed and
in his right mind. And they were afraid. They
also who had seen it told them by what means he
who had been demon-possessed was healed. Then
the whole multitude of the surrounding region of
the Gadarenes asked Him to depart from them,
for they were seized with great fear. And He got
into the boat and returned.
Now the man from whom the demons had
departed begged Him that he might be with Him.
But Jesus sent him away, saying, 'Return to your
own house, and tell what great things God has
done for you.' And he went his way and
proclaimed throughout the whole city what great
things Jesus had done for him.'*
Luke 8: 26-39

I would be remiss if I failed to mention the
ultimate defeat handed down to the devil on the cross.

Jesus offered Himself up as the sacrifice needed to save all who would believe. He became the "Second Adam" and took the authority that satan had usurped from Adam and Eve.

THE DISCIPLES DELIVERED

Not only was this type of deliverance indicative of Jesus' ministry, it was also of His followers. When Jesus sent the twelve Apostles out to preach during His earthly ministry they were <u>commanded</u> to cast out demons.

> *"These twelve Jesus sent out and commanded them, saying: 'Do not go into the way of the Gentiles, and do not enter a city of the Samaritans. But go rather to the lost sheep of the house of Israel. And as you go, preach, saying, 'The kingdom of heaven is at hand.' Heal the sick, cleanse the lepers, raise the dead, **<u>CAST OUT DEMONS</u>**. Freely you have received, freely give. Provide neither gold nor silver nor copper in your money belts, nor bag for your journey, nor two tunics, nor sandals, nor staffs; for a worker is worthy of his food.'"*
> Matthew 10:5-10 (emphasis mine)

On another similar occasion, Jesus appoints seventy of His followers to minister to the surrounding cities. He gives them much the same commissioning as He did in the passage above and assigns them the power necessary to fulfill the task.   Uniquely, we are given a view of the results of this group's preaching.

"Then the seventy returned with joy, saying,
*'Lord, even **THE DEMONS ARE SUBJECT TO***
US IN YOUR NAME.'
And He said to them, 'I saw Satan fall like
lightning from heaven. Behold, I give you the
authority to trample on serpents and scorpions,
and over all the power of the enemy, and nothing
shall by any means hurt you. Nevertheless do not
rejoice in this, that the
spirits are subject to you, but rather rejoice
because your names are written in heaven.'"
Luke 10:17-20 (emphasis mine)

WE MUST DELIVER

This type of deliverance, characteristic of Jesus and his disciples, is also expected of all of us who believe. Though this passage in Mark has been questioned as to whether it belongs in the original Greek text, the underlying message and truth can be corroborated throughout the rest of Scripture and is not foreign to its overall meaning.

"He who believes and is baptized will be saved;
but he who does not believe will be condemned.
*And these signs will follow those who believe: **IN***
MY NAME THEY WILL CAST OUT
***DEMONS**; they will speak with new tongues;*
they will take up serpents; and if they drink

anything deadly, it will by no means hurt them;
they will lay hands on the sick, and they will
recover."
Mark 16:16-18 (emphasis mine)

Any struggle, battle or war can only be effective if
you first know your enemy, and second know where your
enemy is, and third understand their tactics or battle
plans. We covered the first aspect by clearly identifying
satan, the fallen Archangel Lucifer, as the enemy of God
and as such the enemy of His Church.

Where is our enemy? Too often I have heard people
speak of sending the devil back to hell where he came
from. Sometimes they exclaim that, "No devil in hell,"
could make them do so and so. Well, the reality of the
situation is this, satan is not in hell nor can you send him
there. The lake of fire (hell) was prophesied by the
Apostle John as the eternal punishment satan would
receive after the final judgment.

"They went up on the breadth of the earth and
surrounded the camp of the saints and the
beloved city. And fire came down from God out of
heaven and devoured them. The devil, who
deceived them, was cast into the lake of fire and
brimstone where the beast and the false prophet
are. And they will be tormented day and night
forever and ever."
Revelation 20:9-10

We also know that before he fell, he was called
Lucifer and was in God's presence.

"How you are fallen from heaven,
O Lucifer, son of the morning!
How you are cut down to the ground,
You who weakened the nations!
For you have said in your heart:
'I will ascend into heaven,
I will exalt my throne above the stars of God;
I will also sit on the mount of the congregation
On the farthest sides of the north;
I will ascend above the heights of the clouds,
I will be like the Most High.'
et you shall be brought down to Sheol,
To the lowest depths of the Pit."
Isaiah 14:12-15

Well, if he isn't in heaven or hell, where "the devil" is he (excuse me, I couldn't help it)?

"And you He made alive, who were dead in
trespasses and sins, in which you once walked
according to the course of this world,
__ACCORDING TO THE PRINCE OF THE__
__POWER OF THE AIR, THE SPIRIT WHO__
__NOW WORKS IN THE SONS OF__
__DISOBEDIENCE,__ among whom also we all once
conducted ourselves in the lusts of our flesh,
fulfilling the desires of the flesh and of the mind,
and were by nature children of wrath, just as the
others."
Ephesians 2:1-3

We find that he is in the atmosphere. He is not located on earth yet, neither is he in heaven. He is in the space between. Some may have a hard time understanding this, since they have believed some of the myths concerning how satan looks. The evil one is not repulsive. He does not have green eyes, cloven hoofs, and a forked tail. The opposite is true. Satan will access our hearts through the things we desire and love the most. He masquerades in any way he can to lure us into his trap. He was beautiful in heaven as we hear of his majestic form in Scripture (Ezekiel 28). He is also revealed as one who comes as an angel of light (2 Corinthians 11:14).

We are called of God and gifted by His Spirit to engage the enemy and restore the kingdom of God on the earth. One of the most obvious Scriptures regarding this struggle is found in the Apostle Paul's letter to the Church in Ephesus.

> *"Finally, my brethren, be strong in the Lord and in the power of His might. Put on the whole armor of God that you may be able to stand against the wiles of the devil. For we do not wrestle against flesh and blood, but against principalities, against powers, against the rulers of the darkness of this age, against spiritual hosts of wickedness in the heavenly places. Therefore take up the whole armor of God, that you may be able to withstand in the evil day, and having done all, to stand."*
> Ephesians 6:10-13

There is a struggle that is discussed in these verses. It is clearly a personal struggle. The subject is an inferred personal pronoun. *You* are to put on the armor so *you* may be able to stand against these "wiles" that the enemy is using against *you*. Then again, *you* take up the armor so *you* may withstand the evil day, and *you* will stand having done all *you* can.   There is a personal element that we often miss at best or ignore at worst. <u>This revelation is important.</u>

The Greek word translated "wiles" (some places as schemes) is *methodeia* (Strong's #3180) and pronounced *meth-od-i'-ah*.   It's the word from which we get our English word 'method' which is exactly what the word means.   There is a method to the evil one's madness.   The word includes the thought of cunning art, deceit, craft, and trickery.

The scheme of satan to trap us is amazingly devious.   He has crafted a plan.   The plan is not haphazardly thrown together.   It is skillfully and artfully crafted to deceive and trick.   Not to necessarily kill, but to deceive, trick, get us off the purpose of God, and to stop the advancement of the kingdom.   In so doing, he destroys us. The kingdom of darkness has been around a long time.   It is not disorganized as the evil one would have us believe.   Rather, his deceitful kingdom is methodical and methodized.

Satan has a scheme specifically designed for me and he has one specifically crafted for you.   He does not desire to repel us with slanted green eyes and fire engine red skin.   Rather, he desires to entice us.   So, little by little, bait by bait, and scheme upon scheme, he methodically allures us to his snare of destruction.   That's the evil one's crafted method and it works amazingly well.   It works so well that if we are truly honest, deep down, we each know the method by which he approaches us.   Yet, knowing this, we still allow the evil one to draw near.   Amazing!

With the understanding that the evil one methodically crafted a scheme to destroy each of us, let's look at another scripture.

> *"Be sober, be vigilant; because your adversary the devil walks about like a roaring lion, seeking whom he may devour."*
> 1 Peter 5:8

A reason that I reference this verse is because of how I have heard 1 Peter 5:8 taught. People have stated that the devil, the roaring lion, is a toothless bully. The teaching attempts to humorously say that Jesus pulled all the devil's teeth and that he can do nothing to us.

Those types of statements worry me. Paul tells us to arm ourselves against the methodical schemes of the devil. Peter states for us to constantly be alert. Anyone who makes light of the evil one doesn't understand the Scriptures. Jesus told us to pray to be delivered from the evil one. The evil one is dangerous and will devour our lives.

GOD IS GREATER

I have said all of that to get to this place. Yes, the evil one is dangerous. We definitely need to pray about our temptations and constantly ask our heavenly Father to deliver us from the plans of the evil one. But I want to make certain that we all know that greater is He that is in you than he that is out there messing with you!

*"You are of God, little children, and have
overcome them, because He who is in you is
greater than he who is in the world."*
1 John 4:4

There is a balance. I don't care what we face in
life or what scheme the evil one devises; Christ in you is
greater than that scheme. I don't care if the evil one's
scheme worked, and sometimes it will, and you are in the
pit. Christ in you is greater than the devil. I know that
no matter how hopeless or how impossible it may seem in
the natural, you have a Father that is well able to see you
through. Greater is He that is in you than he that is in
the world.

He is the Great I Am. He has everything I need to
get out of the pit and to be victorious. You need to
develop an unshakable confidence in Father (Abba) God.
You've got to be fully convinced that there is nothing too
hard for our God. You've got to know that you know that
you know that He loves you with an everlasting love. He
is personally concerned about every one of us. He will
deliver you from the trap of the evil one.

Let me leave this chapter with some great
thoughts of encouragement from God's Word.

*"But thanks be to God, who gives us the victory
through our Lord Jesus Christ."*
1 Corinthians 15:57

*"For I am persuaded that neither death nor life,
nor angels nor principalities nor powers, nor
things present nor things to come, nor height nor
depth, nor any other created thing, shall be able*

to separate us from the love of God which is in
Christ Jesus our Lord."
Romans 8:38-39

"And the God of peace will crush Satan under
your feet shortly. The grace of our Lord Jesus
Christ be with you. Amen."
Romans 16:20

SECTION THREE

FOURTH *"G"*

GIVE PRAISE

"In this manner, therefore, pray:
Our Father in heaven, Hallowed be Your name.
Your kingdom come.
Your will be done on earth as it is in heaven.
Give us this day our daily bread.
And forgive us our debts, as we forgive our debtors.
And do not lead us into temptation,
but deliver us from the evil one.
For Yours is the kingdom and the power and the
glory forever. Amen"
Matthew 6:9-13

CHAPTER TWELVE

WE GIVE PRAISE BY OUR

SUBMISSION:

"For Yours Is The Kingdom"

Over the years there has been some debate over the inclusion of this doxology at the end of the prayer. The Roman Catholic Church does not use it in its liturgy. I know that from firsthand experience. For several years, I worked at a funeral home. I was actually enrolled in courses to become a licensed funeral director/embalmer and was working my apprenticeship.

The largest Catholic Church in North and South Carolina was very tightly associated with our funeral home. They were extremely precise in their demands and expectations. The Monsignor over the parish was reared in a family that owned funeral homes. We were required to attend very specific training just for this parish and were extremely careful to follow all of their guidelines.

My first service assisting was a little nerve racking, to say the least. When they began the Lord's Prayer, I was feeling pretty good about the day. No "mess-ups" was a good sign. I joined in with full voice and participated boldly. Then it happened. I couldn't believe it. They all stopped after the word "evil." I just barreled right on through and into the doxology with my eyes closed and my spirit wide open.

Stop a second and realize the impact of this moment. I can visualize it right now. Everyone (over 200 people) suddenly went quiet in prayerful expectation, waiting for the priest to continue the solemn service. Here I am in my deep, loud, southern accent proclaiming, "For Thine is the kingdom, and the power and the glory, Forever. Amen." Yeah, it was an embarrassing moment. I felt like Gomer Pyle shouting, "Shazam" at a sudden-death game-winning putt at the Masters Golf tournament in Augusta (on national TV).

Seriously though, there are two main schools of thought regarding the Greek texts that are used for the translation of the New Testament. One is referred to as the "critical text" and the other the "majority text."

The critical method involves the development of the most significant findings. They are held to a very high standard with many different criteria used to decide the various perceived inconsistencies. One of the essential criterions is that they purposely give greater weight to the oldest manuscripts, copies or partials. All of the texts are then used to create one eclectic text from what is deemed to be the most reliable manuscripts.

The majority method is, in the simplest terms, using the Greek texts with the most copies. The concept is that the more copies we have to attest to the writing the stronger the belief that we have the most correct and approved copy. This is especially strong given the lack of a printing press and these had to be copied by hand. It is somewhat weak, in that if the many copies were newer and included the doxology that the oldest copies didn't have, then the question is posed, "does the fact that there are many, make it correct?"

The critical method does not see this doxology present in its earliest manuscripts or partial texts. The majority method finds it in its vast library of early copies. The King James and subsequent New King James Versions are from the *Textus Recepticus* which is near to the majority method at the time.

What is the impact if this doxology was not in the original prayer? Not a thing. Not really anything of any magnitude at least. It does not alter any form of our theology. It does not create a different message or change the heart of the prayer. Those who believe it isn't original point out that it was possibly added in the early church by one of the scribes as an appropriate benediction that is based on other portions of Scripture. It is very similar to David's doxology in 1 Chronicles.

"Yours, O LORD, is the greatness,
The power and the glory,
The victory and the majesty;
For all that is in heaven and in earth is Yours;
Yours is the kingdom, O LORD,
And You are exalted as head over all."
1 Chronicles 29:11

There are many scholars who have taken the time to make their view of this doxology known. I will share two with differing attitudes towards this section.

"If any reliance is to be placed on external evidence, this doxology, we think, can hardly be considered part of the original text. It is wanting in all the most ancient manuscripts; it is wanting in the *Old Latin* version and in the *Vulgate:* the former mounting up to about the middle of the second century, and the latter being a revision of it in the fourth century by JEROME, a most reverential and conservative as well as able and impartial critic. As might be expected from this, it is passed by in silence by the earliest Latin fathers; but even the Greek commentators, when expounding this prayer, pass by the doxology. On the other hand, it is found in a majority of manuscripts, though not the oldest; it is found in all the *Syriac* versions, even the *Peschito* -- dating probably as early as the second century -- although this version lacks the "Amen," which the doxology, if genuine, could hardly have wanted; it is found in the *Sahidic* or *Thebaic* version made for the Christians of Upper Egypt, possibly as early as the *Old Latin;* and it is found in perhaps most of the later versions. On a review of the evidence, the strong probability, we think, is that it was no part of the original text."[1]

"The whole of this doxology is rejected by Wetstein, Griesbach, and the most eminent critics. The authorities on which it is rejected may be seen in Griesbach and, Wetstein, particularly in the second edition of Griesbach's Testament, who is fully of opinion that it never made a part of the sacred text. It is variously written in several MSS., and omitted by most of the fathers, both Greek and Latin. As the doxology is at least very ancient, and was in use among the Jews, as well as all the other petitions of this excellent prayer, it should not, in my opinion, be left out of the text, merely because some MSS. have omitted it, and it has been variously written in others."[2]

Because of the familiarity of this part of the prayer, we are going to study it and apply it to the prayer. Most people in protestant churches today are accustomed to it and consider it part of the prayer. You know I do from my funeral episode. Many have heard the great musical version of the prayer composed by Albert Hay Mollette (my favorite is Andrea Bocelli with the Mormon Tabernacle Choir, on YouTube).

We have dealt quite extensively with the Kingdom of God in chapter four under the phrase, "Your Kingdom Come." As we consider this portion, we are focusing on the last of the 4G's, *Give*. We are giving praise, as is quite evident by the context of this doxology. Because we are talking about God's Kingdom and how we can *Give* Him praise we will spend this chapter dealing with the importance of submission in the Kingdom.

God is the Sovereign of His kingdom. His throne is established on authority, and all the acts of God issue from His throne. All things were and are created by His authority. Even the physical laws of the universe are maintained by His authority. All things to come are also determined, allowed and supported by His divine, sovereign authority.

As we emphasized the origin of satan earlier, it is easy to recognize that rebellion, resulting from his pride, was the cause of his fall. He tried to compete with God. He trespassed against God's holiness and violated God's authority. Rebellion, then, is a principle founded by satan.

Considering its foundation, each of us needs to see the importance of being completely purified from this principle. It is actually possible to preach Christ and also exercise satan's principle. He is not as afraid of our preaching the Word as he is of our submitting to the authority of Christ. The controversy of the universe then is who shall have the authority: God, satan or us.

OBEDIENCE

The greatest demand of the Bible is obedience to God's will. Even the commands and rituals to make sacrifices or offerings and the call to deny ourselves or bear our cross are all intertwined with and subject to the foundation of obedience.

Scripturally, it is clear that there are two overriding principles in the universe from which we must choose.

1. The principle of God's authority.
2. The principle of satanic rebellion.

We cannot effectively follow both. We cannot serve God and harbor a rebellious spirit. Satan laughs when a rebellions person preaches because he is dwelling in the principle of satanic rebellion.

Obedience is the godly principle of submission. Without submission, there can be no real Kingdom. If every subject is forced to comply with the monarch it becomes more of a dictatorship.

The Word of God has much to say about submission and the Kingdom. We must understand this submission in reference to the Kingdom, not in our human orientation of being held down and kept from achieving. When submission is taught, it often is met with resistance. Our soulish man is not keen on surrendering. We will fight until the last second to keep from yielding. Americans are programmed to always think about their rights. Submission requires the acquiescence of those "inalienable" rights to the Sovereign of Heaven.

JESUS

The ultimate example for us to follow is our Lord Jesus Christ. We are told to emulate Him and allow His Spirit to reign within us (the Kingdom). The best illustration of that is given in the New Testament letters to the Church of the Philippians and the Diaspora of Judaic believers in the book of Hebrews.

> "Let this mind be in you which was also in Christ Jesus, who, being in the form of God, did not consider it robbery to be equal with God, but made Himself of no reputation, taking the form of a bondservant, and coming in the likeness of men. And being found in appearance as a man, He humbled Himself and became obedient to the point of death, even the death of the cross. Therefore God also has highly exalted Him and given Him the name which is above every name, that at the name of Jesus every knee should bow, of those in heaven, and of those on earth, and of those under the earth, and that every tongue should confess that Jesus Christ is Lord, to the glory of God the Father."
> Philippians 2:5-11

> "Who, in the days of His flesh, when He had offered up prayers and supplications, with vehement cries and tears to Him who was able to save Him from death, and was heard because of His godly fear, though He was a Son, yet He learned obedience by the things which He suffered. And having been perfected, He became the author of eternal salvation to all who obey Him,"
> Hebrews 5:7-9

Jesus humbled Himself twice: 1) He emptied Himself in His Divinity and 2) He humbled Himself in

His humanity. He was so emptied on earth that no one recognized Him as God except by revelation. His own glory, power, status and form weren't evident. He was treated as an ordinary man. As the Son, He submits to the Father's authority. He declares in John 14:28, *"The Father is greater than I."* His Heavenly Father becomes the emblem of authority and Jesus assumes the symbol of obedience.

The Lord took the place of a slave, accepting human limitations of time and space, which were not applicable to Him prior to His incarnation. He gave up equality with the Father. Because of His great love, He forsook authority and took up obedience, even unto death.

It comes to reason then, that to be filled with Jesus is to be filled with obedience. Christ is the principle of obedience, so anyone who accepts Him must accept the principle of obedience. Also, those who are filled with Christ must also be filled with obedience.

Submission through obedience is the way of Jesus. He was made Lord only after He emptied Himself. He came to earth for this reason. Rebellion came from the created beings (Lucifer, Adam and Eve), obedience must now be established in a created being (Jesus).

He discarded the concept of being disobedient and reclaiming His original authority. He walked humbly in obedience, died, was emptied and was unwilling to fill Himself again.

Because of His submission and obedience, the Father has exalted Him. Jesus returned to glory as Lord! The name of Jesus is most precious among names. At His name, every knee shall bow and every tongue will confess that Jesus is Lord.

We who serve God will eventually meet authority. It may be in the universe, society or our home church.

Problems are bound to arise. We will do well to learn the lessons of submission. Cultivating a spirit of obedience and as you practice it, it gets easier.

SUBMISSION TO GOD

God's kingdom is the coordination of authority. In spiritual work, organization, management or synchronization, submission to authority is the rule. There is no room for isolated individual service; the individual is not the unit. God is establishing the revelation of His Kingdom through the principle of obedience through submission.

According to the passage above from Hebrews 5, Jesus learned obedience through suffering. He never complained. The Lord's obedience is for the sake of the Kingdom of God and the aim of redemption is to further the Kingdom of God.

As we saw in chapter 4, God's Kingdom is established. He is determined to reveal it on the earth, even though men rebel, even though angels rebel!

Jesus' message was that the Kingdom of God is at hand. He came to earth to set up God's Kingdom. His good news (Gospel) is two-fold:

1. Personal – He calls men to receive eternal life through faith.
2. Corporate – He calls men to enter God's Kingdom through repentance.

In all reality, Jesus Himself is actually the Kingdom of God. When He is among us, so is the Kingdom.

AUTHORITIES

God has allowed the institution of certain authorities in the world. We are to submit to them and obey them so as to not cultivate within our spirits an attitude of rebellion. We will investigate these authorities and renew our submissive spirit so that the anointing of God may flow down to us.

IN THE WORLD: All governing authorities are instituted by God. They are delegated by Him and represent His authority. He shows Himself through the system of authority. Our duty is to be subject to God's delegated authority as well as His direct authority.

"Let every soul be subject to the governing authorities. For there is no authority except from God, and the authorities that exist are appointed by God. Therefore whoever resists the authority resists the ordinance of God, and those who resist will bring judgment on themselves. For rulers are not a terror to good works, but to evil. Do you want to be unafraid of the authority? Do what is good, and you will have praise from the same. For he is God's minister to you for good. But if you do evil, be afraid; for he does not bear the sword in vain; for he is God's minister, an avenger to execute wrath on him who practices

*evil. Therefore you must be subject, not only
because of wrath but also for conscience' sake.
For because of this you also pay taxes, for they are
God's ministers attending continually to this very
thing. Render therefore to all their due: taxes to
whom taxes are due, customs to whom customs,
fear to whom fear, honor to whom honor."*
Romans 13:1-7

If we resist God's delegated authority, we are actually resisting God. If we disobey His delegated authority, we incur God's judgment. Jesus was never a party to any rebellion. What the end of those verses is basically saying is that there are four symbols of obedience to earthly authorities:

1. Taxes to whom taxes are due.
2. Revenue (customs) to whom revenue is due.
3. Respect (fear) to whom respect is due.
4. Honor to whom honor is due.

These worldly authorities are to be obeyed. A Christian does this, not only to avoid God's wrath, but also for the sake of conscience. 2 Peter 2:10 admonishes us to be careful not to revile authority.

IN THE FAMILY: God has placed an order of delegated authority in the creation of the family. This is not a discriminatory action on behalf of God, but a principle of order. God's delegated order is (1) the husband, (2) the wife and (3) the children, according to Ephesians 5:21-33. This does not mean that one sex or one person is more important than another, it is just the way God initiated it for our best good.

The husband represents the covering and love of Christ, Who gave Himself for the Church (His bride). The wife represents the Church who lovingly submits to the will of the Lord Jesus. The children honor and obey their parents and the parents care for and teach the children.

We learn obedience and submission in our families. If the children and/or parents are not walking in the order of God, how can there be blessing and peace? Rebellion in a home will cause division among all its members.

IN THE CHURCH: God has set in the Church elders who rule well, those who labor in preaching, teaching, evangelism, prophetic ministry and apostolic oversight. We should all be taught to obey those who have the rule over us in the church (Hebrews 13:17). Younger ones in age should be subject to the older ones. The Kingdom is to be found in the Church. The Church is the contemporary sphere wherein God's authority is exercised and released so that we may learn the lesson of submission and obedience.

The leaders of the Church are expected to develop attitudes of humility and service. It is shameful and sinful for a leader to consciously display his position and authority in such a way as to provoke his membership. He is to be a gentle shepherd looking out for their needs above his own.

We are cautioned to have respect for those that are in spiritual leadership. Often, one of the first things others say to me when I speak on Church authority is, "What if the authority is wrong?" Good question. What if He is? Does that give you permission to now sinfully gossip or rebel? How we respond tells us more about us than it does about the leader. To reject His delegated authority is an affront to God. Submission to the delegated authority requires brokenness and humility.

Let me ask you a couple of questions, "How big is your God?" "How powerful is your God?" Now stop before you jump out and answer to quickly. You may have a pat answer that rolls of the tongue so slippery and swift, but your actions may speak differently. God is more than able to hold the delegated authority accountable and responsible. He has not asked you to step in for Him. Whether the delegated authority is right or wrong is not our concern, it is God's. We have to keep our end of the equation to obey.

Remember in David's life (after being anointed as a boy to become Israel's next King) there was a time when King Saul was after him. The King was wrong. He was acting outside of the leadership of God and the Spirit of God had left him. He chased David for years all across the nation, in and out of caves. Yet, even when the opportunity came to him (actually twice), David would not touch the man God had anointed and placed as King (delegated authority). In fact, when King Saul was mortally wounded by archers in his final battle and asked his armor bearer to finish the job instead of letting the enemy have the pleasure.

The armor bearer would not, so Saul fell on his spear. The armor bearer, supposing Saul dead, fell on his sword and died. An Amalekite found Saul barely alive and killed him at his request. He then ran and told David all that had transpired. I believe he thought he was bearing "Good News" about the death of David's pursuer, opening up the opportunity for David to ascend to the throne of Israel. Yet when David heard this entire story, he order that the Amalekite be executed saying,

*"How was it you were not afraid to put forth your
hand to destroy the LORD's anointed?"*
2 Samuel 1:14

David had learned the lesson of honor, obedience and submission. Even when the authority was wrong, David allowed God to be the Judge and not pick up the offense himself.

Permit me a brief aside as I share an important piece of the story of Saul. King Saul was commanded by God through the prophet Samuel to go to battle against the Amalekites. He orders were to completely annihilate them all because of their great sin against Israel during the Exodus. He was chosen to be God's instrument of judgment and wrath. He fought, but did not follow all of God's commands and left some alive. The following verse explains how God feels about obedience and rebellion.

'So Samuel said:
*'Has the LORD as great delight in burnt offerings
and sacrifices,*
As in obeying the voice of the LORD?
Behold, to obey is better than sacrifice,
And to heed than the fat of rams.
For rebellion is as the sin of witchcraft,
And stubbornness is as iniquity and idolatry.
Because you have rejected the word of the LORD,
He also has rejected you from being king.'"
1 Samuel 15:22-24

God's King was slain by an Amalekite that he refused to kill. Be careful, your disobedience could eventually be the source of you total downfall.

To take it even further, Haman, the trusted advisor to the Emperor of Persia was planning the complete annihilation of the Jewish race. Queen Esther defied Persian law and presented herself before the King. She represented her people and was instrumental in the deliverance of the nation. This Haman was also an Amalekite, another result of Saul's disobedience. Note, the results of your disobedience can ripple through the ages.

Allow God to take care of His appointed, anointed and delegated leaders. They are His responsibility and not yours. You are not to sit in judgment over God's anointed leadership. The only exception to the rule is found in the words of Peter as He stood before the Jewish council (religious leadership).

> "And when they had brought them, they set them before the council. And the high priest asked them, [28] saying, 'Did we not strictly command you not to teach in this name? And look, you have filled Jerusalem with your doctrine, and intend to bring this Man's blood on us!' But Peter and the other apostles answered and said: 'We ought to obey God rather than men. The God of our fathers raised up
> Jesus whom you murdered by hanging on a tree. Him God has exalted to His right hand to be Prince and Savior, to give repentance to Israel and forgiveness of sins. And we are His witnesses to these things, and so also is the Holy Spirit whom God has given to those who obey Him.'"
> Acts 5:27-32

When the commands of the authority were in direct opposition to the commands of Jesus, the choice was made to obey Jesus rather than those who have strayed from God's clear (not felt), precise (not vague) instructions. This is not an "out" to give us permission to disobey or rebel.   There must be an unambiguous consensus that a breach of the direct and irrevocable known will of God has occurred, specifically in relation to His Word. Remember, this is serious and you will be held to account if you foster a rebellious spirit in yourself, your family or church.

Note that, even though there was a legitimate conflict, they still were humble. Submission is a matter of attitude whereas obedience is a matter of conduct. Obedience cannot be absolute: some authorities should not be obeyed. Submission ought to be absolute. Even when making a suggestion, we should maintain an attitude of submission. We should be able to serve a bad king. That is true Biblical submission.

Here the apostles were forbidden by the Jewish council to preach the gospel. They kept a submissive spirit throughout the trial. Even so, they continued on with the Lord's commission. They did not disobey with a quarrelsome attitude or a spirit of strife. There was no shouting or slander. It wasn't out right insubordination. They quietly and softly dissented.

In the case of a conflict between delegated authority and direct authority, remember:

1. Obedience is relative: conduct
2. Submission is absolute: from the heart
3. God alone receives absolute obedience
    without measure

4. Those below God receive qualified obedience
5. Submission is required of us to delegated authority, but we should disobey the order which offends God (not us).

MORE CHURCH: The fullest expression of God's authority is found in the Body of Christ, the church. The Church is the Body of Christ. Christ is the Head. The Head and the body are inseparable. No head will harm its body. For the body to obey the head is natural and agreeable. The two should be so united that obedience through submission includes both the conscious and the automatic.

All the various members of the body are attached in some neurological fashion to the head. Instead of the independent nature we see in our country and across church lines today, each member is inter-dependent on the function of the other members. If I want a bottle of water to drink, my feet and legs have to carry the rest of my members to the refrigerator. There my hand, supported by my arm, shoulder and torso, will open the door and take a bottle out. My eyes will have to determine whether the bottle is water, green tea or hot sauce. My nose will confirm that my eyes were correct when my hand brings the bottle to my mouth. Then my mouth will validate everyone else's decisions as my feet and legs take me back to me seat.

Who was most important in this action? The head is. It coordinated it all, but all of the other parts were equally responsible for their part. Each member had to rise up when their turn came to perform their function.

They also had to submit to the function of other members so they could do their part.

If my legs had not submitted to the brain and allowed my hands to take the lead, I would have walked past the refrigerator. The same needed to happen between the hand and the eye, or I might end up drinking from the bottle of hot sauce.

This inter-dependence is relational because of the connection to the same body led by the head. If the foot rejects the hand, it is the same as rejecting the head. The hand cannot feel color; it needs to accept the authority of the eye. If we accept the authority of the member, we accept the authority of the Head.

"But, speaking the truth in love, may grow up in all things into Him who is the head—Christ—from whom the whole body, joined and knit together by what every joint supplies, according to the effective working by which every part does its share, causes growth of the body for the edifying of itself in love."
Ephesians 4:15-16

We see that Christ is the Head of the Church, His body. We are joined together and knit together by what we supply, by working together in a spirit of love and cooperation. The body is deformed when members do not work properly. When the Spirit of God is at work in the members, the body can become so coordinated as to not even be conscious of being different members, just a whole body.

To resist the help of our brothers and sisters in Christ (members of the Body) is rebellion. God many times uses another member to supply our needs. We can do everything or supply everything. The distribution of functions and gifts is by nature also a delegation of authority. We have to remember that we are but a member. Whoever is gifted has a ministry. We are all gifted. With that ministry comes a level of authority.

Through God's direct and indirect authorities, we will receive spiritual supply. To be subject to one another is restful. The burden is distributed to various members. In truth, there is no burden in obedience and submission. Actually there is emancipation when we submit to authority in other members.

3 POSITIONS OF AUTHORITY

Within the Kingdom of God we find 3 distinct, yet inter-related, levels of authority. These positions are either designated or delegated by God. We need to be aware of these positions and sentient of our attitude toward each position. We are not called to judge if the people God places in these positions are perfect, we are just called to heed our own attitude towards God's decision. It is clear throughout Scripture that to rebel against the delegated authority of God is to rebel against God. Let's quickly summarize these 3 areas of level.

First: God is the absolute Authority. He delegated it to Jesus (Matthew 28:18) Who in turn has delegated areas of authority to man.

Second: Those who are delegated authority and have been placed in authority. They are responsible to watch the souls of those under their care. They are to lead, teach, feed and rebuke the sheep.

Third: Those who are under authority. The responsibility here is to obey, submit, pray and know them. Everyone should be under some form of authority in order to keep accountable.

How does all of this relate? We give praise to God when we place His agenda and plans before our own. Giving Him the final authority, as well as those to whom He has delegated authority, exhibits trust and faith. These in turn give the Master of it all the ultimate worship and exaltation.

Our strength is greatest when we surrender our part to Him and allow the Father to infuse us with His power.

-Dr. Lonnie E. Riley-

CHAPTER THIRTEEN

WE GIVE PRAISE IN OUR

WEAKNESS:

"And The Power"

We have already spent time in earlier chapters discussing the mighty power of God. Our Heavenly Father is omnipotent, meaning almighty or infinite in power. He is more powerful that any of His children can imagine or adequately express in their feeble words. As this doxology moves from expressions of the Kingdom to expressions of His power I am reminded that we *give* praise, we show our great dependence on His power, through our weaknesses. He is given credit for the works done, because He uses people, inadequate humans, to work through. Though we walk in great power by the Spirit of God through Christ, we are not the cause of such power. It is not because we are such special Christians that the supernatural is at work in our lives. It is the plan of God that His people have the strength needed to reach the world and defeat the attacks of the enemy. The least we are "professionally" qualified (or at least that we rely solely on that qualification), the greater the praise is given to God for using His power through us.

The Scriptures are ripe with examples of God using little to accomplish much. Slaves took down the great Egyptian empire. Gideon's 300 men were given an awesome victory over thousands because of God intervention. A young shepherd lad killed a giant warrior. A little boy submitted his lunch of 5 loaves of bread and two fish to Jesus. He blessed it and used it to feed 5,000 having 12 baskets full. God also used 12 young men (mostly teenagers) to lead His new church and ultimately turn the entire world around. There is an old song I remember singing years ago. The refrain goes like this:

"Little is much when God is in it!
Labor not for wealth or fame.
There's a crown—and you can win it,
If you go in Jesus' Name"[1]

I love the way the Apostle Paul put it in his second letter to the Church in Corinth, a church that was enamored by the supernatural and power ministries of the day. He has told them of a thorn (or splinter) in the flesh, an evil angel from satan, that is troubling him. He has asked God three times for deliverance. Here is the story of what happened in his words:

> *"And lest I should be exalted above measure by the abundance of the revelations, a thorn in the flesh was given to me, a messenger of Satan to buffet me, lest I be exalted above measure. Concerning this thing I pleaded with the Lord three times that it might depart from me. And He said to me, 'My grace is sufficient for you, for My strength is made perfect in weakness.' Therefore most gladly I will rather boast in my infirmities, that the power of Christ may rest upon me. Therefore I take pleasure in infirmities, in reproaches, in needs, in persecutions, in distresses, for Christ's sake. For when I am weak, then I am strong."*
> 2 Corinthians 12:7-10

In this discourse the lesson being taught to Paul by God is important. "My strength is made perfect in weakness." That is what we are saying in this chapter. God is not interested in your strength. Your strength does not impress Him anymore than a new born baby's strength impresses Mr. Universe. Your ability is a joke compared to His and what He plans to provide for you. However, if you are walking in the obedience through submission we spoke if in the last chapter, He wants to work wonders through you with His awesome power. He is looking for those who will admit their weakness and rely totally on Him.

This lesson is learned by Paul. He even lets it be known that he will, with gladness, boast about his weaknesses so that the power of God may be revealed to the world. In this dialogue, we understand that these are not just Paul's words; they are the words of the Lord. Jesus is revealing to Paul that whenever he is weak, God's strength is disclosed as complete, total and perfect. This, by the way, is exactly what Jesus did. He laid aside all of His divine power and glory and relied on the leadership of the Father through the anointing of the Holy Spirit. That is how He accomplished all He did.

Paul, wanting to make sure this church was understanding the concept, expands the idea by saying that he takes pleasure in some of the things thee might consider unpleasant like, infirmities, reproaches, needs, persecutions or distresses when it for the sake of Jesus. It finally dawned in on him that he became the strongest whenever he became weak.

The word infirmity is the main word for translated as sick or sickness. It is usually a feebleness of the body (or mind). Paul is not condoning sickness, nor is this a statement against God's desire or ability to heal; it is Paul submissiveness to whatever may come his way in order for God's power to be perfected.

The use of reproaches is interesting. The actual word is related to *hubris*. In ancient Greek, *hubris* had a different meaning than it does today; it referred to actions that shamed or humiliated the victim for the pleasure or gratification of the abuser. It had a strong sexual connotation, and the shame reflected on the perpetrator as well. What types of crimes might have been included in *hubris*? It usually denoted offenses such as assault and battery, sexual crimes or the theft of public or sacred property. Paul is saying in effect that he would undergo the dishonoring, or shame that brought about reproach (criticism, blame, scolding or accusation) in order to show God's strength.

I believe next, that Paul is saying that he is willing to go without to watch God show His provision. When He uses the word "needs" he is speaking to the necessities of life, not just his selfish wants. Too often if our culture we see those who do not fully understand the difference between wants and needs. Paul is here speaking of the baser, more needful things of existence. He is ready to do without those things in order to see God be proclaimed as his Provider of those needs by His power.

The Apostle was even willing to submit to being hounded by, pursued by, harassed by and hunted by unbelievers or evil forces so that God would be able to exercise his magnificent power. This is the main meaning of the word for persecute.

One of the other meanings of persecute that is considerably relevant today is the term, "discriminate against." Many people in this culture are quick to claim that they have been discriminated against and will even take others to court for it. Paul was willing to allow God to flex His muscles (instead of some court) in his defense. That certainly takes a lot of faith and a dying to our own selfish will.

Calamity is not a word we like to have associated with our Christianity. We are not usually anxious to experience grief or misery, pain or sorrow. Our personal anguish or misfortune is certainly not what we correlate as being a "blessing" from God. Even though there are many verses which explain the necessity of suffering for the believer, this is often overlooked in our bless me, prosper me, or open the windows of heaven mentality of many in today's church. But that is what Paul is saying when he uses the word for distress. God is glorified when He delivers us from all these things.

Careful, though, do not attribute to God any type of exploitation or manipulation, He is a loving Father Who wants the best for His children. He is also a loving God Who wants to draw the rest of the world into His fold of faith. They must see that God is both able and willing to take care of their difficulties by His mighty power. They see that when He shows that power through our circumstances.

As the children of our Heavenly Father, we are blessed to have the power of God working in our lives. This power is not of our own merit, it is given to us as a gift from God. Uniquely, the Divine power given to us by Our Father, God is the Holy Spirit of God poured out by the Son of God. As I alluded to earlier, Jesus submitted to this and modeled it before the entire world. Philippians 2 speaks so much about what Jesus gave up, but it also tells of what our Lord received. He is now exalted! Jesus is Lord of all. Every knee will bow to His name. This He did as the ultimate example for us. We must learn to yield our notions of strength and power to God and let Him fill us with His power through the Holy Spirit.

HOLY SPIRIT POWER

This power we are referring to is in us only because the Holy Spirit falls on us. We are weak! That is evident, but we are promised that His strength will work both in and through us by this outpouring if God's Spirit. It is clearly promised by Jesus to His disciples just moments before He ascended into heaven.

> *"And being assembled together with them, He commanded them not to depart from Jerusalem, but to wait for the Promise of the Father, 'which,' He said, 'you have heard from Me; for John truly baptized with water, but you shall be baptized with the Holy Spirit not many days from now.'*
> *Therefore, when they had come together, they asked Him, saying, 'Lord, will You at this time restore the kingdom to Israel?' And He said to them, 'It is not for you to know times or seasons which the Father has put in His own authority.* ___**BUT YOU SHALL RECEIVE POWER WHEN THE HOLY SPIRIT HAS COME UPON YOU**___; *and you shall be witnesses to Me in Jerusalem, and in all Judea and Samaria, and to the end of the earth.'"*
> Acts 1:4-8 (emphasis mine)

Jesus is promising the outpouring of the Holy Spirit (the Promise of the Father) to be given to the disciples. He is equating the coming outpouring to baptism. As John baptized with water, Jesus would be baptizing His followers with the Holy Spirit. When that occurs, He tells them they will receive power. It will not be their power; it will be the power of God.

Power is the word translated from the Greek, "*dunamai.*" Other ways it is translated is strength, mighty work, miracle and even might. As other languages began to develop from a Greek base, words took on certain symbolism over the years. The etymology of our word "dynamite" obviously has its roots in "*dunamai.*" The Promise of the Holy Spirit would be evident by its extremely forceful power.

This correlation of the Holy Spirit with power has been made many times throughout Scripture, and I am sure was not lost in the minds of the disciples. They had heard the great stories and made those correlations immediately.

One of the most famous (if not infamous) judges in the pre-king era of Israel was Samson. Samson is known by many as the most powerful man to have ever lived. He was incredibly strong and had many powerful acts attributed to him. The Philistines were trying to capture him and each time they tried, he overtook them. Whenever a great act of strength was about to take place, the Bible says, "And the Spirit of the LORD came mightily upon him." When he was eventually captured, it was because the LORD had departed from him because he had broken his Nazarite vows. Even in his death, it was God's power that helped him destroy the heathen temple and kill thousands of Philistines with one act.

About 100 years before the capture of Jerusalem and the Jewish nation by Babylon, Isaiah prophesied in Judah. One of his contemporary prophets was a mighty man named Micah. He is one who has the awesomely terrible responsibility to foretell the destruction and captivity. Yet he also continually speaks of God's mercy and faithfulness. One of the most prominent Old Testament prophecies regarding the birth of the Messiah is in this little book, declaring Bethlehem as the birth place of Jesus (5:2). Micah credits the great power he had in his prophetic role to the Spirit.

*"But truly **I AM FULL OF POWER BY THE**
SPIRIT OF THE LORD, And of justice and
might, To declare to
Jacob his transgression And to Israel his sin."*
Micah 3:8 (emphasis mine)

After the people of Israel have lived through their
Babylonian captivity, God begins the drawing of His
people back to the Holy Land. The work to rebuild the
temple begins, but is halted because of opposition from
Syria. During this time, the people were encourage by
the prophesies of Zechariah. On one occasion, he has a
word to the governor of Jerusalem, essentially stating
that he (Zerubbabel) would complete the temple project in
the power of God's Spirit.

*"So he answered and said to me: 'This is the word
of the Lord to Zerubbabel: '**NOT BY MIGHT
NOR BY POWER, BUT BY MY SPIRIT**,' Says
the Lord of hosts.'"*
Zechariah 4:6 (emphasis mine)

The most blessed woman of all time experienced this
empowerment. When Mary was just a teen-aged girl she,
was visited by the angel, Gabriel, and told that she was
the chosen one of the LORD. God favored her and she
would give birth to the Messiah. This news was no doubt
overwhelming to her, but she still had to ask how this
could happen since she was a virgin. Then he gave this
answer:

*"And the angel answered and said to her, '**THE
HOLY SPIRIT WILL COME UPON YOU**,*

AND THE POWER OF THE HIGHEST WILL
OVERSHADOW YOU; therefore, also,
that Holy One who is to be born will be called the
Son of God.'"
Luke 1:35 (emphasis mine)

Jesus had emptied Himself of all the power and glory that He held in His position in heaven. Still, He was able to walk in astounding power. During His earthly ministry He: healed the blind, the lame, and the bleeding, walked on water, turned water into wine, calmed the sea, cast demons out and much more. He operated out of the power of the Spirit, not out of His own position as God.

*"Then Jesus returned in **THE POWER OF THE***
***SPIRIT** to Galilee, and news of Him went out*
through all the surrounding region."
Luke 4:14 (emphasis mine)

CHRIST'S STRENGTH

The strength that Jesus had while ministering on this earth is available to each of His followers, you and me.

"Most assuredly, I say to you, he who believes in
Me, the works that I do he will do also; and
greater works than these he will do, because I go
to My Father."
John 14:12

Not only are we promised the Holy Spirit and His power, we now have the actual power of Jesus at work in and through of us. Yes, Jesus emptied Himself and took on the form of a man, but God has highly exalted Him. He now sits on the right hand of God in power.

He actually desires to work through us in faith. Paul writes again to the Church in Philippi about the strength he has in Jesus:

> *"I can do all things through Christ who*
> *strengthens me."*
> Philippians 4:13

"All things" is a very broad statement. He had prefaced that remark by thanking the church for their gift, mentioning that he had learned to be content in Christ, no matter what his circumstances. He knew how to be poor and to be rich. He also was acquainted with hunger and need as well as being full and abounding. He learned that he could do it all by the strength he gained through Jesus. We too can do all things *through Christ who strengthen us*!!

As Americans, we are accustomed to viewing the world through strength. For the first 25 years of my life, our nation was constantly on alert as we walked a tight line with the Soviet Union. Everyone called it the cold war. Even though the Soviet Union was strong and forceful, most people I knew believed we were stronger.

Then the unbelievable happened, this great nation fell apart. The USSR was dissolved and our stalemate was over. We are the greatest country in the world. We have the strongest military. On and on you can hear the proud pundits as they wax loud and strong about the might and power of the U.S.A. The "greatest nation ever," they say.

Somehow, that egotism has infiltrated not only our patriotic thoughts, but our spiritual ones as well. We believe that we are so powerful and that nothing can stop us, hurt us or even slow us down. We are God's new chosen people and there can be no stopping our progress. We are so favored that all we have to do is "speak" the word and it happens. Please don't misunderstand me; I believe that the Church of Jesus Christ is powerful. That we can walk in extraordinary power. That the supernatural should become "natural" for His children. We must always understand that this great power is not of our own doing. It is because of Jesus. We are weak, He is strong.

> *"For though He was crucified in weakness, yet He lives by the power of God. For we also are weak in Him, but we shall live with Him by the power of God toward you."*
> 2 Corinthians 13:4

WEAKNESS : POWER

My son, Joshua, has always been a math whiz. He loves numbers. I began to teach him about them before he reached the age where he went to Kindergarten. By the time he was only 4 years old, I would have him come to my side at family gatherings and show his mathematical prowess. I would shoot off a problem including addition and subtraction some 10 numbers long and he would have the answer ready immediately. The next year, when he was only 5, he could do the same with problems that included multiplication and division. These were concepts that most 3rd to 5th grade children were wrestling with. He was taking high school math classes when he was only in middle school, and took college level classes in High School. Joshua went on to graduate from college with a degree in mathematics and at present works for a bank where he daily enjoys seeing the importance of such math. (He also enjoys pointing out that he knows more than dad these days.")

One of the concepts that he learned is his mathematical studies is that of ratios. The relationship between two numbers can be expressed as a "ratio." Such relationships can be direct or indirect in proportion. As direct, a ratio increases or decrease based on the individual increase or decrease. The ratio of 2:4 is the same as the ratio 4:8 or 8:16 and so on. This ratio is a double ratio. The first number, doubled, is the second number.

Sometimes there can be inverse ratios as well; the more of one thing, creates less of the other. That is the type of ratio we have in regards to the power of God. The weaker we are, the greater His power is shown to be. The less we have, the more He can provide. Here are a couple of verses that show this inverse ratio.

"He gives power to the weak, And to those who have no might He increases strength."
Isaiah 40:29

"Beat your plowshares into swords And your pruning hooks into spears; Let the weak say, 'I am strong.'"
Joel 3:10

This authority is not something that we can boast about. It is not because we are so holy and righteous that we are able to walk in such power. It is not related to the volume of Scripture we have memorized or our grasp of theological concepts. It is not directly connected to how many weeks we have perfect attendance in Sunday school or men's/women's prayer groups. The strength does not come from anything we have done, it's nearly the opposite. The less we qualify, according to our standards, the greater the glory that is given to God. We can see it in the Scriptures that speak of the early church and the disciples.

> *"So when Peter saw it, he responded to the people:*
> *'Men of Israel, why do you marvel at this? Or why*
> *look so intently at us, as though by our own power*
> *or godliness we had made this man walk?'"*
> Acts 3:12

The Apostle Paul seemed to have a unique understanding of this ratio. As we saw at the first of the chapter, he especially made it known to the church at Corinth. This was a congregation that had experienced its problems. They were divisive over their leadership, they had allowed corruption to enter the ranks, they abused the Lord's Supper and were out of control in their services. They loved the power of God flowing through them as they exercised the gifts of the Spirit, but they didn't know how to control themselves. They began to think more highly about themselves than they should. Here is some of the additional counsel given to them by Paul.

"But God has chosen the foolish things of the world to put to shame the wise, and God has chosen the weak things of the world to put to shame the things which are mighty;"
1 Corinthians 1:27

This reveals God's way. God has made the choice, Paul says, to use weakness to overcome the mighty in worldly estimation. God's design is that we allow ourselves to be used by Him to confound the wise and powerful.

"I was with you in weakness, in fear, and in much trembling."
1 Corinthians 2:3

Paul even reminds them of his time with them at his first meeting there in Corinth. He started this ministry there and, though Acts tells us of some great and powerful things that happened there, Paul confesses his own personal weakness. God used that weakness to begin this great work.

*"But we have this treasure in earthen vessels, that the excellence of **THE POWER MAY BE OF GOD AND NOT OF US**."*
2 Corinthians 4:7 (emphasis mine)

Clearly he is stating that the treasure the Gospel of Christ, His light being shined on our dark souls, of being used by God, is related to God's power easily being recognized as coming from Him, and not from us. This "earthen vessel" is in respect to our created condition. Adam was created from the dirt of the ground. We are "dirt made" beings being used by the God of the universe, showing His great power in us for His glory.

> *"No, much rather, those members of the body*
> *which seem to be weaker are necessary."*
> 1 Corinthians 12:22

I love the Epistle to the church at Ephesus. This was a magnificent city, second only to Rome, in the empire. The renowned temple of Diana (Artemis) was located there, creating a huge spiritual battle over the area. The demon spirits had enjoyed uninterrupted control over the area, but the light of Christ was beginning to shine in the darkness. Those evil spirits had developed strong holds over the region as well as in the individual lives of the citizens of Ephesus.

When he was imprisoned in Rome, Paul writes to the church and encourages them to walk in the power of God, not their own.

> *"And what is the exceeding greatness of His power*
> *toward us who believer, according to the working*
> *of His mighty power which He worked in Christ*
> *when He raised Him from the dead and seated*
> *Him at His right hand in the heavenly places."*
> Ephesians 1:19-20

These verses are part of the prayer Paul told them he was praying for them. He desired that their eyes be opened in such a way that there was great spiritual understanding (again because of the great spiritual battle that was waging for this city).

Part of this understanding was that they recognize the power of God at work in them. Not their own power, but God's power. Not just any kind of power, but that which God exhibited when He raise Jesus from the dead.

> *"And you He made alive, who were dead in*
> *trespasses and sins, in which you once walked*
> *according to the course of this world, according to*
> *the prince of the power of the air, the spirit who*
> *now works in the sons of disobedience."*
> Ephesians 2:1-2

Here, Paul is reminding them of the enormous change that has taken place in their lives by the power of God. They were on the other side. The prince of the power of the air, satan, had ruled them by his power in the spirit realm. No more. They were delivered, but that has caused conflict and the demonic realm is ready to fight back.

> *"Of which I became a minister according to the*
> *gift of the grace of God **GIVEN TO ME BY THE***
> ***EFFECTIVE WORKING OF HIS POWER.***"
> Ephesians 3:7 (emphasis mine)

As the Apostle was writing to them about the call that God has placed on his life, he reminds them of God's grace that has been so freely given to them. He talks of the mystery of God, that the Gentiles might be acceptable as children of God. This was of no small importance to this former "Pharisee of the Pharisees," trained in Judaism by the great teacher Gamalial. His religious training created a "law" mentality. Only by keeping the law of God, as given to Moses, could anyone be considered holy or worthy. No Gentile could ever meet those demands without turning his/her back on their past and embracing Judaism as a convert (Proselyte). Paul recognizes that this shift in his thinking and acting it is done by the "effective working of His power." Only God can work these types of changes in everyone.

Paul again tells them how he is interceding for them and again it involves understanding the power of God at work in their lives and in their city. He knows that they have to be strong, but that strength must come from within through the power of God.

"That He would grant you, according to the riches
of His glory, to be strengthened with might
through His Spirit in the inner man."
Ephesians 3:16

As he finished this prayer, he writes one of my favorite verses in Scripture:

"Now to Him who is able to do exceedingly
abundantly above all that we ask or think,
according to the power that works in us,"
Ephesians 3:19-21

I have noticed over the years that most people tend to just quote the first half of this verse. It's easy to see why, that will get you all pumped up. I often go into Bible bookstores and look at the beautiful paintings and prints they have framed. Usually this great verse is only quoted in part. I love preaching on that part. Let me give you a little taste of my excitement. This verse would be great if it only said, "God is able to do all that we ask or think." It just solidifies the message and the ability into our minds. It would be even better adding in the "Above" all that we ask or think. Yeah, above sounds great. Then we add "Abundantly" to the above all and it's getting wilder in here. But it actually adds another word, "Exceedingly" – Abundantly – Above – All!! I might have to take a break so I can shout and run around my kitchen table here.

But there is the second part of the verse that lays some of the outcome at our feet. "According to" should make us stop and think. God can do all this that we ask or think in accordance to or with the power that is working in us. We need His power at work in us in order for Him do it. This is not something that we work up, it has to do with surrender and allowing Him to work through our weakness.

As he concludes his epistle, he focuses again on the need, in that demonic stronghold, for the correct type of strength.

"Finally, my brethren, be **_STRONG IN THE_**
_LORD__, and in the_ **_POWER OF HIS MIGHT_**_._
Put on the whole armor of God, that you may be
able to stand against the wiles of the devil. For
we do not **_WRESTLE_** *against flesh and blood,*
but against principalities, against powers,
against the rulers of the darkness of this age,
against spiritual hosts of wickedness in the
heavenly places. Therefore take up the whole
armor of God, that you may be able to
WITHSTAND *in the evil day, and having done*
all, to **_STAND_**_."_
Ephesians 6:10-13 (emphasis mine)

We are not just to be strong in our own might, but he definitively asserts that our strength must come from the Lord and our power from His might. The battle is spiritual. The enemies he names are the ranks of demonic spirits under the command of the devil.

Our strength is greatest when we surrender our part to Him and allow the Father to infuse us with His power. I can remember as a young boy getting ready to cut open a watermelon in the back yard. We had a picnic table and I can remember trying to move the table so we can fit more lawn chairs around it. I just needed to move one end around. I tried to pick it up and swing it around, but it was too heavy for me. Suddenly, from behind, my dad reached around me and "we" picked it up without a problem and we slid it right where we (he) wanted it. I might have been able to do it ½ inch at a time. My strength would have grown less and less as I kept trying. But when my father showed up, it all changed. I was no stronger than before. But his strength (in spite of my weakness) allowed me to think I had helped move the table. The reality was that dad's muscle got it done; I was just the one who started it. If you had been around, there would have been no doubt in your mind who actually carried the weight and performed the act.

That is simplistic, but who says it has to be difficult or confusing? God works through (or in spite of) our feeble efforts. He is looking for willing vessels (earthen vessels) through which to send the current of His divine power. When we try to work in our own power, we may get some things done (a ½ inch at a time). However, as we allow our Heavenly Father to the situation, He places His hands over ours and lifts the obstacle out of the way and accomplishes the supernatural. When that happens, all glory is given to Him, because everyone knows that we don't have that type of strength, might or power.

CHAPTER FOURTEEN

WE GIVE PRAISE BY OUR

RECOGNITION:

"And The Glory Forever, Amen"

Finally, we *GIVE* praise by our recognition of the glory of God. He should always strive to give Him the glory. If you study the Westminster Shorter

Catechism, one of the first questions asked is, "What is the chief end of man."

The answer given is, "Man's chief end is to glorify God, and to enjoy Him forever." God deserves the glory. He deserves the credit, gratitude, acknowledgment, thanks, appreciation and tribute.

All of that sounds great and Scriptural, but what does that look like in our daily lives? How are we to *GIVE* glory to God? There are several ways that are practical and easily definable according to the Scriptures. We will consider the following ways of *GIVING* glory to God:

1. In our body
2. In our spirit
3. With our mind
4. With our mouth
5. In all we do
6. Even in Heaven

In keeping with our method of study, let's look carefully at the meaning of the word glory. In the Greek it is the word "dox'-ah (δόξα). Perhaps you have even sung the "Doxology" at your church before. This is the same word. It is translated "glory" 145 times in the New Testament and "glorious" another 10 times. The other 12 times it is used it is translated honor (6), praise (4) or dignity (2). It is from the base word "dokeo" (to think, or to think good of). Its overall meaning is to think highly of with dignity, glory, honor, praise or worship.[1] Though both Old and New Testaments deal with the concept of the physical glory of God as it is expressed among His people, this is not the meaning in this text. The glory of God in the tabernacle, temple and on the mount of transfiguration is not our focus. We are speaking here of the credit God receives from His creation. The praise given to Him by those He has saved and redeemed. The honor that is bestowed upon Him through the acts and words of those who name Him as Father, Lord and Master.

IN OUR BODY

Did you ever think that you could *give* glory to God with your body? Most of my developmental years I was surrounded by people who found their relationship best expressed by the external things. For example here is a quick list of a dozen things considered unacceptable if you were going to be called a Christian in their denomination or if one follows their more legalistic theology.

1. Guys can't have long hair
2. Girls have to put their long hair up
3. Boys can't wear faded jeans
4. Women can't wear pants
5. You always have to wear long sleeves
6. You can't wear jewelry (even wedding bands)
7. Women have to wear hosiery
8. You can't drink any alcohol
9. No make up for girls
10. No cussing
11. Do not smoke
12. Don't wear shorts

This is just off the top of my head. There were many other things that could possible fill another book if I took the time to really think about it. It is understandable, then, for me to gravitate towards legalism when I think about glorifying God in my body. But as I have tried to understand these things in light of the New Covenant in Jesus' blood, the love and grace of God and a classical hermeneutic, I have found myself not holding to legalism as the main way of showing glory to God in my body. Let's see how the Apostle Paul framed these words in his letter to Corinth.

> *"Flee sexual immorality. Every sin that a man does is outside the body, but he who commits sexual immorality sins against his own body. Or do you not know that your body is the temple of the Holy Spirit who is in you, whom you have from God, and you are not your own? For you were bought at a price;* **THEREFORE GLORIFY GOD IN YOUR BODY** *and in your spirit, which are God's."*
> 1 Corinthians 6:18-20 (emphasis mine)

At 10 years old I became very interested in art. My parents were open-minded to my pursuit enough to actually pay for private art lessons. It started out like coloring in a book. Then I began to draw shapes with chalk. Water color was the next logical step and finally I was working with oils like the big boys, the masters. I look back on those old paintings and realize that they are not so great, but my parents and family always made a big deal out of the works I completed. Even as I am writing this at my kitchen table, there is an oil painting I did hanging on the wall behind me. What makes this piece worth hanging isn't just my signature at the bottom, besides the sentimental value, it has a nice frame. A so-so picture can become great with the right framing around it. This frame should draw attention to the painting. It should help us see the value of the work. It should attract, but not to itself.

In this verse we must understand how Paul "frames" these words so that we can understand the total context (picture).

The main picture here is that your body is God's. As a Christian you were bought (redeemed) with the price of the life of the Messiah (Jesus). It is clear from the verses leading up to the statement that he is making reference to immorality. Sexual sins are a sin against the body. By keeping yourself away from sexual sin, you are giving glory to God in your body. You are validating His claim as Lord and Creator when you submit this area of your life to Him. Paul also dealt with the body part in his letter to the Church in Rome.

> *"I beseech you therefore, brethren, by the mercies of God, that you present your bodies a living sacrifice, holy, acceptable to God, which is your reasonable service."*
> Romans 12:1

Any student of the Bible will be able to tell you about the sacrificial rules and laws of the Old Testament. There are certain animals to be sacrifice. They are only acceptable in a certain condition. There are special days and rites to be followed in order for sacrifices to be recognized, acknowledged and ultimately received, by God.

Paul is drawing his readers a picture of that sacrificial system when he makes this comparison. We are to present to God. Give to Him our bodies. Not just our spirit and soul, our bodies. How? As living sacrifices. He's not asking for us to be killed and placed on an altar and set on fire, he is begging (beseeching) that we voluntarily surrender our bodies as a sacrifice. This should be considered as acceptable and holy (set apart) unto Him. We surrender and He received our surrender. Of course, one of the big problems with "living" sacrifices is that we have the tendency to try to crawl off the altar. This is an on-going, daily battle to remain surrendered to God on His altar so that we can fulfill our reasonable service to Him.

Though I have heard many sermons on the evil of smoking and drinking, which at times stretched the limit of Scriptural understanding, I cannot remember an occasion where I heard preaching on gluttony with the same "hell-fire" passion. Could it be that is because most of the preachers were well-fed and very round? They would have to be the first to the altar if they had expounded on that topic. Yet the Scripture is even clearer on that topic than smoking (actually not specifically condemned, but generically so) or drinking (as wine is all through the Bible).

I found over the years, that even those who have managed to keep themselves from the "dirty dozen" I listed at the beginning of the chapter do not necessarily always give God the credit for their abstinence. However the Holy Spirit leads you to glorify God in your body, please don't make it a hard and fast rule for all believers to follow. He is working on you and your surrender to Him. Others need to work on other areas of submission. Love one another, pray for one another and obey God's direction for YOU!

IN OUR SPIRIT

Perhaps this part is a little more difficult to comprehend. In my theological understanding, we are a complex trinity. We are made of three distinct, yet interrelated parts. We are a spirit, we have a soul and we live in a body. In the realm of surrender we are told that our bodies are to be living sacrifices, our souls are to be saved and our spirits are made alive in Christ. Let's look at the 1 Corinthians verses again with the emphasis placed on our spirits.

> *"Flee sexual immorality. Every sin that a man does is outside the body, but he who commits sexual immorality sins against his own body. Or do you not know that your body is the temple of the Holy Spirit who is in you, whom you have from God, and you are not your own? For you were bought at a price; therefore **GLORIFY GOD** in your body and **IN YOUR SPIRIT**, which are God's."*
> 1 Corinthians 6:18-20 (emphasis mine)

Our spirits are the part of our being with which God communicates. It is the element that is filled with the Holy Spirit, is resurrected and made new through His power. God designed that we be spiritual beings. Adam's uniqueness was in the fact that he was a spirit. That uniqueness died when he sinned. We are all given that fallen (dead) nature through our connection to him. We are "dead" in our trespasses and sins.

The original concept was that God would commune with our spirits, which would communicate to our souls and that to the body. Without this great model in place, we often allow our minds or our emotions and sometimes our self-will to dominate. At other times we just allow the body to dictate our actions.

How then are we, as resurrected spirit beings, to glorify God in our spirits? I believe we can glean the appropriate answer from the words of Jesus as the Apostle John penned them.

> *"But the hour is coming, and now is, when the true worshipers will* **WORSHIP THE FATHER IN SPIRIT AND TRUTH; FOR THE FATHER IS SEEKING SUCH TO WORSHIP** *Him.*
> *God is Spirit, and those who worship Him must* **WORSHIP IN SPIRIT** *and truth."*
> John 4:23-24 (emphasis mine)

The backdrop of this passage is very interesting. Jesus had insisted that He and His disciples travel through the territory of Samaria. The disciples were told by Jesus to go into a town and get some food. While they were gone, a lady came to the well near where Jesus was sitting. As she began to draw water, Jesus asked her for a drink. This led to a full discussion on the water of life that eventually caused her to believe in Him. Part of the discussion was about worship.

Worship can be divisive at times. The Jews believed that the true temple of God was in Jerusalem and that this was the only acceptable place to offer sacrifice and worship God. The Samaritans had their own mountain for worship and sacrifice. This lady tries to lure Jesus into this dialogue. These verses are His insightful answer to her. God wants us to worship Him in spirit.

By worshipping God, we bring glory to Him. He is lifted up and praised. Glory is attributed to Him when we move beyond just our physical or soulish (emotion, intellect and volition) worship to the realm of the spirit. When we are in tune with Him and His spirit, we begin to see all things with a new, fresh outlook.

WITH OUR MIND

In my opinion, the greatest creation of God is our minds. It is such an untapped resource of nearly limitless capacity. It can be channeled (when submitted to the reign of our spirit) in such a way as to bring great glory to God. It is the central control of our actions, reactions, emotions and will. You couldn't move your eyes across this page if your mind was not engaged in the process.

As a stroke victim, I am well aware of the power of the mind and the injury that can occur to the mind as well. Though I suffer no lasting physical effects (i.e. paralysis, slurred speech or poor muscle coordination), I often struggle with issues that seem more neurological. It took me quite a while to be able to speak well again. Though I welcomed the challenge to overcome any of the physical effects through both physical and occupational therapy, I was less than enthusiastic when it was time for speech therapy. This would increase my frustration and anxiety each time she came into my room. I had real problems communicating. I have just as much problem focusing when there was the slightest bit of noise or distraction in the room. My speech therapist would use flash cards of pictures and I was supposed to tell her what the picture was. Now this was not some Freudian ink blot picture test, this was a simple picture of a cat. Now I have known how to say and spell cat for years. (Even in several languages). But I couldn't for the life of me get the word "cat" out when she flashed that card. I felt stupid and helpless.

My writing was also affected as well as my ability to recall numbers. I am so thankful for my wife; she encouraged me and stood by me through all of this frustration. I am much better today. Since then I have exceeded everyone's expectations (except my wife and kids). I spent three years as a music pastor and five years as a senior pastor. I went back to school for a season to study funeral directing, I became a certified crematory operator, I have owned two business and this is my fifth book. All of that has happened since my stroke. God has blessed me immensely. Most people cannot tell that I even had a stroke.

The mind is a powerful and "beautiful" thing. It is at its apex when it has submitted itself to its Creator, the God of the universe. Reason is an important function of the mind. Mankind stands apart from all the rest of creation because of his ability to reason. However, this capacity to reason has also been a steady downfall of the human race.

Eve fell prey to faulty reasoning when she listened to the serpent. Cain's rationalization and anger proved too much for him to handle and he became the first murderer. Over the ages there have many numerous groups of people who have thought of themselves as greater than other groups. This has opened the door to slavery. Military leaders have analyzed the battlefield and built great dynasties that were ultimately destroyed.

Each empire had its development of the mind to some degree, the most notable being the Hellenistic

(Greek). Rome capitalized on Greek wisdom and inserted much of it into its culture. After the fall of Rome, the world was in a great state of flux and reasoning took a back seat to surviving through the dark ages.

In the 17th and 18th centuries, the age of enlightenment began. As never before, the entire globe awoke from its intellectual slumber and tried to make sense of its existence, purpose and faith. Different countries and cultures defined and refined their stance on everything from social/political issues to music and the arts.

Great minds were discovered in most areas of thought. Consider these leaders of the Age of Enlightenment:

Sir Isaac Newton	John Locke
Mozart	Beethoven
Rousseau	Thomas Jefferson

This list could continue for pages, but you can see some of the evolution of thought represented in only these six individuals. Sadly, as this enlightenment happened, the foundation of Scripture was eventually considered suspect and a slow but distinct break from Biblical standards began.

Critical thinking is necessary, but what one can reason is not the end. The thought process that elevates only its thoughts, and perhaps those of others, with no regard to the Creator is built on sinking sand that will eventually collapse. With no Scriptural foundation, the entire process was without direction and we see some of the most outlandish concepts being delivered on nearly every sphere of life. This appeared in the fact that the political, economic, development, archaeological and religious realms all coming to different conclusions because they did not have a common point of reference, God.

Then the most outrageous of claims began to be made, that God Himself was not real. They claimed that He was the creation (rather than Creator) of man's under evolved reasoning abilities. Jesus' life, death and resurrection became a crutch, a figment of the imagination of weaker and less intelligent people. Only what could be studied, quantified and measured was considered of any real value. Slowly God was being pushed out of the mind of those with any education.

Thus we can see the need for the timeless truth as declared by Paul in his letter to the Romans:

> *"And do not be conformed to this world, but be* ***TRANSFORMED BY THE RENEWING OF YOUR MIND****, that you may prove what is that good and acceptable and perfect will of God."*
> Romans 12:2 (emphasis mine)

Over the centuries, we have developed our thinking processes based on those individual's work who did not give God His proper place in reasoning. We must renew our minds in order to understand the full scope of God's intent. God does not desire that we return to the Dark Ages, nor does He want us to underutilize the great gift He gave us in the mind. On the contrary, He wants us to develop and grow. He longs that we see the majesty of the mind He created for us.

I believe we will be able to use parts of our brain that we have never cognitively accessed when we are in His presence. This renewing process will begin by changing the foundation of our reasoning process. Our house of wisdom must be held in suspect if it cannot abide the foundation of Scripture.

Paul also speaks to the Roman Church about the importance of being with one mind, thinking the same things in regard to God, Jesus, The Holy Spirit, our purpose and eternity. When we are like-minded toward one another, we can bring great glory to God.

> *"Now may the God of patience and comfort grant you to be like-minded toward one another, according to Christ Jesus, **THAT YOU MAY WITH ONE MIND** and one mouth **GLORIFY THE GOD AND FATHER OF OUR LORD JESUS CHRIST**."*
> Romans 15:5-6 (emphasis mine)

This brings glory to God, because it is the result of the surrender of human reasoning. Mankind, no matter how highly he thinks of himself, is the creation of God and in no way God's equal. When we realize this and come together with this same mentality, God is seen and proved to be the Wisdom of all.

WITH OUR MOUTH

We are beginning to understand that out of the mouth of a person flows what he really believes. Some people have considered such little misstatements as "Freudian slips," but though they are not necessarily a person's reasoned thoughts; they are part and partial of what they have allowed into their minds. Even the

Psalmist realized the importance of the connection between thoughts and speaking.

> *"Let the words of my **MOUTH** and the meditation*
> *of my heart   Be acceptable in Your sight,*
> *O LORD, my strength and my Redeemer."*
> Psalm 19:14 (emphasis mine)

Whatever we allow our mind to focus on will eventually be spoken. As we reason internally over issues and thoughts, we will in due course speak it out. We can, and should, give glory to God with our mouth. We should exalt Him and His name forever. His grace and mercy should always be on our lips. We should sing from our hearts of the goodness of God. He is worthy of all honor and glory, and we are lifted in all areas of our life when we verbally submit our praise to Him.

The longest book in the Bible is the book of Psalms. All 150 of these are to be sung or spoken in adoration to our God. The longest chapter in the Bible (119), as well as the shortest (117), is in the Psalms. So is the center chapter of all Scripture, Psalm 118. Consider how the author's of these chapters saw the importance of bringing glory and praise to God with our mouths.

> *"I will bless the Lord at all times; His praise shall*
> *continually be in my mouth."*
> Psalm 34:1

> *"He has put a new song in my mouth— Praise to*
> *our God; Many will see it and fear, And will trust*
> *in the Lord."*
> Psalm 40:3

"O Lord, open my lips, And my mouth shall show forth Your praise."
Psalm 51:15

"My soul shall be satisfied as with marrow and fatness, And my mouth shall praise You with joyful lips."
Psalm 63:5

"Let my mouth be filled with Your praise And with Your glory all the day."
Psalm 71:8

"I will greatly praise the Lord with my mouth; Yes, I will praise Him among the multitude."
Psalm 109:30

"All the kings of the earth shall praise You, O Lord, When they hear the words of Your mouth."
Psalm 138:4

"My mouth shall speak the praise of the Lord, And all flesh shall bless His holy name Forever and ever."
Psalm 145:21

Again, Paul places an emphasis on speaking the same together as the Church as well as being of one mind. The same Scripture in Romans instills this concept:

*"Now may the God of patience and comfort grant you to be like-minded toward one another, according to Christ Jesus, **THAT YOU MAY***

__WITH__ one mind and __ONE MOUTH GLORIFY__
__THE GOD AND FATHER OF OUR LORD__
__JESUS CHRIST__."
Romans 15:5-6 (emphasis mine)

We are encouraged and expected to lift our voice of
praise to God. We are to glorify Him verbally alone and
in one accord, as one mouth, even in the quoting of this
great prayer together.

IN ALL WE DO

"Therefore, whether you eat or drink, or whatever
you do, __DO ALL TO THE GLORY OF GOD__."
1 Corinthians 10:31 (emphasis mine)

No matter how hard we try, we cannot truly
compartmentalize our physical or mental lives from the
Spiritual. Our body, soul and spirit are intertwined. The
only way to separate our soul and spirit from our body is
through what we know of as death! In our life, we daily
see the interaction of the tripartite nature. If we learn to
live with the correct/biblical view of the flow of our
decision, then we will begin to see ways to give God glory
in everything. Whatever we are doing, we can do it in
such a way as to bring honor, glory or recognition to our
Heavenly Father.

This is verse has been pulled out and used for
many legalistic justifications. Some of the rules the
church used to have (as we mentioned earlier) were based
on man's over-development of this verse. But, in our day
and age, this verse seems to have received little to no

attention. We must realize that we are God's emissaries on the earth. We are called His ambassadors. Whatever we do, how we speak and how we react are all reflected on to Him. We represent Him to those who know we are believers. The so called, "Prince of Preachers" is an English Baptist minister named C. H. Spurgeon. He was a great speaker and full of the power of the Spirit. His church grew into the largest attendance in the world at that time. He is often quoted in sermons, books, articles and theological treatise. I have often found his position on smoking cigars somewhat humorous and provoking. After speaking once, he was followed by Dr. Pentecost who was to help make the message practical and offer a type of response to the message. He used the topic of smoking as an example of the "little sins" that will harm you. To that, Mr. Spurgeon rose and said,

> "Well, dear friends, you know that some men can do to the glory of God what to other men would be sin. And notwithstanding what brother Pentecost has said, I intend to smoke a good cigar to the glory of God before I go to bed to-night.
>
> "If anybody can show me in the Bible the command, 'Thou shalt not smoke,' I am ready to keep it; but I haven't found it yet. I find ten commandments, and it's as much as I can do to keep them; and I've no desire to make them into eleven or twelve.
>
> "The fact is, I have been speaking to you about real sins, not about listening to mere quibbles and scruples. At the same time, I know that what a man believes to be sin becomes a sin to him, and he must give it up. 'Whatsoever is

not of faith is sin' [Rom. 14:23], and that is the real point of what my brother Pentecost has been saying.

"Why, a man may think it a sin to have his boots blacked. Well, then, let him give it up, and have them whitewashed. I wish to say that I'm not ashamed of anything whatever that I do, and I don't feel that smoking makes me ashamed, and therefore I mean to smoke to the glory of God."[2]

Just as it would now, this caused quite a stir among the church. Here we see that Spurgeon was using this same verse in order to reason out his desire to smoke cigars. Either way it can be used for control or license, holiness or grace. As this controversy swelled into a crescendo of popular discussion, Spurgeon decided to respond to the issue by writing to the editor of the local newspaper:

"To the Editor of the Daily Telegraph.

SIR,

YOU cannot regret more than I do the occasion which produced the unpremeditated remarks to which you refer. I would, however, remind you that I am not responsible for the accuracy of newspaper reports, nor do I admit that they are a full and fair representation of what I said. I am described as rising with a twinkling eye, and this at once suggested that I spoke flippantly; but indeed, I did nothing of the kind. I was rather too much in earnest than too little.

I demur altogether and most positively to the statement that to smoke tobacco is in itself a sin. It may become so, as any other indifferent action may, but as an action it is no sin.

Together with hundreds of thousands of my fellow-Christians I have smoked, and, with them, I am under the condemnation of living in habitual sin, if certain accusers are to be believed. As I would not knowingly live even in the smallest violation of the law of God, and sin in the transgression of the law, I will not own to sin when I am not conscious of it.

There is growing up in society a Pharisaic system which adds to the commands of God the precepts of men; to that system I will not yield for an hour. The preservation of my liberty may bring upon me the upbraidings of many good men, and the sneers of the self-righteous; but I shall endure both with serenity so long as I feel clear in my conscience before God.

The expression "smoking to the glory of God" standing alone has an ill sound, and I do not justify it; but in the sense in which I employed it I still stand to it. No Christian should do anything in which he cannot glorify God; and this may be done, according to Scripture, in eating and drinking and the common actions of life.

When I have found intense pain relieved, a weary brain soothed, and calm, refreshing sleep obtained by a cigar, I have felt grateful to God, and have blessed His name; this is what I meant, and by no means did I use sacred words triflingly.

If through smoking I had wasted an hour of my time—if I had stinted my gifts to the poor—if I had rendered my mind less vigorous—I trust I should see my fault and turn from it; but he who charges me with these things shall have no answer but my forgiveness.

I am told that my open avowal will lessen my influence, and my reply is that if I have gained any influence through being thought different from what I am, I have no wish to retain it. I will do nothing upon the sly, and nothing about which I have a doubt.

I am most sorry that prominence has been given to what seems to me so small a matter—and the last thing in my thoughts would have been the mention of it from the pulpit; but I was placed in such a position that I must either by my silence plead guilty to living in sin, or else bring down upon my unfortunate self the fierce rebukes of the anti-tobacco advocates by speaking out honestly. I chose the latter; and although I am now the target for these worthy brethren, I would sooner endure their severest censures than sneakingly do what I could not justify, and earn immunity from their criticism by tamely submitting to be charged with sin in an action which my conscience allows.

Yours truly,

C. H. SPURGEON.
Nightingale Lane, Clapham, Sept. 23."[3]

In an effort to stop the development of a "Pharisaic system which adds to the command of God the precepts of men," Spurgeon used this dialogue to focus on God, not just on an issue. Today, one would be hard-pressed to find a minister who smokes, mainly because of the known health risks and the desire to treat the body as the temple of God. Yet the understanding of giving glory to God in all that we do is definitely not lost in this story. We are not exempt at any moment in life from representing God and bringing praise, honor and glory to Him. We should be walking, talking, working, living, praying, praising, fasting, and witnessing glory givers.

The Greek word "Doxa" appears in the Kings James Version of the New Testament 168 times in the following ways:

Glory	145
Glorious	10
Honor	6
Praise	4
Dignity	2
Worship	1[4]

Just from the sheer number of instances of use it is clear that we are to live our lives in such a way as to give glory, honor, praise, dignity and worship to our glorious God.

EVEN IN HEAVEN

The giving of glory to God is not just for this life only. Even a cursory reading of the book of, "The Revelation of Jesus Christ," (commonly just called

Revelation) shows the lasting and eternal giving of glory to God. The word glory is used 18 times in those 21 chapters. Much of it is directly related to expresses praise and honor to God as part of the worship if heaven.

Giving glory now, on this earth and in this life, are but precursors of the existence we will have before God. He is glory and will receive the glory from all creation. Jesus will be glorified for His wonderful act of love and devotion. All of heaven and earth will exalt Him as the King of kings and the Lord of lords.

FOREVER

The concept of "forever" or "eternal" is hard for us to comprehend. Each of us in America has at least two documents that prove we existed, our birth certificate and our death certificate. Both of these are date and time specific, down to the minute. If you look at your birth certificate you will find the month, day, date, year and time you may your screaming entrance into this world. That is considered you beginning (technically and spiritually it was at conception, but this is how we measure it). For the first couple of years your age is much more specific. At first your parents told people you were 5 days old, 21 days old etc. Then you were aged in weeks or months. Finally you are looked at in terms of years. At present, I am 53 years old; I would receive some bizarre looks if I went around telling people I am 642 months old.

At some point, unless some rapture or end time event happens, we will all breath our last and die. Someone, usually in the medical field, will decide exactly when that happened and it will be entered onto the official death certificate date and time. You age will be calculated in years, months and days.

I don't share that with you to be morbid, but to prove the point that we all think within the constraints of time. We know someone's beginning and end. We have all experience the passing of time.

I can remember sitting in second grade at Waverly Terrace Elementary School, just two blocks from my childhood home in Columbus, GA, staring at the clock. I was waiting for the final bell so I could hit the play grounds after school. I would run home and report in, then be outside at the school yard and playgrounds with my friends.

I remember getting out of school at 3:15. The last 15 minutes of the day seemed to pass so slowly. I would watch the second hand on that huge round clock. If there wasn't any noise, you could hear each second "click" as the hand moved. I watched it and if you had asked me then, I would have sworn that it was in slow motion.

Our lives have been marked by time in other ways. We spent years in elementary school, then middle school and finally high school. Then some of us spend more years in colleges.

Our jobs keep track of how many hours we work and how many days until we get paid. Our careers are marked by the years of experience we have in our profession. Even the government says we can retire at a certain age (in years) and at what age we can receive help with medical expenses.

Our history is marked in centuries and millennium. In 1492, Columbus sailed the ocean blue. July 4, 1776 is Independence Day in the United States. There are a host of other important historical dates, most recently is the attack on our country on September 11, 2001.

With all of this emphasis in and around us on time and events one can easily understand the difficulty we have with expressing "forever" or "eternal." Even some of the numbers are hard for us to comprehend. Jesus died 2,000 years ago! That is beyond my grasp.

Our minds will one day be expanded to appreciate this concept, but not while we are here and alive. The thought that before there was anything or anyone, God existed is enough to cause us to blow a gasket (intellectually). We are not wired that way. Then to think that everyone who has ever lived is still out there in an eternal place of either blessing or damnation, and that we will also spend "forever" with our creator is a paradigm that is impossible to understand because we don't have a frame of reference.

The actual Greek word that has been translated here as "forever" is "aiōnios" (αἰώνιος).[5] It is usually translated as eternal or everlasting. The root word is "Aion (Aeon)" and age means an infinitely long time.[6]

This word sums up giving the recognition to God for His kingdom, power and glory. It also acknowledges that there will be no end to either of the three. His kingdom, His power and His glory are each perpetual and infinite. Angels and demons alike are aware of this truth. Our purpose on earth is to live our short lives (in comparison) in the awareness that the faith decisions we make while here will determine the type of eternal existence we will experience.

THE POWER OF THE AMEN

At the boarding school I attended for High School, we had some very unique and precious traditions. One of my favorite, looking back, involved our meal time. When the time came for a meal, let's say lunch, we were able to take our books and papers to our room after the last bell. Then the boys would all congregate just outside the chapel and wait for the bell. This wasn't a school type of buzzer, there was an actual bell. Someone (I never knew who) pulled the rope and rang it to let everyone know it was time to eat. This hungry mob of young men would race toward the building and enter the left door and the girls would enter the one on the right.

As you entered the dining hall there was singing. The choir director/music teacher (Ms. Reed) would be standing at the head of her table singing. All the other students and teachers would join in for a rousing rendition of some gospel tune. Each person went to his/her assigned table and stood behind a chair until the song was finished.

Ms. Reed would then call on someone to pray a prayer of blessing of the meal. You could hear a pin drop, hoping you wouldn't be the one called upon. It was a rather large dining hall, so it was usually difficult for everyone to hear the prayer, but I can speak from experience that the guys were paying extra special attention to hear one word. That one word would create a reaction like "sick'em" to a dog or "souie" to a pig. Once we heard that word it was time to dig in. You know the word. *AMEN!*

We find ourselves now at the end of a long road of studies and hopefully changes in our paradigm about this prayer. The final word is not just a religious way of ending a prayer. *Amen* means more than just "the end" or a fancy way of saying, "Goodbye." It is definitely more than appeared in the case above which was more like a code word for, "let's eat." It has a profound meaning in general and a unique use in particular in the New Testament.

The basic meaning of *AMEN* is, "So be it," or "Let it be done." To respond to a sermon, speech, or prayer with, "Amen" is to say both individually and collectively an agreement and a commitment to making it come to pass. Though there are similar words in Aramaic or Syriac, the basic use of the word is said to be Hebrew origin. This is one of the unique words of the Bible where there is no translation, but rather a transliteration as in the word "Hallelujah." The Hebrew pronunciation of the word was imported into the Greek of the early Church. Then it entered Latin and was then introduced to other Western languages.

Amen occurs first in Numbers 5:22 when a woman suspected of adultery responds to the Priest, "Amen, Amen." The word appears in the Old Testament around 30 times. The Hebraic root of the word and the application of it in Judaism are extremely exceptional. From an actual Hebrew scholar, we can better understand both the religious and the cultural importance of the word, *Amen*. Dr. Samuel Lebens is the chair of the Association for the Philosophy of Judaism, and has published a very interesting article on the significance of *Amen*.

"In different contexts, the word 'Amen' seems to mean slightly different things. Rabbi Yehuda bar Siman said that in response to the Priestly Blessings, the word 'Amen' contains three of its regular meanings all bound up together (Devarim Rabba Parshat Ki Tavo 1).

The first of the three meanings of 'Amen' is the legal function of taking an oath upon the utterer. The book of Numbers (chapter 5) describes a ceremony in which the priest, acting as a legal functionary, reads out the words of an oath on behalf of a certain woman; the woman merely has to say 'Amen' and the oath becomes hers. When you say 'Amen' to the priestly blessings, you are taking an oath-like responsibility upon yourself. You are, as it were, swearing to become the sort of person who is worthy of receiving the blessings that are here on offer. You are, in short, committing to becoming a better Jew.

The second of the three meanings of 'Amen' is the function of accepting upon yourself the negative conditions of a transaction. When you sign the rental agreement, you accept upon yourself the condition that if you break something, you're going to pay a big surcharge. If you decide to sign, that's because you've considered your options, and you think that the risk is worth taking. When the Jewish people entered the land of Israel, they were to enact a ritual that Moses described in Deuteronomy 27. In the ritual, the Levites would describe the blessings and the curses associated with the Torah; the blessings that would accrue if we observed its statutes and the curses that would accrue if we didn't. In response to each curse, the entire nation said, 'Amen.' In so doing, they were accepting that having the Torah is worth the consequences of not keeping it. When you say 'Amen' in response to the Priestly Blessing, it means that you accept that the burden of the Torah is worth it – you've read the small print, and you're willing to sign up.

Finally, the third meaning alluded to by the Midrash, is that 'Amen' can mean 'let it be so.' When you say 'Amen' to the Priestly Blessing, you express the hope that the divine grace and the divine peace described in the blessing really will descend upon you."[7]

There are a greater number of instances where the AMEN is used in the New Testament. There are over 50 instances just in the Synoptic Gospels with another 25 in the Gospel of John.

Also unique to the New Testament is the use of *AMEN* at the beginning of a saying as it introduces a new thought rather than the traditional use that responds to words of a previous speaker or thought. The King James Version uses the translation, "Verily, verily, I say unto you" in those instances, but it is the same word. So in effect Jesus was saying, "Amen, Amen, I say unto you."

We use *Amen* most often as a word of agreement. If the minister is preaching and says something with which you agree, you may respond by saying, "Amen." At times, when the preacher knows that agreement will activate the word in your spirit, he may ask for an, "Amen" from the congregation.

Saying, "Amen" means more than just ascent to the words that have been said, it is an activation of those words into your life. There is power in the words we speak and it is important "when" we speak them. This is why it is important to listen more than we speak. We must know what we are activating into our life. Understanding what you are saying, "So be that unto me" may cause us to be slow in responding.

"For all the promises of God in Him are Yes, and
in Him Amen, to the glory of God through us."
2 Corinthians 1:20

This is a great verse of activation. All of the promises of God in Him (Jesus Christ) are in agreement (yes) and activated (amen) for God's glory through us. There are three people spoken of in the verse, God, Jesus and us. God has given many promises and they are all available to be fulfilled in your life, activated by you through agreement. This is done because of the completed work of Jesus for us. Allow me to expand on this a moment.

In the book of Deuteronomy chapters 27 & 28, Moses is directed by God to divide the people and place them on two mountains with the Levites (priests) in the valley between. It is interesting to note that when the Levies begin to pronounce the curses of the law, they all shout, "Amen." However, when they pronounce the blessings, it is silent. No "Amens" are said. The reason for the silence in that they knew in their own strength they would not be able to fulfill the law and they couldn't experience the promise if they disobeyed. They were able to agree with the curse because they knew of their sinfulness, but not the blessing.

We can agree with the blessing because it is not in our strength or obedience but in Him that we can receive the promises of God. We can activate our faith in and through Jesus so that we may receive the promises of our Father. Here is one interesting note in regard to cursing and blessing (Amen). The last word in the Old Testament is "curse" and the last word in the New Testament is "Amen." Before Jesus' work on the cross, the curse was upon mankind. Jesus took the curse (cursed is anyone who hangs on a cross) for us. Now we are able, in Him, to say "Amen" to the blessing.

Finally, remember that Jesus revealed that one of His names is "the Amen." He is the, "So Be It" of God.

"And to the angel of the church
of the Laodiceans write,
'These things says the Amen, the Faithful and
True Witness, the Beginning of the creation of
God:'"
Rev. 3:14

Afterword

DON'T STOP! Often people are tempted to skip sections like this thinking it is just a summary or restatement of what they have already read. NOT SO! I have some things that must be said in order for all that you have read to make its maximum impact on your life.

In this modern age, technology is always changing. If you buy a computer, it seems out of date by the time you take it out of the box. Nearly every time your cell phone contract is up for renewal (usually every 2 years) there are new, better, faster and fancier phones ready to lure you back into the contract. Many times the cell provider will allow you to get the newest phones mid-way through your contract if you sign up for an extension to your contract.

New inventions are always taking our technology to the next level. Companies are constantly competing for our business and attention, so they need the newest gadget that will turn our heads. One of my best friends, Jim Odom, works in the robotics industry. His company designs automated machines, usually out of forklifts, that will do repetitive functions. The forklift will go to a certain part in the warehouse and pick up a stack of pallets that are loaded down with heavy material and transport them to another section of the warehouse and create a stack there. This will happen at whatever intervals the machine is programmed to do it. Many of these machines will automatically move materials all day and be charged all evening. This is all possible because of its programming. It reduces cost, liability and there is no need for the constant oversight of a manager. It also doesn't require several people to learn how to work a forklift. Even his company's technology is changing rapidly.

I say that to help you realize that the title of this book, though appropriate when written, may soon seem "out of date" or "old school." 4G communication is the thing now, but soon it may be 5G. Bobby Doty, Vice President of Business accounts at my bank, and my friend, wisely suggested I include another G in this conclusion so that we aren't dated. Everyone knows there's always room for more. This is the desert plate. My son, Randall, used to tell us how full he was at dinner. He just couldn't eat any more. Then Kim would talk about some cake, or a bowl of ice cream and he would jump to attention. "I thought you were full," she would say. He would reply, "There is always room for ice cream." So, no worries mate. I've got your fifth G so we can remain fresh for a little while longer.

5TH "G"
GROUP

One item that has not been delved into during the length of this study must be addressed or the entire work would be a mockery of the gravest sort. There will no doubt initially be much support and agreement, however as we submerge ourselves into the deeper psyche of the modern church we will inevitably find resistance if not revilement towards this extra "G".

The unspoken topic is found in the plurality of the majority of the possessive pronouns. "Our" Father, Give "Us" this day "Our" daily bread, forgive "us" "Our" as "We" forgive "our, Lead "us" Deliver "Us".

Clearly this prayer was not taught as in individualized way. It is not "MY Father who is in Heaven." NO! It is always in the plural. Just like all of Christianity is not to be an individualized relationship. It finds its greatest witness or testimony in the fact that it takes place in a congregation of believers.

The writer to the Hebrews clearly shows the importance of the community of believers:

"And let us consider one another in order to stir up love and good works, not forsaking the assembling of ourselves together, as is the manner of some, but exhorting one another, and so much the more as you see the Day approaching."
Hebrews 10:24-25

Why is this plurality of believers of such importance? What happens in the congregation that sets it apart from the individualized, personal, intimate worship of God? How has the move away from practicing our Christianity in community by deciding to go it alone with nature or in solitude affected His church? There are several critical areas that our independence from one another has caused harm to His body.

OUR TESTIMONY

Jesus was extremely clear when sharing with the disciples just before His crucifixion that their witness would be tied to their relationship with one another. There is meant to be, by God's design, a recognizable difference in the Church's love for each other as opposed to the love people see and experience outside of this fellowship.

> *"A new commandment I give to you, that you love*
> *one another; as I have loved you, that you also*
> *love one another. By this all will know that you*
> *are My disciples, if you have love for one another."*
> John 13:34-35

It is extremely interesting that the way they loved each other would be how "all" would know they were His disciples. It had nothing to do with their vast knowledge of Scripture. There is no mention of great healing and miraculous events. The only way Jesus declared the world would know, is by the way we love each other.

We cannot truly love one another if we are not in fellowship with each other. Can we truly "Agape" each other without the help of the Holy Spirit through our collective, corporate worship?

HIS PRESENCE

Yes, I have experienced God's presence alone. I have felt His leadership and encountered Him while standing on the sea shore near my home. Many people throughout Biblical history have spent amazing quiet times with the Father with no one else present. However, Jesus did make an unambiguous statement regarding His presence to the disciples.

"Again I say to you that if two of you agree on earth concerning anything that they ask, it will be done for them by My Father in heaven. For where two or three are gathered together in My name, I am there in the midst of them."
Matthew 18:19-20

In order to qualify for this unique promise of His presence, we must be meeting together. It does not require hundreds or thousands, but it does require more than just one.

This reminds me of the three Hebrew young men who were cast into the fire because they refused to bow to an idol. After a while, the king looked inside the furnace and realized that the Son of God was in the fire with those young men who didn't die, or even get burned.

We can see throughout Scripture that there are differing aspects of God that are revealed at certain times as His glory is made manifest. Jesus is promising a distinct manifestation will take place when His people are gathered together in His name.

It is in our best interest to consistently and continually join together in order to create the atmosphere where we receive this manifestation.

RESTORATION

*"Brethren, if a man is overtaken in any trespass,
you who are spiritual restore such a one in a
spirit of gentleness, considering yourself lest you
also be tempted."*
Galatians 6:1

The Church is to show gentleness in helping anyone who has sinned be restored. We can't fulfill this essential function without being in fellowship through the love of Christ. We, by our very nature, will strive to control and force people into our mold of thinking and behavior. We need to be in relationship with one another so that we can trust each other during these times of restoration.

BEAR BURDENS

"He ain't heavy, he's my brother." That's an old spiritual song, but it shares a provocative truth. We are to help carry one another. As the family of God our responsibility is to assist our brothers and sisters in carrying their burdens.

*"Bear one another's burdens, and so fulfill the
law of Christ."*
Galatians 6:2

Sharing the load is part of our duty. Going it alone not only keeps you from having access to someone when you need it, it also leaves some needy Christians in a position of weakness because you aren't there to help.

PRAYER

We are also expected to join with each other in prayer. We should have our own daily time alone with our Father where we commune with Him. That is obvious. But what is also unmistakable is our responsibility to unite our prayers and stand together in agreement.

"Confess your trespasses to one another, and pray for one another, that you may be healed. The effective, fervent prayer of a righteous man avails much."
James 5:16

We cannot continue to stand in a position of spiritual warfare alone. We are to join arms together and hold one another up in the Spirit. It is not a solitary position when we storm the heavenlies in prayer, it is a collective. There is power in agreement. We must, as the verse says, not only confess our sins to one another, but to pray together and we will see the miraculous hand of God bring healing to our brothers and sisters in the Lord. We are seeing the body fall prey to sickness because of our unwillingness to join together and see God move in our congregation.

ANOINTING

As we saw earlier in the book, there is power in the unity of the body. When we are together and submit to one another in love, there is power and anointing according to the Psalmist.

> **Behold, how good and how pleasant it is**
> **For brethren to dwell together in unity!**
> *It is like the precious oil upon the head,*
> *Running down on the beard,*
> *The beard of Aaron,*
> *Running down on the edge of his garments.*
> *It is like the dew of Hermon,*
> *Descending upon the mountains of Zion;*
> *For there the LORD commanded the blessing—*
> *Life forevermore.*
> Psalm 133

We are not able to be in this type of unity if we don't share our time of worship with the purpose of God clearly set before us. When we have that unity, it produces an anointing that creates an atmosphere for the demonstration of the supernatural power of God. God, in Christ, intends for us to be unified so that the power of Almighty God might be displayed in our midst. The blessing of God is commanded where there is unity. Many are living without that blessing when they are not united with a fellowship of believers.

ACCOUNTABILITY

God has made it clear throughout the whole of Scripture that we are to hold each other accountable. I have written an entire book on this topic, _Yes You Can, You Just Need Help!_ There is a divine mandate to help each other become people of integrity through personal accountability. We cannot do that without a purposeful submission to the body of Christ.

We can find strength and comfort in this submission. According to the Teacher in Ecclesiastes, these types of relationships will bring several blessings.

> _Two are better than one,_
> _Because they have a good reward_
> _for their labor._
> _For if they fall, one will lift up his_
> _companion._
> _But woe to him who is alone when he falls,_
> _For he has no one to help him up._
> _Again, if two lie down together,_
> _they will keep warm;_
> _But how can one be warm alone?_
> _Though one may be overpowered by another,_
> _two can withstand him._
> _And a threefold cord is not quickly broken._
> Ecclesiastes 4:9-12

First, he mentions that there is a good reward for the labor when two are working together. They help each other from falling and by aiding the other if one does fall. The cool of loneliness is not effective because they are together. They help one another from being overpowered in the battle.

This accountability can take many forms as in a mentor/mentee relationship, an accountability group, couples helping each other, spouses agreeing together or two individuals in a developing accountability relationship. The context of that relationship is to be found in a strong commitment to Scriptural truths with which all of the parties agree. This should take place in the development of the congregation.

TEACHING

One of the five-fold ministry gifts that the Apostle Paul mentions that is given to the Church by our Lord Jesus Christ is that of a teacher.

"And He Himself gave some to be apostles, some prophets, some evangelists, and some pastors and teachers, for the equipping of the saints for the work of ministry, for the edifying of the body of Christ, till we all come to the unity of the faith and of the knowledge of the Son of God, to a perfect man, to the measure of the stature of the fullness of Christ; that we should no longer be

*children, tossed to and fro and carried about with
every wind of doctrine, by the trickery of men, in
the cunning craftiness of deceitful plotting, but,
speaking the truth in love, may grow up in all
things into Him who is the head—Christ— from
whom the whole body, joined and knit together by
what every joint supplies, according to the
effective working by which every part does its
share, causes growth of the body for the edifying
of itself in love."*
Ephesians 4:11-16

All of these gifts, but that of a teacher in particular, involves the development of people together. Teaching requires more than just some sporadic interaction. It is not just a periodic motivational speech.

To teach requires that someone must be learning. To learn means that the material must be presented thoughtfully and purposefully is such a way as to develop the confidence of the student that he/she is assimilating the information so that they can recall it for testing and utilization in a real world context. By its very nature, teaching requires regular meaningful interaction. This takes place in our churches through our coming together regularly.

BODY

Other thoughts arise from the Scripture we just quoted. The church is compared to the function of a body. Jesus is said to be the head of this body and that we are His body. Bodies are made of many members and parts.

A body cannot function if it is not an interrelated incorporation of all those members and parts. My body would not work if my right leg was in my upstairs bedroom, my left leg was in the kitchen, my right arm was in the spare bedroom and my left arm was in my living room. The parts and members must be connected to the head and interrelated to one another.

CALLING/SENDING

From the beginning of the Church we can see how God has called certain people to fulfill His will in specific ways and that is recognized by the Church entity. How that calling is acknowledged by the body is important and the subsequent sending of ministers into the ministry is also important. Consider these verses regarding Paul and Barnabas:

"Now in the church that was at Antioch there were certain prophets and teachers: Barnabas, Simeon who was called Niger, Lucius of Cyrene, Manaen who had been brought up with Herod the tetrarch, and Saul. As they ministered to the Lord and fasted, the Holy Spirit said, 'Now separate to Me Barnabas and Saul for the work to which I have called them.' Then, having fasted and prayed, and laid hands on them, they sent them away."
Acts 13:1-3

It is easy to see the involvement of the church in this process. There was a calling of the men by God, then a recognition of that calling by the Church and finally a sending out of those called by the church through corporate fasting, prayer and the laying on of hands. This is far from an independent act.

EVALUATION

Those verses in Ephesians also speak about being tossed by the wind of doctrine, the trickery and craftiness of others. The tossing by the wind gives the word picture of an anchorless ship that is without a pilot at the helm. It is tossed left and then right. It rises and falls. There is no stability. We are cautioned to not allow this to happen.

This is spoken of in the context of the body. We are supposed to help evaluate how each other is interpreting the Scriptures and what doctrines we are following. If we are not in fellowship with a congregation and just "go to church on television," who is holding the message you receive to account?

It also seems as though the Spirit is opening the eyes of many these days with fresh, new revelation. Many Christians are excited about this move and have a tendency to follow those who preach these new things. How are we to evaluate these new revelations without talking with someone we trust? We need the context of relationship in order to discuss these matters and keep ourselves on track.

Let me ask you this question, how do you know you are walking in the truth? There have been so many strange and wrong interpretations of the Bible over the years. What makes your view correct? The Scripture says us for us to "try the spirits." We hear Paul's words to

Timothy admonishing us to "study to show ourselves approved." It is best "tried" in the accountability of a congregation of spirit-filled, spirit-led disciples.

ENCOURAGEMENT

"And let us consider one another in order to stir
up love and good works, not forsaking the
assembling of ourselves together, as is the manner
of some, but exhorting one another, and so much
the more as you see the Day approaching."
Hebrews 10:24-25

The overlying emphasis on this verse is not just an admonition to refrain from forsaking the assembling, but rather an incentive to encourage one another. Consider the four positive implications of this verse.

First: Consider one another. This means to look out for one another. The same Greek word is also translated behold, perceive or discover. Basically we need to keep an eye out for each other. God never intended for His Church to be made of Lone Rangers. He expects us to be watchful of one another.

Second: Stir one another. The King James Version used the word, "provoke." As I child, so my sisters tell me, I would often provoke them at the dinner table until they reacted and got in trouble. Here the writer is using the word in a positive light. We are to stir each other (provoke) to action. We are to motivate or stimulate one another to love (agape) and to perform good works. If we are trying to live our Christian life alone, we have a tendency to become "belly button inspectors."

That means we are always looking inward and not fulfilling the mission of God. We are to love each other as a testimony and do good works out of that love. The term "Good works" reminds me of the New Testament commendation, "Well done, good and faithful servant."

Third: <u>Assemble with one another</u>. Though it is said in the negative, the message is clear, "Keep meeting together." We are not to be like the others who have abandoned the assembly of the saints. We must gather together for these other purposes. This is not a legal or overbearing requirement to be at the Church every Sunday, Sunday night, Wednesday night and every other meeting in between. He is speaking about the "manner" of others. The custom of some to forsake or leave the fellowship, not miss an occasional Church service.

Fourth: <u>Exhorting one another</u>. This is an interesting word, exhort. We commonly think of it as an act of urging one another, pressing, insisting or pushing someone. That is not the actual meaning here. The majority of the time that this Greek word is used, it is translated, "beseech" as in Romans 12:1. It is also translated as comfort, desire, pray and entreat. I like to use the work *"Encourage"* to try and summarize all of the above. The Church is not just a bless me club, nor is it a place of torment and damnation (like so many who want to control others have tried to make it), it is a community intended to stir up and encourage. We all need both as we strive to fulfill God's will and to do His work in the world.

We should not seek to complete His plan in solitude. He has designed that we work together and create a model of His eternal Kingdom. The way this portion reads, we should be both giving and receiving the encouragement, "Exhorting one another." I will submit to you, that these four areas of thought are just as important as the weekly "sermon" or "message." These actions are pivotal in creating the climate for God's Spirit to move.

GROUP

I have always admired and respected the concept of American individualism. You know what I mean, the rugged, "I pulled myself up by my own boot straps," mentality and made myself into the success I am. I enjoy a full vocal rendition of "I did it my way" as much as any other red blooded American. But contrary to those statements are the statements of the Scripture. We are not encouraged or even allowed to "do it our way." God demands our submission to His way. The way He has implemented is that we be in communion and fellowship with one another.

As you allow the truths of this book to permeate your spirit, remember that each of the areas we have studied are meant to be fulfilled in the context of the body life of the Church. This group you have identified yourself with is the force through which God has moved to reach the world that He loves so much.

No doubt there have been seeds of truth in the chapters or sections of this study that have impacted your spirit. As you pray this prayer, let the Holy Spirit take those seeds and plant them into the good soil of your heart. Let Him cultivate around them and keep the weeds (the cares of this world) from choking the seed. Allow Him to nurture you, encourage you and develop you into a strong and faithful member of His Kingdom.

Now, before we are totally finished, let us once more pray together as our Lord taught us:

Our Father in heaven,
Hallowed be Your name.
Your kingdom come.
Your will be done
On earth as it is in heaven.
Give us this day our daily bread.
And forgive us our debts,
As we forgive our debtors.
And do not lead us into temptation,
but deliver us from the evil one.
For Yours is the kingdom
And the power
And the glory
Forever.
Amen."

Notes

Introduction

1. Charles L. Allen, *All Things Are Possible Through Prayer* (Fleming H. Revell Company, 1958) page 13
2. C. Peter Wagner, *Prayer Shield* (Ventura, CA, Regal Books, 1992) page 99
3. Adam C. Clarke, *Adam Clarke's Commentary On The Bible: The Gospel Of Matthew Chapter 6 Verse 9* (Bible Explorer 4, 2006)
4. H. Richard Niebuhr quoted in Philip Yancy, *What's So Amazing About Grace?* (Grand Rapids, MI: Zondervan, 1997), 13-14

Chapter One

1. Frederick Martin Lehman, *The Love Of God* (Public Domain)
2. Jack Frost, *Father's Heart Conference,* (My Notes: 1997)
3. Jack Frost, *ibid*
4. Richard J. Foster, *Celebration of Discipline* (San Franciso, CA: Harper & Row, 1988)

Chapter Two

1. Merriam-Webster.com/dictionary/sovereignty
2. The Holy Bible, New International Version (Holman Bible Publishers, 1986)

Chapter Three

1. Strong, *Strong's Exhaustive Concordance of the Bible*

Chapter Four

1. Myles Munroe, *Rediscovering the Kingdom* (Destiny Image Publishers, Inc., 2004) Page 26
2. Archives.gov/exhibits/charters/declaration_transcript.html
3. Abrahamlincolnonline.org/lincoln/speeches/gettysburg.htm
4. Myles Munroe, *Rediscovering the Kingdom* (Destiny Image Publishers, Inc., 2004) Page 27
5. Ibid, page
6. The New Spirit Filled Life Bible
7. merriam-webster.com/dictionary/eschatology

Chapter Five

1. twelvetribes.com/articles/crusades-gods-will
2. archive.org/stream/meinkampf035176mbp/meinkampf035176mbp_djvu.txt
3. merriam-webster.com/dictionary/will
4. James Strong, *Strong's Exhaustive Concordance Of The Bible* (World Bible Publishers, Iowa Falls, Iowa)
5. gotquestions.org/Gods-will.html#ixzz2ovegzSKm
6. Charles L. Allen, *God's Psychiatry* (Fleming H. Revell Company, Old Tappan, New Jersey, 1953) Page 109
7. battlecryprayerboard.org/gods-will-is-his-word-10-ways-god-reveals-his-will-for-us/

Chapter Six

1. God's Psychiatry p113
2. Celebration of Discipline p40
3. TREVOR'S SONG P106-107

Chapter Seven

1. christianinconnect.com/1john.htm
2. biblestudytools.com/lexicons/greek/kjv/hamartia.html

Chapter Eight

1. answers.yahoo.com/question/index?qid=20060924225420AAiIakm
2. mayoclinic.org/forgiveness/ART-20047692
3. Ibid

Chapter Ten

1. Strong's Exhaustive Concordance
2. Ibid
3. Ibid
4. Ibid
5. Ibid
6. Ibid

Chapter Eleven

1. Strongs
2. Adam Clarke's Commentary
3. Barnes' Notes on the New Testament
4. cyberhymnal.org/htm/m/i/mightyfo.htm

Chapter Twelve

1. Jamieson-Fausset-Brown Bible Commentary
2. Adam Clarke's Commentary

Chapter Thirteen

1. Little is Much When God is in it, Refrain, Words & Music: Kittie L. Suffield, 1924

Chapter Fourteen

1. Strong's Talking Greek & Hebrew Dictionary
2. http://www.spurgeon.org/misc/cigars.htm
3. Ibid
4. Strong's Talking Greek & Hebrew Dictionary
5. Ibid
6. http://dictionary.reference.com/browse/aeon
7. http://www.haaretz.com/jewish-world/the-jewish-thinker/the-power-of-amen-on-yom-kippur-1.466490

Index

Abed-Nego, 273
Abraham, 80, 81, 83, 84, 90,
    99, 108, 133, 135, 140,
    197, 227, 228, 230,
    263, 264, 265, 266,
    271
Achan, 248, 252-254, 256, 261
Adam, 32, 80, 98, 106, 113,
    173, 175, 176, 177,
    178, 179, 181, 248,
    249, 250, 271, 280,
    281, 286, 305, 333,
    345
Adam (second), 99, 286
Adonai, 83, 88, 89, 91, 93
Ahab, 81
Ai, 253
Allen, Dr. Charles L., 15, 141,
    152
Amelekite, 310, 311, 312
Apostles, 25, 26, 117, 118, 119,
    133, 151, 188, 286,
    312, 313, 377
Aramaic, 364
Ark of the Covenant, 24, 60, 86,
    255
Augustine, 124-125
Babylon, 273, 326
Bahamas Faith Ministries
International, 107
Bathsheba, 255, 256
Batman, 13
Beam, T.A., 155
    Trevor's Song, 155
Beethoven, 349
Ben-hadad, 81

Bethlehem, 166, 167, 168, 238,
    326
Biblical references: Acts **1:1**,
    117; Acts **1:2**, 117;
    Acts **1: 3**, 103, 117;
    Acts **1:4-8**, 325; Acts
    1:4, 118; Acts **1:5**,
    118; Acts **1: 6**, 103,
    118; Acts **1:7**, 118;
    Acts **1:8**, 55, 118; Acts
    2:23, 131; Acts **3:12**,
    332; Acts **4:28**, 131;
    Acts **5:27-32**, 312;
    Acts **8: 12**, 103; Acts
    13:1-3, 379; Acts
    15:13-18, 255; Acts
    19: 8, 103; Acts **28:**
    23, 103; Acts **28: 30-**
    31, 104; Amos **9:11**,
    255; 1 Chron. **29:11**,
    70, 299-300; 1 Chron.
    29:12, 70; Col. **1:9**,
    132; Col. **1:13**, 104;
    Col. **1:14**, 56, 186;
    Col. **1:16**, 283; Col.
    2:1, 187; Col. **2:10**,
    54; Col. **2:13**, 186;
    Col. **2:15,** 283; Col.
    3:3, 54; Col. **3:12-14**,
    201, 218-219; 1 Cor.
    1:27, 333; 1 Cor. **2:3**,
    333; 1 Cor. **4:20**, 104 ;
    1 Cor. **6:19**, 53; 1 Cor.
    6:18-20, 342, 345;
    1 Cor. **10:13**, 260;
    1 Cor. **10:31**, 354;
    1 Cor. **11:25**, 216;

1 Cor. **12:22**, 334;
1 Cor. **12:27**, 53; 2
Cor. **1:20**, 160, 367; 2
Cor. **4:7**, 333; 2 Cor.
5:21, 114; 2 Cor. **5:18**,
55; 2 Cor. **5:20**, 55; 2
Cor. **9:7**, 36; 2 Cor.
11:14, 290; 2 Cor.
12:7-10, 321; 2 Cor.
13:4, 330; Deut. **3:2**,
137; Deut. **6:4**, 87;
Deut. **7:9**, 85; Deut.
10:17, 85; Deut. **27**,
367; Deut.**28**, 367;
Eccl. **4:9-12**, 376; Eph.
1:5, 54, 132; Eph.**1:7**,
186; Eph. **1:11**, 134;
Eph. **1:19-20**, 334;
Eph. **2:1-2**, 335; Eph.
2:1-3, 179, 289; Eph.
2:4-7, 37, 53; Eph.
2:12, 116; Eph. **3:7**,
335; Eph. **3:16**, 336;
Eph. **3:19-21**, 336;
Eph. **3:19**, 53; Eph.
4:11-16, 377-378; Eph.
4:15-16, 151, 315;
Eph. **4:18**, 116; Eph.
4:30-32, 214, 218;
Eph. **5:17**, 131; Eph.
5:21-33, 308; Eph.
6:10-13, 290, 337;
Exod. **6:2-3**, 84; Exod.
13:21, 242; Exod.
14:1-4, 234-235; Exod.
15:13, 242; Exod.
15:26, 91; Exod. **20:7**,
78; Exod. **21:23-25**,
194; Exod. **33:12-17**,
233; Exod. **33:20**, 180;
Exek. **3:1**, 240; Exek.
4, 241, Exek. **5**, 241;
Exek. **28**, 290; Gal.
1:3-5, 279; Gal. **1:4**,
131; Gal. **6:1**, 373;

Gal. **6:2**, 374; Gal. **6:7**,
209; Gen. **1:1**, .87;
Gen. **1:26-28**, 175;
Gen. **3:1-6**, 249-250;
Gen. **5:1-3**, 178; Gen.
5:32, 137; Gen. **12:1-3**,
227; Gen. **12:4**, 137;
Gen. **14:18-20**, 83;
Gen. **16:13**, 84; Gen.
17:2, 84; Gen. **18:14**,
75; Gen. **21:33**, 85;
Gen. **22:5**, 264; Gen.
22:8, 264; Gen. **22:15-
18**, 265; Gen. **49:25**,
84; Heb. **2:11**, 55;
Heb. **4:16**, 54, 172;
Heb. **5:7-9**, 303-304;
Heb. **7:26-27**, 184;
Heb. **8:7-13**, 217; Heb.
9:11-15, 184-185; Heb.
10:14, 43; Heb. **10:24-
25**, 371, 380; Heb.
11:6, 152, 225; Heb.
11:16, 55; Heb. **11:17-
19**, 265; Heb. **12:14-
15**, 215; Heb. **13:17**,
309; Hos. **1**, 241; Isa.
60:1, 180; Isa. **6:5**,
180; Isa. **6:7**, 180; Isa.
14:12-15, 73, 289; Isa.
20:2-3, 240; Isa. **40:11**,
244; Isa. **40:29**, 331;
Isa. **49:10** , 244; Isa.
57:18 , 244; Isa. **58:11**,
244; Isa. **61:1-3**, 116;
Isa. **63:14**, 245; James
1:2-3, 259; James
1:12-15, 260; James
5:16, 374; Jer. **27**, 241;
Jer. **31:34**, 56; Jer.
32:27, 75; Job **42:2**,
134; Joel **3:10**, 331;
John **1:12**, 53, 185;
John **1:16**, 116; John
3:3 , 102; John **3:5**,

102; John **3:16**, 35, 36, 52, 56; John **3:17**, 35, 56; John **3:18**, 56; John **4:23-24**, 346; John **5:19**, 106; John **5:22**, 36, 56; John **6:32-58**, 164-166; John **6:35**, 163; John **6:38**, 106; John **8:12**, 163; John **8:32**, 210; John **8:36**, 210; John **10:9**, 163; John **10:11**, 163; John **11:25**, 164; John **11:41-42**, 18; John **12:47**, 56; John **2:49**, 106; John **13:34**, 40, 372; John **13:35**, 40, 372; John **14:6**, 164; John **14:10**, 106; John **14:12**, 328; John **14:13-14**, 92; John **14:28**, 304; John **15:1**, 164; John **15:15**, 53; John **15:16**, 55, 92; John **16:23-24**, 92; John **16:26** , 36; John **16:27**, 36, 52; John **17:11, 21-23**, 212-213; John **17:23**, 53; John **18: 36**, 103; 1 John **1:9**, 56, 183, 187; 1 John **2:5**, 38; 1 John **2:13**, 277; 1 John **2:14**, 277; 1 John **2:20**, 116; 1 John **2:27**, 116; 1 John **3:1**, 38, 53; 1 John **3:12**, 277; 1 John **4:4**, 293; 1 John **4:7-8**, 38; 1 John **4:8**, 33; 1 John **4:9**,… 39; 1 John **4:10**, 39; 1 John **4:11**, 40; 1 John **4:12**, 40; 1 John **4:13-16**, 40-41; 1 John **4:17**, 41, 116; 1 John **4:18**, 41,54; 1

John **4:19**, 42; 1 John **4:20-21**, 42-43; 1 John **5:18**, 55; Josh. **1:5**, 224; Josh. **6:18-19**, 252; Josh. **7:20-21**, 253; 1 Kings **16:24**, 91; 1 Kings **18:36-37**, 18; Luke **1:35**, 327-328; Luke **2:49**, 26; Luke **4:14**, 328; Luke **4:17-19**, 274-275; Luke **4:18**, 116; Luke **4:43** , 102; Luke **5:12-13**, 160-161; Luke **8:1** , 102; Luke **8:12**, 277; Luke **8: 26-39**, 284-285; Luke **9:1** , 102; Luke **10:17-20**, 287; Luke **11:1**, 15; Luke **15:11-32**, 33; Luke **17: 20**, 102, 115; Luke **17:21**, 115; Luke **22:20**, 216; Luke **22:31-32**, 267; Luke **23:46**, 27; Mal. **1:6**, 93; Mal.**1:7**, 93; Mal. **1:8**, 93, 94; Mal. **1:13**, 94; Mal. **2:10**, 87; Mal. **4:2-3**, 94; Mark **4:15**, 277; Mark **14:24**, 216; Mark **16:16-18**, 287-288; Matt. **3:1**, 99; Matt. **4:17**, 100; Matt. **4:23**, 100; Matt. **5:3**, 100; Matt. **5:10**, 100; Matt. **5:13**, 55; Matt. **6:6**, 28; Matt. **6:9-13**, 17, 22, 148, 296; Matt. **6:14-15**, 193; Matt. **6:25-34**, 153-154; Matt. **6:33**, 101; Matt. **7:9-11**, 29; Matt. **7:11**, 154; Matt. **7:21**, 101, 124; Matt. **10:5-10**, 286; Matt. **10:7**, 101;

Matt. **12: 28**, 101, Matt. **13:19**, 277; Matt. **13:38**, 277; Matt. **18:3**, 156; Matt. **18:19-20**, 372; Matt. **18:35**, 196; Matt. **21:22**, 161; Matt. **25:34**, 108, 120, 121; Matt. **26:26**, 168; Matt. **26:28**, 216; Matt. **27:46**, 27-28, 87; Matt. **28:18**, 99, 316; Micah **3:8**, 327; Micah **5:2**, 326; Micah **7:18**, 56; Num. **5:22**, 364; Num. **20:6-1**, 235-236; 1 Peter **2:2**, 151; 1 Peter **4:11-13**, 267-268; 1 Peter **5:8**, 292; 2 Peter **1:3**, 160; 2 Peter **2:10**, 308; 2 Peter **3:9**, 132; 2 Peter **3:18**, 151; Phil. **2**, 324; Phil. **2:9-11**, 92-93; Phil. **3:20**, 54; Phil. **4:13**, 55, 329; Prov. **3:5-6**, 244; Prov. **16:9**, 244; Prov. **18:21**, 49; Ps. **5:8**, 242; Ps. **9:2**, 84; Ps. **19:14**, 352; Ps. **23**, 239-240; Ps. **25:5**, 242; Ps. **27:11**, 242; Ps. **31:3**, 243; Ps. **32:8**, 243; Ps. **34:1**, 352; Ps. **37:25**, 169; Ps. **40:3**, 352; Ps. **40:8**, 130; Ps. **42:9**, 86; Ps. **48:14**, 243; Ps. **51:5**, 173; Ps. **51:15**, 353; Ps. **61:2**, 243; Ps. **63:5**, 353; Ps. **71:8**, 353; Ps. **97:9** , 73; Ps. **109:30**, 353; Ps. **117**, 352; Ps. **118**, 352; Ps. **119**, 352; Ps. **119:133**, 243; Ps. **133**, 214, 375; Ps. **138:4**, 353; Ps. **139:10**, 243; Ps. **139:24**, 243; Ps. **143:10**, 243; Ps. **145:21**, 353; Rev. **3:14**, 368; Rev. **1:11**, 187; Rev. **11:15**, 121; Rev. **20:9-10**, 288; Rev. **21:1**, 120; Rev. **21:2**, 120; Rev. **21:3**, 120; Rev. **21:4**, 120; Rom. **1:18-32**, 178; Rom. **3:23**, 172, 178; Rom. **4:7**, 185; Rom. **5:1**, 53; Rom. **5:1-5**, 199-200; Rom. **5:5**, 36, 39; Rom. **5:8**, 36; Rom. **6:23**, 74, 183; Rom. **8:1**, 185-186; Rom. **8:1-2**, 54; Rom. **8:28**, 144, 231; Rom. **8:31**, 54; Rom. **8:31-39**, 30-31; Rom. **8:35**, 54; Rom. **8:35-39**, 282-283; Rom. **8:38-39**, 293-294; Rom. **12:1**, 137, 343, 382; Rom. **12:2**, 133, 137, 350; Rom. **13:1-7**, 307-308; Rom. **13:8-10**, 201; Rom. **14:17**, 104; Rom. **15:5-6**, 351, 353-356; Rom. **16:20**, 294; 1 Sam. **2:3**, 85; 1 Sam. **15:22-24**, 311; 1 Sam. **16:11-13**, 137; 2 Sam. **1:14**, 311; 2 Sam. **11:2-5**, 256; 1Thess. **4:3**, 132; 2Thess. **1:3**, 151; 1 Tim. **2:3-4**, 132; 2 Tim. **1:7**, 54; 2 Tim. **1:12**, 198; 2 Tim. **2:13**, 219; Zech. **4:6**, 327

Blake, William, 220
Bocelli, Andrea, 301
Boom, Corrie Ten, 220
Calcutta, 174

Canaan, 80, 81, 271
Christophany, 105
Clarke, Adam, 18, 277
Columbus, 361
Communication, 13, 14, 23, 24,
    57, 62, 68, 150, 370
Confederacy, 211
Daniel, 118, 133, 134, 273
David, King of Israel, 117, 130,
    133, 137, 140, 197,
    236-240, 248, 254-
    256, 261, 272, 273,
    299, 310, 311
Declaration of Independence,
    108
Diaspora, 304
Doty, Bobby, 10, 370
Eden, Garden of, 271
Egypt, 81, 84, 137, 167, 209,
    217, 228, 230, 231,
    234, 235, 272, 300
Eli, 86
Elijah, 18, 118
Elisha, 105, 118
Emancipation Proclamation,
    211
Esau, 81
Eschatology, 119, 134
Esther, 274, 312
Eucharist, 24, 167, 168
Eve, 173, 175, 176, 177, 178,
    179, 248-252, 254,
    261, 271, 280, 281,
    286, 305, 348
Ezekiel, 25, 118, 240, 241
Fear, 41, 42, 43, 54, 57, 68, 94,
    105, 112, 155, 180,
    239, 272, 281, 282,
    285, 304, 308, 333,
    352
Forgiveness, 64, 116, 121, 128,
    140, 172, 174, 182,
    183, 185, 186, 189,
    190, 192, 193, 194,
    196, 200, 201, 202,
    203, 204, 206, 207,
    208, 209, 210, 211,
    212, 213, 214, 215,
    218, 219, 220, 280,
    312, 358
Foster, Robert, 57, 154
Frost, Jack 44, 45, 46, 52
Gabriel, 327
Gaither Vocal Band, 31
Gamalial, 335
Georgia, 13, 128, 196, 211
Gethsemane, Garden of, 142,
212
Gettysburg Address, 108-109
Gideon, 320
Goliath, 272, 273
Graham, Dr. Billy, 173
Hadassah, 274
Halloween, 48, 78
Ham, 65, 271
Haman, 274, 312
Hashem, 89, 93
Herodian Temple, 24
Hitler, Adolf, 126, 140
    Mein Kampf, 126
Holy Spirit, 40
Hosea, 241
Houston, Texas, 15
Ichabod, 86
Independence Day, 361
Iraq, 14
Isaac, 81, 84, 90, 197, 263-265,
    266
Isaiah, 86, 118, 180, 240, 326
Ishmael, 230
Jacob, 81, 84, 197, 229, 230,
    272, 327
James, 206, 251, 259, 261, 275
Japheth, 65, 271
Jefferson, Thomas, 349
Jehovah, 81, 88, 90, 164
Jeremiah, 241
Jericho, 252, 253
Jerusalem, 26, 118, 119, 120,
    121, 126, 238, 240,

255, 273, 312, 325,
326, 327, 346
Jesse, 236
Jesus, 14, 15, 16, 17, 18, 19, 24,
25, 26, 27, 31, 33, 34,
35, 36, 37, 39, 40, 41,
42, 43, 50, 53, 55, 56,
57, 60, 77, 78, 81, 86,
87, 91, 92, 93, 99, 100,
101, 102, 103, 104,
105, 106, 107, 111,
114, 115, 116, 117,
118, 120, 121, 131,
132, 134, 138, 139,
142, 143, 151, 153,
154, 156, 161, 163,
164, 165, 166, 167,
168, 169, 172, 178,
185, 188, 189, 193,
194, 195, 196, 197,
198, 199, 201, 203,
207, 210, 212, 213,
214, 215, 216, 218,
219, 248, 250, 251,
257, 262, 266, 267,
270, 274, 275, 279,
281, 283, 284, 285,
286, 287, 292, 293,
294, 303, 304, 305,
306, 308, 309, 312,
313, 316, 320, 322,
324, 325, 326, 328,
329, 330, 335, 342,
343, 346, 350, 351,
353, 354, 359, 360,
362, 366, 367, 368,
371, 372, 373, 377,
378
Jethro of Midian, 233
Jews, 25, 103, 126, 165, 166,
301, 346
John the Baptist, 99, 133
Jordan River, 99, 252
Joseph (Jacob's son), 133, 229-
232, 236, 272
Joseph (Jesus' father), 26, 133,
165
Joseph of Arimathea, 142
Joshua, 81, 252, 253
Judaism, 25, 118, 335, 336, 364
King James Version, 62, 88,
194, 276, 299, 360,
367, 382
Korea, 14
Lazarus, 18
Lebens, Dr. Samuel, 364
Lehman, Frederick Martin, 31,
32
Lincoln, President Abraham,
108, 211
Locke, John, 349
Longfellow, Henry Wadsworth,
220
Lot, 271, 272
Luther, Martin, 220, 282
Mary (Jesus' mother), 26, 133,
327
Mary (Magdalene), 267
Mayo Clinic, 202, 209
Mercy Seat, 25
Meshach, 273
Mollette, Albert Hay, 201
Monroe, NC, 44, 45
Mordecai, 274
Mormon Tabernacle Choir, 301
Moses, 65, 78, 79, 81, 85, 88,
103, 112, 117, 133,
137, 140, 164, 177,
189, 197, 224, 232-
236, 238, 252, 255,
272, 335, 365, 367
Mother Teresa, 174
Mount Carmel, 18
Mount Moriah, 90, 263
Mozart, 349
Munroe, Dr. Myles, 107, 111,
113
Myrtle Beach, SC, 79, 206
Nantahala River, 225
New King James Version, 299

New Life Christian Fellowship, 45
New Spirit Filled life Bible, The, 115
Newton, Sir Isaac, 349
Niebuhr, H. Richard, 19
Noah, 65, 133, 137, 271
Paradigm Shift, 24-26, 44, 91, 118, 362, 364
Passover, 26, 169, 272
Paul, 36, 37, 38, 42, 81, 104, 119, 131, 133, 142, 143, 151, 178, 187, 213, 214, 216, 218, 231, 256, 275, 279, 290, 292, 320, 321, 322, 323, 324, 329, 332, 333, 334, 335, 336, 342, 343, 350, 351, 353, 377, 379, 380
Pentecost, 267
Peter, 81, 151, 160, 187, 197, 266, 267, 275, 292, 312, 332,
Pharisee, 15, 25, 102, 115, 335
Pope John Paul II, 126
Pope Urban II, 125
Potipher, 230
Prayer, 14, 15, 16, 17, 18, 19, 24, 25, 47, 57, 60, 62, 64, 78, 85, 91, 92, 95, 98, 130, 138, 141, 142, 150, 152, 153, 155, 157, 158, 161, 167, 172, 190, 192, 193, 194, 196, 198, 212, 218, 223, 224, 247, 248, 253, 257, 260, 263, 266, 269, 273, 275, 276, 279, 297, 298, 299, 301, 304, 332, 334, 336, 354, 363, 364, 371, 374, 375, 379, 383
Priceline.com, 232

Prodigal Son, 33-35
Purim, 274
Revelation, 81, 359, 360
Riley, Ella Mae, 9
Riley, Jason, 11, 14, 225, 262, 263
Riley, Joshua, 225, 330-331
Riley, Kim, 11, 79, 80, 143, 192, 370
Robertson, Frederick William, 220
Roman Catholic Church, 125, 174, 297
Rousseau, 349
Ruth, 236
Sadducee, 15, 25
Samson, 117, 326
Samuel, 85, 87, 117, 133, 137, 237, 238, 311
Sarah, 75, 81, 84
Saul, King, 237, 238, 272, 310, 311, 312
Saul (Paul), 81, 380
Seth, 178
Shadrach, 273
Shatner, William, 232
Shekinah Glory, 24, 25, 60
Shem, 65, 271
Shiloh Place, 52
Silas, 275
Skype, 13
Sodom, 271
Solomon, King, 273
Soviet Union (USSR), 329
Spurgeon, C.H., 355-359
Supreme Court, 74
Syriac, 364
Ten Commandments 38
Textus Recepticus, 299
Torah, 25, 89, 91, 365, 366
Tutu, Desmond, 220
Twain, Mark, 220
Tyson, Mike, 72
United States Marine Corps, 14
Ur (Chaldea), 80, 271

Uriah, 255, 256
Vietnam, 14
WWII, 14
Wagner, Dr. C. Peter, 17
Westminster Shorter
Catechism, 339-340
Wiggins, Ann, 11, 251
Wilde, Oscar, 219, 247
Worley, Dr. Randall, 200
Yes You Can, You Just Need
        Help, 377
YouTube, 31, 301
Zechariah, 327
Zerubbabel, 327

FREEDOM MINISTRIES INTERNATIONAL

The heartbeat of Lonnie and Kim is to help the church understand the revelations of:

➢ The Glory of God
➢ The Power of Prayer
➢ The Finished Work of the Gospel
➢ Freedom from legalism through grace.

The Riley's are available for teaching, speaking, conferences, revivals and concerts.

For information on scheduling, or to receive their newsletter and e-blasts, visit their website at: www.fmintl.org

Dr. Riley's Other Books

DR. LONNIE E. RILEY

THE POWER
of

PRAYING FOR
YOUR PASTOR

How to effectively intercede for your spiritual leader.

Dr. Riley's Other Books

DR. LONNIE E. RILEY

THE
EXTRAORDINARY
POWER OF
1%

40 Motivational Studies
That Can Change Your Life
1% At A Time.

Dr. Riley's Other Books

Yes, You Can!

You Just Need Help

A Guide to
Personal Accountability

DR. LONNIE E. RILEY

Author of *The Extraordinary Power of 1%*

WHAT'S *LOVE* GOT TO DO WITH IT?

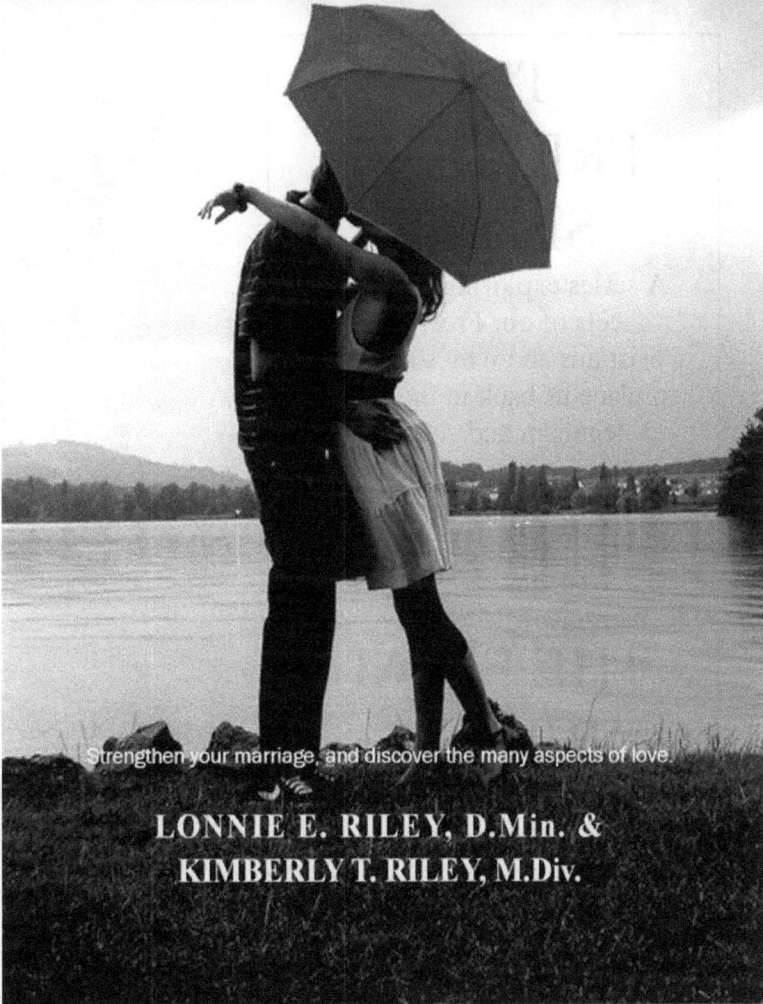

Strengthen your marriage, and discover the many aspects of love.

LONNIE E. RILEY, D.Min. &
KIMBERLY T. RILEY, M.Div.

COMING

SOON

THE FREEDOM SERIES

A series exploring the many facets of our Freedom as Christians and why some want to place us back in the box of legalism and control.

DR. LONNIE E. RILEY

The Freedom Series

THE FINAL RIP OFF $15.95

You will discover ways of saving money on final expenses and also understand some of the common abuses in the funeral industry from an insider's viewpoint.

The Final

R.I.P. Off

DR. LONNIE E. RILEY

ABOUT THE AUTHOR

Dr. Lonnie E. Riley is the President Elect of Coastal Christian College & Seminary, a new higher educational institute in Myrtle Beach, SC. He is a prolific author, song writer and teacher. As an experienced church planter (starting or aiding in 5 congregations) he has a unique perspective on evangelism, church growth and the methodology that the Church as a whole is utilizing in these last days. He and his wife, Kimberly, reside in Myrtle Beach.

www.ingramcontent.com/pod-product-compliance
Lightning Source LLC
Chambersburg PA
CBHW070337090426
42733CB00009B/1220